Dealing with Losers

Dealing with Losers
THE POLITICAL ECONOMY OF POLICY TRANSITIONS

Michael J. Trebilcock

UNIVERSITY PRESS

Oxford University Press is a department of the University of Oxford. It furthers the University's objective of excellence in research, scholarship, and education by publishing worldwide.

Oxford New York
Auckland Cape Town Dar es Salaam Hong Kong Karachi Kuala Lumpur Madrid
Melbourne Mexico City Nairobi New Delhi Shanghai Taipei Toronto

With offices in
Argentina Austria Brazil Chile Czech Republic France Greece Guatemala
Hungary Italy Japan Poland Portugal Singapore South Korea Switzerland
Thailand Turkey Ukraine Vietnam

Oxford is a registered trademark of Oxford University Press in the UK and certain other countries.

Published in the United States of America by
Oxford University Press
198 Madison Avenue, New York, NY 10016

© Oxford University Press 2014

All rights reserved. No part of this publication may be reproduced, stored in a retrieval system, or transmitted, in any form or by any means, without the prior permission in writing of Oxford University Press, or as expressly permitted by law, by license, or under terms agreed with the appropriate reproduction rights organization. Inquiries concerning reproduction outside the scope of the above should be sent to the Rights Department, Oxford University Press, at the address above.

You must not circulate this work in any other form
and you must impose this same condition on any acquirer.

First printing in paperback, 2015.
ISBN 978-0-19-045694-8 (paperback : alk. paper)

Library of Congress Cataloging-in-Publication Data
Trebilcock, M. J.
  Dealing with losers: the political economy of policy transitions / Michael J. Trebilcock.
     pages cm
  Includes bibliographical references and index.
  ISBN 978-0-19-937065-8 (hardback : alk. paper)
 1. Policy sciences—Economic aspects. 2. Political planning—Economic aspects.
 3. Transaction costs. 4. Social policy. 5. Economic policy. I. Title.
 H97.T737 2014
 330—dc23
                                                                      2013038173

Note to Readers
This publication is designed to provide accurate and authoritative information in regard to the subject matter covered. It is based upon sources believed to be accurate and reliable and is intended to be current as of the time it was written. It is sold with the understanding that the publisher is not engaged in rendering legal, accounting, or other professional services. If legal advice or other expert assistance is required, the services of a competent professional person should be sought. Also, to confirm that the information has not been affected or changed by recent developments, traditional legal research techniques should be used, including checking primary sources where appropriate.

(Based on the Declaration of Principles jointly adopted by a Committee of the American Bar Association and a Committee of Publishers and Associations.)

You may order this or any other Oxford University Press publication
by visiting the Oxford University Press website at www.oup.com.

{ TABLE OF CONTENTS }

Acknowledgments ix

1. **Introduction: The Places in-Between** 1

2. **Framing the Issues: Normative Discourses, Political Imperatives** 9
    I. Normative Theories of the Case for and Against Compensation or Mitigation of Transition Costs 9
        A. *Efficiency Theories* 9
        B. *Utilitarianism* 13
        C. *Social Contract Theories* 14
        D. *Communitarianism* 14
        E. *Corrective Justice* 15
        F. *Libertarianism* 16
    II. The Role of Compensation and other Mitigation Transition Strategies in Positive Theories of the Political Process 17
        A. *The Economics of Politics: Public Choice Theory* 17
        B. *The Implications of Public Choice Theory for Transition Policies* 18
        C. *The Limits of Public Choice Theory* 19
    III. Alternative Explanations of Political Behavior 20
        A. *Structural Explanations* 20
        B. *Institutional Explanations* 20
        C. *Psychological Explanations* 22
        D. *Ideational Explanations* 24
        E. *The Implications of Alternative Explanations of Political Behavior for Transition Policies in the Political Process* 26
    IV. Conclusion 29

3. **Public Pensions: Reconciling Fiscal Sustainability with Intergenerational Equity** 31
    I. Introduction 31
    II. Public Pension Plans and the Sustainability Problem 32
    III. Policy Responses to the Sustainability Problem 33
    IV. Options for Dealing with the Losers 37
    V. Public Choice and Normative Analysis 39
    VI. Conclusion 41

4. **Reforming the US Home Mortgage Interest Deduction** 43
    I. Introduction 43
    II. How Does the MID Work? 44

A. The Election to Itemize   44
   B. The Mechanics of the MID   45
   C. The MID in the Context of Other Tax Treatment of Housing   46
 III. History of the Deductibility of Home Mortgage Interest   46
   A. Origins of the MID   46
   B. The Politics Leading to the Codification of the MID   48
 IV. The Policy Case Against the MID   48
   A. Justifications for Subsidizing Homeownership   49
     i. Positive Externalities from Consuming More or Better Housing   49
     ii. Positive Externalities in Choice of Renting versus Owning a Home   49
   B. Justifications for Not Subsidizing Homeownership—Negative Externalities   50
   C. The MID Is Ineffective in Addressing Externalities   50
   D. The MID Is Inefficient and Inequitable   51
     i. Efficiency Critiques of the MID   51
     ii. Equity Critique of the MID   53
 V. Reform Options   53
   A. Affected Constituencies   54
   B. Current Developments and the Availability of Insurance   55
   C. Classes of Strategies for Reforming the MID   56
     i. Cold Turkey: Cancel the MID Overnight   56
     ii. Replace the MID with a Credit   56
     iii. Grandfathering   57
     iv. Capping the Deductibility of the MID (and Other Itemized Deductions)   57
     v. Phaseouts of the MID Over Time   58
     vi. Raising the Standard Deduction   58
 VI. Conclusion   59

5. Trade Liberalization: Gradualism, Reciprocity, Reversibility   **63**
 I. Introduction   63
 II. Measuring Adjustment Costs   64
 III. History of Adjustment Cost Policies   65
 IV. Normative Rationales for and Against Intervention   66
   A. Economic Efficiency   66
   B. Distributive Justice   68
   C. Communitarianism   68
 V. Political Considerations   69
 VI. Policy Instruments   71
   A. Gradualism   72
   B. Reciprocity   73
   C. Reversibility   73
   D. Labor Market Adjustment Policies   75
     i. Passive Policies: The Safety Net   75
     ii. Active Policies: The Trampoline   76
     iii. Trade-Specific Adjustment Programs   78
     iv. Other Policies   79
 VII. Conclusion   80

Table of Contents vii

6. Agricultural Supply Management: Unraveling the Transitional Gains Trap   81
   I. Introduction   81
   II. Dairy Supply Management in Canada   82
      A. The Structure of Canada's Dairy Supply Management Scheme   82
      B. The Effects of Canada's Dairy Scheme   84
      C. The Politics of Dairy—The Necessity of Compensation   86
         i. Public Choice Theory   86
         ii. Public Sympathy   87
         iii. Political Geography   88
         iv. Transitional Gains Trap   88
   III. Overcoming Challenges to Reform   88
      A. Persuading the Public   89
      B. Policy Options for Compensation and Mitigating Opposition to Reform   90
         i. Minor Reform   90
         ii. Options for Dismantling Supply Management   91
         iii. Options for Compensation and Transition Assistance Policies   92
   IV. Normative Considerations Regarding Compensation and Transition Programs   93
   V. Conclusion   94

7. Liberalizing Immigration Policy: The Gains and Strains of Accommodating More and Diverse Newcomers   97
   I. Introduction   97
   II. Stylized Facts About Immigration Policies in Receiving Countries   98
   III. Normative Critiques of Prevailing Immigration Policies   99
      A. Economic Perspectives   99
         i. Labor Market Effects in Host Countries   100
         ii. Fiscal Effects in Host Countries   101
         iii. Implications for Existing Immigration Policies   102
      B. Non-economic Perspectives   104
         i. Communitarianism   104
         ii. Liberalism   106
         iii. Implications for Existing Immigration Policies   107
   IV. Rethinking Immigration Policies   107
      A. Independent Applicants   108
      B. Family Preference Immigration   111
      C. Refugees and Asylum Seekers   111
      D. Illegal Immigrants and Temporary Workers   112
   V. Conclusion   114

8. Climate Change Policy: Managing More Heat in the World's Kitchens   119
   I. Introduction   119
   II. Policy Instruments   120
   III. Ethical Considerations   122
      A. Liability for Past Emissions   122
      B. Justifying Different Emissions Levels   124

IV. Political Factors 125
　　　　A. Structural 125
　　　　B. Institutional 126
　　　　C. Ideational 128
　　　　D. Psychological 129
　　V. Transition Strategies 131
　　　　A. Taxes and Permits 131
　　　　B. Carbon Tariffs and Equity 132
　　　　C. Revenue Neutral Carbon Pricing 132
　　　　D. Grandfathering and Exemptions 133
　　　　E. Price Ceilings, Floors, and Collars 134
　　　　F. Information and Exhortation 134
　　　　G. Framing 135
　　VI. Conclusion 135

9. Institutional Reform and Development: The Perils of Utopianism   139
　　I. Introduction 139
　　II. Path Dependence Theory 140
　　III. Rule of Law Reform and Development 141
　　IV. Democratic Reform and Development 143
　　V. Property Rights and Development 145
　　VI. Conclusion 149

10. Conclusion: Taking Transition Costs Seriously   151
　　I. Introduction 151
　　II. The Virtues of Incrementalism and Compromise 153
　　III. Lessons from Experience 155
　　IV. Conclusion 158

　　Notes 161
　　Index 207

{ ACKNOWLEDGMENTS }

In writing this book, I have incurred a number of debts of gratitude: first, to a number of very talented research assistants—Evan Rosevear, Chapters 2 and 8; Noel Semple, Chapter 3; Emily Satterthwaite, Chapter 4; Lara Guest, Chapter 5; Chris Barker, Chapter 6. Evan Rosevear's contributions as a political scientist have been particularly invaluable. I am also indebted to several colleagues, friends, and reviewers for comments on earlier drafts of several chapters: Carolyn Tuohy (Chapter 2); Ron Davis (Chapter 3); Ben Alarie and David Duff (Chapter 4); Derek Ireland (Chapter 6); Yoram Margalioth, Andrew Green, and Don Dewees (Chapter 8); James Baillie and two anonymous reviewers for Oxford University Press on the entire manuscript. I am also indebted to my close friend, collaborator, and former colleague, Ron Daniels, for sowing the seeds of the idea of this project over dinner in Harvard Square in the Fall of 2011. Finally, I am greatly indebted, as always, to my superbly efficient assistant, Nadia Gulezko, for handling many of the logistics of this project, and to the highly professional editorial staff of the Oxford University Press for shepherding the book through the publication process on an expeditious time-table.

{ 1 }

Introduction: The Places In-Between[1]

I have spent much of my professional career researching, writing, and teaching about the policy reform process in a wide range of policy contexts. I have also, in many contexts, been an active participant in this process, in one capacity or another. I have repeatedly been struck in many, if not most of these contexts, by the realization that diagnosing the ills of the status quo, and imagining better policy alternatives, at least in their broad contours, are often not especially controversial. However, the real challenges, in many cases, relate to getting from "here" to "there." Over time, existing policies develop their own encrustations of institutions, vested interests, adaptive preferences, and expectations that render the trajectory of getting from here to there a major part of the policy challenge. This book is about that challenge, which I attempt to illuminate both at a general level and through concrete illustrations developed in seven brief policy reform case studies.

As most parents of small children who have embarked on long vacation trips can attest, one of the most recurrent and frustrating questions is "are we there yet?," to which the common, enigmatic, and no doubt equally annoying answer is typically "we're getting closer." This book is about the "here" and the "there," but most particularly the importance of taking seriously, in political economy terms, "the places in between."

The long fight to end slavery, led by William Wilberforce, among many others, culminated in Britain with the enactment of the *Slavery Abolition Act* in 1833. This act made provision for a payment of 20 million pounds (almost 40 percent of the British budget at the time) in compensation to plantation owners in many British colonies—about $21 billion (US) in present day value. Moreover, only slaves below the age of six were initially freed while others were redesignated as "apprentices," who were to be freed in two stages in 1838 and 1840.[2] Wilberforce and many other abolitionists accepted that compensation and phased implementation were required to ensure enactment of the legislation,[3] particularly by the House of Lords where plantation owners were strongly represented among the aristocracy.[4]

Whenever governments change policies—whether tax, expenditure, or regulatory policies—even when the changes are on net socially beneficial, there will typically be losers. These losers will have made investments of one kind or another, physical, financial, or human, predicated on, or even deliberately induced by, the pre-reform set of policies. Very few policy changes make somebody better off and nobody worse off according to their own subjective valuations (the economists' concept of Pareto efficiency). Rather, policy changes reallocate social benefits and costs in different ways.[5] The issue of whether and when to mitigate the costs associated with policy changes, whether through explicit government compensation, grandfathering, phased or postponed implementation, is ubiquitous across the policy landscape.

A few selective, but far from exhaustive, examples serve to illustrate this point. First, take the case of land use regulations or controls. Sometimes relevant levels of government see fit to change these regulations. They may increase building setbacks from property lines or road allowances. They may impose height restrictions on buildings in residential or mixed-use neighborhoods. They may change zoning laws from mixed-use to residential. In most of these cases, existing property owners will be exempted from these requirements, and their existing uses treated as legal "non-conforming uses." In a similar vein, in tight residential housing markets, sometimes rent controls are imposed on existing rental properties, but the construction of future rental buildings is often exempted from these controls in order to incentivize new rental construction and alleviate supply constraints.

To take another example, environmental regulations are often subject to change, reflecting new scientific knowledge of environmental risks, or at least public perceptions thereof. Energy efficiency requirements for motor vehicles are but one example where regulations have become more stringent over time. Typically, these do not apply to the existing fleet of motor vehicles but to motor vehicles manufactured in the future, and often with a lead time in order to allow manufacturers to adapt to more stringent requirements. Similarly, in the case of climate change policies, often countries adopt relatively long time horizons for phasing in requirements for renewable energy generation, or carbon taxes, or cap-and-trade regimes on an implementation schedule designed to become more stringent over time, while avoiding disruptive and costly changes to existing forms of production or consumption.

Another example, particularly apt in a contemporay US policy context, relates to proposals to reform gun control laws. Even strong proponents of stricter gun control laws in proposing comprehensive background checks on all purchasers of guns or proposing the prohibition of assault rifles or magazines in excess of a certain capacity recognize that such restrictions can only feasibly apply to prospective purchases of weapons, and not existing owners of weapons, who would be effectively grandfathered under these reform proposals.

A yet further example relates to professional qualifications. In many professions, including law, medicine, and dentistry, entry requirements have become increasingly stringent over the past century. Yet, in applying these more stringent requirements, existing professionals are, in effect, grandfathered, subject perhaps to continuing professional education requirements.

Another, and quite different, international example is found in post-conflict nation-building exercises, where a major challenge is addressing what should be

Introduction: The Places In-Between 3

done with respect to atrocities committed in the past by various antagonists in the conflicts that have afflicted a nation. Here, more or less judicious combinations of truth and reconciliation commmissions, lustration policies designed to disqualify certain officials from previous repressive regimes from future public office, and residual classes of cases where the most egregious past atrocities are remitted to either domestic or international criminal tribunals for prosecution, are often adopted. Such combinations of policies are obviously designed to draw a qualified line in the sand between what has happened in the past and new rules of civic engagement and collective governance going forward.[6]

The seven brief case studies that I develop in this book are all designed to illustrate in greater detail, and in widely disparate policy contexts, the central importance of transition cost mitigation strategies, particularly those aimed at specific subgroups of populations, in advancing politically feasible reform options. Although these case studies are, to some extent, idiosyncratic in that (with the exception of mortgage interest deductibility) they reflect areas of public policy in which I have had a previous engagement either as a scholar or policy participant, they are also major contemporary (and in many cases contentious) areas of policy debate.

In the public pension context discussed in Chapter 3, where many countries have in the past adopted pay-as-you-go, self-sustaining public pension schemes, the sustainability of these schemes is or has been threatened, first by significant increases in life expectancy of pension beneficiaries (and hence the scale of their entitlements), and second by declining fertility rates, which have reduced the size of the working age population whose contributions finance current entitlements. Simply reducing entitlements across the board is likely to be perceived as widely unfair by current pensioners and imminent retirees, who have limited or no capacity to adjust to such a reduction in entitlements, while raising contribution rates substantially on existing workers to finance shortfalls in the system would be widely perceived as unfair to them and an implicit tax on new job creation. Raising the existing retirement age incrementally, along with modest benefit reductions and contribution increases, may yield the most politically feasible set of burden-sharing options.

Chapter 4 focuses on the reform or abolition of mortgage interest tax-deductibility in the United States. This policy is widely viewed, at least by economists, as inefficient in overstimulating demand for homeownership and encouraging over-leveraging by homeowners, as well as being inequitable in conferring disproportionate benefits on higher income taxpayers in higher marginal tax brackets, for whom the deduction is more valuable. However, abolishing or reforming this provision is likely to entail significant direct transition costs for homeowners, given that the value of the deduction has been largely impounded in house prices, as well as imposing indirect costs on the housing sector more generally. A gradual, back-ended phaseout of the deduction, accompanied by a much more finely targeted form of time-limited assistance to first-time home buyers with below-average household incomes may be the most politically feasible reform option. This case study illustrates a broader set of issues with many kinds of tax reforms. Although the starkest forms of retroactivity would be widely rejected as unfair (e.g., raising tax rates on income that has been previously taxed), reforms that raise rates on future income (or capital gains) have a retroactive effect on investments made prior to the changes and are predicated, at least to some extent, on the existing tax rules.

Chapter 5 addresses the politics of negotiating new international trade liberalization commitments, multilaterally, bilaterally, or regionally. In this context, a significant focus of negotiations will typically be on demands by various of the negotiating parties for exclusions or dispensations for certain sectors or for gradual rates of reduction over time in prevailing levels of protection, such as tariffs or quotas. More generally, gradualism in implementing liberalization commitments over time, safeguard provisions to permit reinstatement of previous protections in the event of unforeseeably large import surges that cause serious injury to domestic industries or their workforces, and reciprocity where contraction of import-competing sectors is offset by expansion of export-oriented sectors that are facilitated by reciprocal liberalization commitments, are all designed to moderate the transition costs, both real and publicly perceived, associated with trade liberalization commitments.

Chapter 6 focuses on a particularly acute manifestation of the centrality of transition costs as an impediment to trade liberalization: agricultural protectionism. This case study focuses on a specific example of this phenomenon—dairy supply management in Canada—but many other countries also provide exceptional forms of protection to their agricalutural sectors through trade restrictions and domestic and export subsidies. These forms of protection (like mortgage interest deductibility) tend to be impounded in land or quota values, so that dismantling these schemes is likely to entail very substantial losses for the current generation of farmers. The intractability of the transition cost problem in the agricultural sector largely explains the very limited progress that has been made in international trade negotiations in liberalizing trade in agricultural products. Progress is only likely to be made with credible political commitments to phase out these forms of protection very gradually over time, but in some cases accompanied by one-time explicit forms of (partial) compensation for losses incurred. The opaqueness and complexity of many of these schemes poses a major challenge for policy reformers in overcoming public ignorance, apathy, and possibly even antipathy, in underwriting such a strategy.

Chapter 7 focuses on liberalizing immigration policy in many industrialized countries, a policy option that shares some affinities with the liberalization of international trade: immigration involves cross-border movement of people, whereas international trade primarily involves cross-border movement of goods (and services). However, liberalizing immigration policy raises some distinctive challenges, including non–wage-related immigration where immigrants are induced to migrate not principally because of greater employment opportunities in the receiving countries, but because of more generous social welfare systems, whose sustainability may be threatened with an unconstrained influx of immigrants seeking to make claims on such programs. More open immigration policies also attract concerns over labor market effects on domestic low-skilled workers, and over the erosion of important cultural, political, or community values in the receiving country as a result of larger influxes of immigrants who do not share these ideals.

Notwithstanding these concerns, over recent decades an increasingly fierce international competition for highly specialized talent has emerged in many sectors, and unduly restrictive immigration policies constrain the competitiveness and innovative potential of the sectors that are hampered by restrictive regulations in their ability to compete for this talent. Hence, progressive liberalization of entry restrictions on highly skilled foreign workers as either permanent residents or temporary workers with a clear path to permanent resident status and ultimately citizenship would seem the highest priority. In the case of less skilled or unskilled foreign workers who are able and willing to fill gaps in local labor markets, a more cautious process of liberalization would seem warranted so as to minimize the risks to less well-endowed domestic workers of wage erosion or job displacement. In the case of countries with large numbers of illegal or undocumented immigrants, such as the United States with an estimated 11 million such immigrants, deportation on a massive scale seems totally infeasible. In moral terms, this is because of the enormous human costs entailed in many cases for the immigrants in question. Politically, it is because of the enormous direct costs involved for government and its taxpayers in implementing such a program. And economically, such a policy would entail substantial upward pressure on wages due to the elimination of a large pool of low-wage workers. Thus, some form of conditional but realistically achievable amnesty seems unavoidable.

In Chapter 8, I turn to perhaps the most daunting regulatory challenge of our age: climate change policy. In the nature of the problem, concerted action by all countries, developed and developing, that are major emitters of greenhouse gases (principally CO_2) is required in order to ameliorate this problem, but to date a formal international agreement among such countries on appropriate abatement policies has proven elusive. Although unilateral policy reforms, such as increasingly stringent carbon taxes or cap-and-trade regimes, are often advocated and relatively more practicable to implement, concerns naturally arise that these will simply lead to carbon leakage or migration to other countries whose industries are not similarly regulated, or indeed relocation of businesses from countries adopting such unilateral policies to countries lacking such policies. In practice, unilateral action alone is likely to have little or no impact on the environmental problem that motivates it, and it may entail a loss of competitiveness, investment, and employment in countries invoking such policies.

These concerns have led to proposals that unilateral action on climate change, in the form of carbon taxes or cap-and-trade systems, should be accompanied by border tax measures ("carbon tariffs") that impose similar burdens on imports, in effect "taxing" consumption of carbon-intensive products, wherever the carbon is produced, with a remission of such burdens where countries of origin adopt similar domestic measures themselves, with a view to the evolution over time of an internationally harmonized carbon tax (or cap-and-trade equivalent). Although such proposals raise a number of difficult legal and geopolitical challenges, it is clear that mitigating various kinds of transition costs is absolutely critical to policy progress on the climate change problem.

My final case study (Chapter 9) focuses on institutional reform in developing countries. Over the past two decades or so, scholars, policymakers, and international aid agencies have tended to converge on a consensus that the quality of a country's institutions—political, bureaucratic, and legal—are a crucial determinant of that country's future development trajectory, a view captured in the mantra "institutions matter," or "governance matters." Unlike the previous six case studies, which were not predicated on fundamental reforms to a country's institutions, in this context institutional reform is viewed as a predicate to more effective policy formulation and implementation. However, despite the investment of vast resources by the international community in institutional reforms in developing countries, experience to date has been mixed to poor, as exemplified by the faltering efforts to institute democracy and the rule of law in countries such as Iraq and Afghanistan and similar efforts in various Middle Eastern countries (such as Egypt and Libya) following the so-called "Arab Spring." It is now increasingly recognized that the contingencies of a country's history and culture—captured by the concept of "path dependence"—delineate both the feasible scope of institutional reform and its advisable contours. More specifically, various kinds of switching costs from the status quo are likely to impede reforms. In terms of political economy, switching costs may be high for those within and outside existing institutions (however socially dysfunctional) who benefit from the institutional status quo and hence will resist reforms. Switching costs may also reflect individual learning costs in adapting to a new regime and the loss of network effects and institutional complementarities that may have evolved around existing regimes. Switching costs may also reflect the scarcity of financial and specialized human resources required to implement new institutional regimes. Finally, switching costs may reflect deeply embedded cultural beliefs or practices—norms of appropriateness—that are highly resistant to change. Regardless of the salience of any particular factor in a specific context, strategies for mitigating switching costs are likely to be a precondition to major progress on institutional reform in developing countries.

As the foregoing examples and the case study synposes make evident, explicit compensation of losers from policy changes constitutes a tiny proportion of the larger universe of transition mitigation strategies employed or available. Nevertheless, much of the scholarly literature that addresses transition costs from policy change has focused on explicit compensation, largely influenced by the complex and sometimes incoherent case law emanating from the US Supreme Court in applying the Fifth Amendment of the US Constitution (the so-called "Takings Clause"), which provides that private property may only be taken by the state for public use and with just compensation. In legal jurisdictions that lack constitutionally entrenched expropriation procedures, statutory laws raise many of the same legal issues, as do expropriation provisions in bilateral investment treaties (BITS) or regional trade agreements such as NAFTA with respect to the treatment of foreign investors. However, transition mitigation strategies other than explicit compensation are not directly engaged by any of these provisions. Moreover, in many respects, debates over the scope of these provisions are addressed to the question of appropriate constraints on government behavior, perhaps enforced by courts or similar arbitral bodies sanctioned by domestic constitutions or statutes or international treaties. A much less well-developed body of literature focuses not on the obligation to compensate as a legal or constitutional constraint on government action, but rather as a strategy for expanding the politically feasible scope for socially desirable policy changes by muting or mitigating the resistance of losers to these changes—the principal focus of this book. In the absence of effective transition mitigation strategies, the status quo becomes the default option, which for a broad cross section of the citizenry is likely to be less congenial than various reform proposals that include transition mitigation strategies. My intended audience for this book is politicians and their constituencies, not the judiciary.

In Chapter 2, I sketch the principal strands of both normative and positive theories of the political process as they bear on the full menu of transition cost mitigation strategies, including compensation, grandfathering, postponed implementation, or graduated implementation. Although voters and interest groups in the political process who perceive themselves as material losers from a proposed policy change are likely to invoke arguments from material self-interest, as discussed in the second part of Chapter 2, they are also likely to appeal to normative values (of the kind sketched in the first part of Chapter 2) in order to engage the support of other citizens or interest groups who share their values but not their interests. Hence, normative and positive theories of the political process exhibit significant interdependencies, which are important to illuminate early in this book with a view to exemplifying them in more detail in particular policy contexts in the case studies that follow.

{ 2 }

Framing the Issues: Normative Discourses, Political Imperatives

The range of normative viewpoints reflected in the scholarly literature on the transition cost compensation or mitigation issue, even among scholars who share the same general disciplinary or theoretical orientation, is startling. I will describe and comment briefly on the leading normative perspectives in turn. By "normative" I mean perspectives or theories that purport to advise governments on what policies they should adopt in this context as a matter of efficiency, fairness, justice, or some other conception of right or wrong. In contrast, positive theories of government merely purport to explain or describe what factors move governments to adopt certain policies, whether right or wrong in a normative sense. I review such theories in the second part of this chapter, along with their implications for transition cost mitigation strategies.

I. Normative Theories of the Case for and Against Compensation or Mitigation of Transition Costs

A. EFFICIENCY THEORIES

An efficiency perspective emphasizes the importance of adopting public policies designed to maximize the total value of social resources, as reflected in the preferences or utility functions of all the members of the society in question. In other words, the guiding criterion is maximizing social welfare.[1] Given problems of accurate revelation of underlying preferences or utility functions, and aggregation of these into a coherent and stable social welfare function in applied policy contexts,[2] this typically entails a presumption in favor of voluntary market transactions, subject to a reasonably well-established list of caveats pertaining to various kinds of market failure, such as monopoly, externalities, information failures, and public goods. Thus, one version of an efficiency perspective on the compensation issue is to inquire whether private markets fail in all or some contexts in allocating the risk of policy changes.

The most prominent proponent of this perspective on compensation issues is Louis Kaplow, who contends that no law or policy should rationally be presumed to be eternal and immutable.³ In his view, the uncertainty of government policy is broadly equivalent to more conventional instances of market uncertainty, such as the success or failure of a new product or the actions of one's competitors. Thus, for Kaplow government transitions warrant the same treatment as market transitions: no transition relief.

Kaplow focuses on the two primary economic consequences of changes in government policy: the effect on incentives to engage in the affected activities and the imposition of risk. An efficient level of investment is induced where investors bear all the costs and benefits of their decisions. Thus, the encouragement resulting from the assurance that compensation or some other form of mitigation will be provided in the event of policy change results in excessive prior investment in the affected activity by shifting part of the long-run costs of private investment to the public, thus distorting an otherwise efficient decision-making process. To the extent that investors are risk-averse, market mechanisms often provide efficient options for striking an optimal risk-incentive trade-off, for example, through discounting the value of assets acquired that may be subject to depreciation in value through future policy changes, or through buying explicit market insurance or through other risk diversification strategies.

Kaplow acknowledges that private insurance markets are subject to failures, such as (1) moral hazard (once insured, parties have incentives to increase their risky behavior); (2) adverse selection (only higher-risk parties are likely to buy private market insurance, which will lead to higher insurance premiums that price less risky parties out of the market); and (3) transaction and information costs (especially for low probability policy contingencies). Nevertheless, it is his contention that governments are unlikely to improve on how markets, including insurance markets, balance risk and incentives, and in many (probably most) cases are likely to strike a less socially efficient balance between risks and incentives. In his view, other transition mechanisms, such as grandfathering, delayed implementation, and phased-in implementation, raise many of the same problems as explicit compensation in distorting risk-incentive trade-offs, while at the same time attenuating the benefits of the policy change in question through exceptions or delays.

Kaplow emphasizes that his analysis assumes that government behaves optimally in undertaking policy reforms in terms of maximizing social welfare and is not influenced in its policy choices by the transition policy in force. In effect, he assumes that all policy changes will be socially optimal.⁴ He concedes that in a complete analysis one would relax these assumptions and consider when government policy is or is not likely to be optimal, how it deviates from optimality when it is not, and how transition policy may affect the choice of underlying substantive policies: "Such is the subject of an entire discipline, political science (or as some prefer, political economy or public choice) and is obviously beyond the scope of this investigation."⁵ He acknowledges that the analysis of private actors with regard to incentives and risk bearing is substantially more developed than is the analysis of government behavior, including how such behavior is affected by transition policy. In the latter respect, he acknowledges that "most analysis—including by this author—has been fairly black box, and has not taken full advantage of recent decades of work by political scientists and other pertinent scholars."[6]

In contrast to Kaplow, scholars adopting a more political economy–oriented perspective on the compensation issue argue that an expansive case for compensation for transition costs may be justified, precisely in order to ensure that policy changes that governments adopt are in fact social welfare–enhancing. For example, a Kaldor-Hicks conception of efficiency is satisfied when society is, on net, better off from a policy change when the winners from the change are in a position to compensate the losers such that the losers would be indifferent to the change after compensation, and the gainers, even after paying compensation to the losers, would still derive a benefit. However, typically under a Kaldor-Hicks conception of efficiency compensation is not in fact paid to the losers; rather, the scale of the benefits to the winners is compared to the scale of the losses to the losers, and if the former exceeds the latter the policy change should proceed.

Critics of this conception of efficiency argue that policymakers, in undertaking the cost-benefit analysis implicit in the Kaldor-Hicks conception of efficiency, face incentives to undervalue the costs of the policies they are promoting, given that they do not bear these costs, and perhaps to overvalue the benefits. Hence, the concern is that policymaking, in the absence of an actual compensation principle (ideally one that is consensually determined, albeit subject to the "holdout" or monopoly problem that some claimants may present), is likely to reflect a form of "fiscal illusion." To combat this tendency, some scholars argue that governments should be required explicitly to compensate the losers—something closer to the Pareto conception of efficiency that requires that a policy change only proceed if it makes at least one individual better off without making anyone worse off—and face the political consequences of explicit budgetary outlays on this account. This, it is assumed, would discipline any tendency of policymakers to adopt policy changes that are not in fact social welfare–enhancing.[7] These might be characterized as "Pareto reforms," rather than "cost-benefit reforms."[8]

However, as John Quinn and I have pointed out,[9] and as Kaplow himself notes,[10] policymakers, whether legislators, regulators, or bureaucrats, rarely capture directly most of the benefits of the policy changes they promote, nor are they likely to bear most of the costs. As such, it is not clear that an explicit government compensation requirement is likely to change government behavior. Conversely, it might actually increase rent-seeking behavior by special interest groups as they will be incentivized to promote socially undesirable policies, recognizing that they will be compensated in the event that these policies are subsequently withdrawn or modified.

A more subtle political economy argument for compensation policy argues that in a majoritarian political system, there may be contexts in which a majority of voters (or their representatives) will find it in their interests "to gang up on" or "single out" a small minority of their fellow citizens, who are not sufficiently numerous or well-organized to be politically influential, to bear most of the costs of policies that the majority favor—a form of Tyranny of the Majority.[11] On the one hand, this might lead to the adoption of policies that are not socially optimal because they confer modest benefits on the majority at great expense to the minority. On the other hand, even where the policies are socially optimal (in a social welfare framework), a "singling out" policy that requires politically marginal interests to bear most of the costs of these policies is likely to strike many people as an abuse of government power. This is most evident in the classic eminent domain case: a local resident's house is taken and the land used to build a public school. Even if the social benefits from this alternative land use exceed the costs to the existing resident, it will strike most people as unfair that the local resident should bear all the costs of this policy transition. Kaplow, drawing on Blume and Rubinfeld,[12] considers that this kind of case may justify government compensation on the grounds that private insurance may be unavailable for reasons related to moral hazard, adverse selection, or transaction costs.

However, it is not clear to me that these insurability problems are any more severe in this context than coverage for many other low probability, independent events such as fire or theft.[13] Moreover, despite Kaplow's objections to broader compensation commitments for policy change by way of analogy to the poor risk-incentive properties of government compensation for natural disasters,[14] it seems obvious that private insurance coverage is less likely to be available, or at least to be prohibitively expensive, for highly correlated (and undiversifiable) risks that many regulatory changes (and natural disasters) entail.[15] It is also argued that policy changes are often likely to be of a sui generis character, precluding pricing based on actuarial experience.[16] Relatedly, Shavell argues that grandfathering may be efficient relative to other risk mitigation strategies if the costs of adapting investments made in compliance with a prior regulatory regime and ongoing compliance costs with a new regime exceed the social benefits (e.g., a municipality increasing the minimum distance a building must be set back from a street).[17] Moreover, adverse selection problems may sometimes favor the mandatory pooling of risks to prevent risk pools from unraveling. Examples might include unemployment, disability, or healthcare insurance.

Thus, concerns over the cost and availability of market insurance appear to have a much broader application than eminent domain, while not directly addressing the issue of "singling-out" as an abuse of government power. Whether or not it is true that markets are relatively efficient in allocating risks of both market and policy uncertainty for either sharply focused or more dispersed losses, through contractual arrangements or explicit insurance, the fact remains that applying Kaplow's "no compensation" presumption, private parties, one way or another, in the case of policy changes, are left bearing all the costs of policy changes (including where they are insurable or diversifiable), even if one assumes them to be on net socially desirable. Whether it is fair that they should do so moves the discussion into a quite different normative domain. As the economist William Fischel notes, "Why has economics not been especially helpful in resolving the 'takings' issue? Part of the answer is that the issue involves fairness as well as efficiency... To move from the conclusion that just compensation promotes efficiency (or inefficiency) to the recommendation that it ought to be paid (or not paid) is to impose the culture of economics on the culture of society at large."[18]

B. UTILITARIANISM

Although utilitarian perspectives on the compensation issue share much in common with efficiency perspectives, they do not necessarily converge in this context. The most prominent proponent of a utilitarian perspective on compensation for transition costs is Professor Frank Michelman.[19] Michelman's formula for compensation, while complex, revolves around three elements. First is the idea of Demoralization Costs (D). The costs are defined as the disutilities to uncompensated losers and their sympathizers beyond material losses, and the lost future production from impaired incentives or social unrest that would arise if no compensation were paid. He asserts that individuals who suffer harm as a result of state action experience a special kind of disappointment and anxiety when they have reason to suspect that they have been singled out as the victims of uncompensated losses. Thus, demoralization costs, for Michelman, include both uncertainty costs and disaffection costs. Second, Settlement Costs (S) are the costs, chiefly administrative, of operating a compensation program, that must be borne to avoid demoralization costs, which may in many cases be substantial in tracing out second, third, and fourth order effects of policy changes (much like determining the ultimate incidence of a tax). Third, Efficiency Gains (E) are the excess of the gains produced by government acts over the material losses inflicted by them, not including (D) or (S).

According to Michelman, government should compensate losses if demoralization costs exceed settlement costs; conversely, governments should not compensate losses if settlement costs exceed demoralization costs. Presumably, if demoralization costs exceed both efficiency gains and settlement costs, government should not proceed with the policy reform in question. As Fischel points out, Michelman's approach adopts an intermediate position between Pareto and Kaldor-Hicks conceptions of efficiency. It is more permissive than the Pareto conception in that it would approve some government actions without actual compensation if settlement costs exceed demoralization costs, while it is less permissive than the Kaldor-Hicks conception, which does not, in principle, require compensation at all.[20] It differs from Kaplow's perspective in that Michelman assigns significant weight to the private costs of policy changes, whether insurable or not, which Kaplow is prepared largely to ignore, or by assumption to treat as exceeded by the social benefits of the policy reform in question.

Although Michelman's decision rule has intuitive attractions, operationalizing it presents formidable challenges. Valuing each of the three key components in his formula in robust and defensible ways, and avoiding the political manipulation of these valuations so as to favor particular political constituencies or special interests, raise major institutional challenges.

C. SOCIAL CONTRACT THEORIES

Although there are many different variants of social contract theories, Rawls's version of this theory is the most prominent contemporary representative.[21] Broadly, the argument is that behind a Veil of Ignorance parties would choose a concept of justice that evaluates possible institutional arrangements in terms of the interests of the least advantaged or worst off members of the community. As no one knows what his or her own personal situation might be under any specific arrangement behind the veil of ignorance, each must consider the possibility that he or she might end up as the worst off individual in the community. Rawls asserts that parties would choose a rule of distribution that permits inequalities only if that rule provided a guarantee that all would be better off than under a rule requiring strict equality in distribution.

Rawls's theory of justice has provoked an enormous body of scholarly literature, which I do not intend to review here. In the context of this project—the issue of compensation or mitigation of transition costs—his theory appears to be of relatively limited application. In the general run of cases that have arisen both in the jurisprudence on takings and in the scholarly commentary, the claimants for compensation can rarely make the case that they are among the least advantaged members of the community (although some past urban renewal projects, for example, have had disproportionate impacts on low-income communities; trade liberalization may prejudice low-paid, low-skilled workers in certain sectors, discussed in Chapter 5; and more liberal immigration policies may similarly put at risk workers with few alternative opportunities, discussed in Chapter 7). Rather, the justification for compensation or mitigation is that these claimants would otherwise have to bear a grossly disproportionate share of the costs of policy change. A prime example of this is the classic eminent domain case, where a government or government agency wishes to acquire an existing resident's home on which to construct a public school. Here, the existing resident's wealth, before and after the taking, is largely, if not totally, irrelevant to his or her claim to compensation. Even if the resident is a multimillionaire, with many other assets, intuitively most people would think that his or her case for compensation is not significantly diminished. Similarly, in a case where a highway service station is demolished for the construction of a new highway, it seems unlikely to be relevant, either as a matter of law or considered normative intuition, whether it is a "mom and pop" enterprise or is owned by a multinational oil company.

D. COMMUNITARIANISM

Unlike individualists, communitarians see the individual as incomplete and unintelligible outside his or her social relationships and social context. In other words, an individual's identity, preferences, and life decisions are determined in part by community and group affinities. Like proponents of distributive justice, communitarians emphasize outcomes such as equity and economic security. The two outlooks differ, however, in that outcomes are important to communitarians not because equality is an end in itself, but because it is a means of achieving social solidarity. Thus, fairness and community solidarity entail sharing broadly both the burdens and benefits of citizenship.[22] In particular, policy changes that involve fracturing existing communities are likely to be resisted, at any event, without policies that ease the costs of transition for affected community members, ideally to other options within the same community. Communitarian values have been particularly influential in justifying trade protectionism generally and agricultural protectionism in particular as well as restrictive immigration policies. These matters are discussed more fully in Chapters 5, 6, and 7 respectively.

E. CORRECTIVE JUSTICE

Corrective justice, as explicated most prominently by Ernest Weinrib,[23] is a quantitative equality in which one person's gain necessarily entails another's loss, so the doing of injury by one entails the suffering of injury by another. The premise is that all individuals are juridical equals and ends in themselves, whom others cannot treat as mere means or instruments for their purposes or desires. On this view, breach of contract or tortious injury constitutes one individual's interference with the rights of another, creating an inequality in the relation between the doer of the wrong and the sufferer, which can be corrected or rectified by the doer's returning to the sufferer the value of what has been taken, thereby re-establishing the initial equality between the two. This initial equality is not defined in terms of equality of resources or status, but by equal rights to noninterference with one's person and property.

For example, drawing implicitly on this normative vein of reasoning, Levmore suggests that compensation is required when government intervention is seen as a substitute for private purchase.[24] Hence, when a government tears down a private home in order to build a public school, compensation is necessary because a private party, in a parallel situation, would have had to purchase the right to act in that way even if that party's proposed use has a higher social value than the incumbent's use. The initial equality between the doer (the government) and the sufferer (the private homeowner) is restored through rectification, whereby the doer returns to the sufferer the value of what has been taken. This view seems compelling in a range of compensation cases, although it is less helpful in cases where policy changes do not directly appropriate private property rights but rather diminish their value through regulatory or tax changes, which may alternatively be sharply focused on one or a few investors or a very broadly defined class of investors, and where the private party encroachment analogy is less apt. A corrective justice perspective might also suggest a predisposition against compensation when the conduct of the bearer of the loss from policy change has precipitated the change for welfare-enhancing reasons (for example, hazardous products or "noxious uses" in the "takings" case-law), in contrast to the innocent resident whose home is taken for a public school.

F. LIBERTARIANISM

On libertarian theories of the state,[25] the role of the state is confined to protecting preexisting private property rights and enforcing voluntarily entered contracts, along with a limited police power to regulate force, fraud, and a restricted category of socially harmful activities, often referred to in the takings literature as "noxious uses." There may also be a limited role in providing public goods, such as highways and other infrastructure, which on some libertarian theories may justify taxing citizens on the demand side, in order to overcome collective action or free-rider problems. On the supply side, eminent domain powers may be justified as a means to resolve holdout or monopoly problems, especially among multiple landowners affected by the proposed government use (e.g., a highway or railway track).[26]

The most prominent contemporary proponent of this perspective on the compensation issue is Richard Epstein. In his well-known and controversial book, *Takings*,[27] he argues from a Lockean view of private property rights that "all regulation, all taxes, and all modification of liability rules are takings of private property *prima facie* compensable by the state,"[28] subject only to a narrowly defined police power justification and a similarly restrictive interpretation of the public use condition that would limit it to classic public goods. On his view, most of the New Deal legislation and regulations adopted by the United States in the 1930s were unconstitutional as uncompensated takings.[29] Conversely, policy changes involving the removal of restrictive laws, for example, deregulation of the telecommunications, airline, and trucking industries, would not, presumably, attract compensation (although some libertarians seem to take an opposing view).[30]

Epstein's views have been challenged from a number of perspectives—from even more austere libertarians who view his interpretation of the "Takings" Clause as permitting an excessive role for the state,[31] to scholars on the left who view it as negating any redistributive role for the state,[32] to scholars who challenge his interpretation of Locke's natural rights theory of property rights,[33] to scholars who view his interpretation as confusingly and loosely eliding natural rights and utilitarian theories of property rights,[34] to constitutional theorists who object to his "originalist" theory of the US Constitution both generally and internally, including his assertion that the Founders actually intended to espouse such a minimalist theory of the State.[35]

A more sympathetic view of Epstein's position is that, contrary to Kaplow's assumption that most policy changes are socially desirable, in a representative democracy factionalism and rent-seeking by special interests may often predominate over the greater social welfare.[36] This interpretation of his theory shares much in common with the Pareto efficiency or "fiscal illusion" rationale for a broad compensation principle and reflects a Public Choice view of the political process (as discussed below), but is susceptible to similar objections in the present context. That is, uncertainty as to the impacts on the behavior of government officials of a requirement of on-budget financial outlays for the cost of policy changes, as well as a strong status quo bias in the distribution of welfare resulting from the near-veto that would be held by propsective losers, risks taking some classes of losers too seriously. It also implies a massive role for judicial review in economic policymaking that may be seen as anti-democratic.[37] Nevertheless, it is difficult to reject Epstein's argument that the relatively sharp dichotomy maintained in the US constitutional case law on the Fifth Amendment between physical encroachments and regulatory takings is indefensible and often incoherent. Taking a substance-over-form approach, clearly physical takings and regulatory takings involve only differences in degree (and sometimes not even that in cases of minor physical encroachments, which are typically compensable, compared to regulatory "wipe-outs," which often are not).[38]

Reflecting on this tangled skein of sharply divergent normative arguments as to the proper scope of a compensation principle for transition costs, ranging from Kaplow's strong "no compensation" presumption to Epstein's "always compensation" presumption, one can hardly be surprised at the sometimes incoherent jurisprudence on this issue, the sharply divergent scholarly commentary, and the multitude of political responses observable in different jurisdictions. That actual compensation or transition cost mitigation practice in the real world is light years removed from either Kaplow's or Epstein's polarities is suggestive of an important range of determinants that their (and other) normative analyses neglect. As Shaviro notes, "The literature's tendency towards corner solutions, in which [rule] change ostensibly justifies transitional adjustment either almost always or almost never, should excite skepticism."[39]

II. The Role of Compensation and Other Mitigation Transition Strategies in Positive Theories of the Political Process

A. THE ECONOMICS OF POLITICS: PUBLIC CHOICE THEORY

Public Choice Theory is derived from a series of seminal works by economists, including most prominently, Anthony Downs,[40] Mancur Olson,[41] James Buchanan and Gordon Tullock,[42] and George Stigler,[43] which essentially model the political process as an implicit marketplace for public polices where policies are demanded and supplied reflecting various quid pro quos, shaped by an overriding political support maximization imperative. Although economic analysis has traditionally conceived of the role of government as a *deus ex machina* that eliminated one or another unfortunate allocative consequences of market failure, economics became compelled to confront the logic of its own behavioral postulates. If parties to private market transactions are for the most part to be presumed to be rational actors attempting to maximize their self-interest, whether in the form of increased profits or increased utility, then at least two important, albeit obvious, implications are likely to follow from this presumption with respect to collective behavior. First, many, perhaps most, individuals are unlikely to have any ex ante preference for market allocations of resources over collective allocations of resources, but will presumably choose to invest resources in pursuing economic self-interest through either market activity or political activity, depending on where their net gains are likely to be the greater. Second, just as with private markets whose functioning is presumed to be dominated by self-interest, so in political "markets" one should assume that relevant actors—voters (demanders), politicians (suppliers), bureaucrats, and the media—tend to be motivated principally by self-interest and not by some collective commitment to the broader public interest.[44]

Thus, to attain or retain political office, politicians will find it rational to fashion policies that exploit various political asymmetries: between marginal voters (uncommitted voters in swing electorates) and inframarginal voters; between well-informed and ill-informed voters; and between concentrated and diffuse interest groups facing differential political-mobilization costs (collective action problems). Moreover, because of short electoral cycles, they will favor policies with immediate and visible benefits that defer costs to later time periods or render them less visible (e.g., by moving them off-budget). Bureaucrats will be motivated to promote policies that maximize their power, pay, and prestige. Regulators will seek a quiet life by coming to accommodations with the interests they are supposed to be regulating and perhaps also by enhancing their prospects of employment in the regulated industry after their tenure as regulators (the "capture" theory of regulation). The media, in order to maximize readership or viewing audiences, thereby enhancing advertising revenues, will trivialize complex policy issues, rely on ready-made sources of information that reflect the biases of established interests, sensationalize mishaps unreflective of systemic policy failures, and turn over issues at a rapid rate with minimal investigative follow-up in order to cater to readers' and viewers' limited attention spans (rational ignorance).

B. THE IMPLICATIONS OF PUBLIC CHOICE THEORY FOR TRANSITION POLICIES

Public Choice theory suggests various implications for the politics of transition cost mitigation. Reflecting some strains in pluralistic theories of democracy,[45] political markets contain some implicit adjustment processes that, over time, may tend to offset gains and losses secured or sustained by different interests on particular issues. Where there is a non-uniform distribution of intensities of preferences among the voters on different policy issues, politicians are likely to fashion policies that appeal to impassioned or highly mobilized minorities at the expense of less organized, less passionate majorities. Given a whole range of issues that must be addressed by government over time with differing configurations of high intensity and low intensity voter interests surrounding each issue, it may be the case that a group of losers on one issue, because it is a low intensity majority, will win on other issues where it is a highly intense minority—a process often facilitated by logrolling among citizens' political representatives. However, there is at least one type of collectively imposed loss that is systematically less likely to be washed out by logrolling over the long run. Losses that are both large in relation to the loser's net worth and substantially larger than the losses that usually result from legislative decisions are less likely to be canceled out by prior or subsequent gains derived from the political market (e.g., the classic eminent domain case such as the taking of a private residence for a public school).

Where the prospective losers from a major regulatory or policy change face a strategic choice between accepting explicit compensation or opposing the change, it will often be rational for them to oppose the change, particularly if ex ante compensation is unlikely to address all the uncertainties associated with the particular losses induced by the change. If the gainers from the policy change are required to underwrite the explicit costs of compensation, here the position is reversed: they face a certain up-front cost, in terms of compensation payments, and uncertain long-term benefits from the regulatory change and the possibility of future political reversal (the problem of time inconsistency). Faced with potentially equivocal positions by losers and gainers with respect to an explicit compensation strategy, politicians are likely to ask themselves whether, through a highly visible expenditure policy in some completely unrelated policy context, greater political returns can be realized than compensating losers from regulatory or other policy changes. To the extent that it is politically desirable to mitigate transition costs, low-visibility, off-budget strategies such as grandfathering or phased or delayed implementation are likely to be preferred, and are generally likely to be biased in favor of concentrated and politically well-organized interests. Conversely, the compensation or mitigation of isolated, widely dispersed, or temporally attenuated losses is less likely to attract political support.

C. THE LIMITS OF PUBLIC CHOICE THEORY[46]

Public Choice theory offers many valuable insights into the policymaking process and is an important antidote to wishful thinking or utopianism in considerations of democratic politics. It does, however, have a number of important limitations. First, its behavioral postulates are ambiguously specified: does it assume purely self-regarding behavior on the part of all relevant actors, or a broader concept of utility-maximization that might include an almost infinite number of other values, including altruism (albeit at the risk of loss of predictive capacity, or even tautology)? Second, despite the vast differences in institutional regimes across different societies, Public Choice theory takes a jurisdiction's existing institutions as given, and has poorly developed explanations of how particular institutions initially emerged, evolved over time, and may change in the future. Third, and relatedly, Public Choice theory has a poorly developed framework for identifying the factors that may disrupt existing political equilibria and lead to major policy changes over time.

More eclectic positive theories of the political process attempt to grapple with these issues, although, it should be acknowledged, at the price of loss of parsimony and explanatory or predictive crispness. I briefly review such theories below.

III. Alternative Explanations of Political Behavior

In canvassing the myriad approaches to explaining the political and policy process, I have adopted a typology of explanations of political behavior developed by Craig Parsons.[47] It is one of several possible organizing schemes,[48] but one that seems well suited to the task at hand. According to Parsons, explanations of political behavior can be classified as one of four types: structural, institutional, psychological, and ideational.[49] I briefly discuss each in turn.

A. STRUCTURAL EXPLANATIONS

Structural arguments largely rely on immutable constraints on policy options, such as geography, natural resources, and the contingencies of history. Although they may also in part rely on dynamic constraints on resources, for the purposes of these explanations, it is assumed that they are not manipulable by participating actors over the temporal scope of the policy issue in question—that is, they are taken as exogenous.[50] Explaining action as a direct function of these exogenous constraints implies that there is little role for interpretation and assumes, at the very least, an intersubjective rationality that guides individual decision-making. As these rational decision-making processes are not (as yet) empirically demonstrable, most scholars rely on evidence of behavior supportive of rationality combined with logical claims, and broadly "rational-looking" decision-making. It is within this school of scholarship that a standard Public Choice account would fall, as would a standard Marxist account. Explanations of contemporary economic performance derived from, for example, historical settler mortality rates at the time of conquest[51] or the legal regime transplanted to a colony are also of this type.[52]

B. INSTITUTIONAL EXPLANATIONS

In general, institutions are understood as organizations and sets of rules that constrain and channel the behavior of the actors operating within them. By many accounts they shape incentive structures and, in turn, raise the costs of some options to the point of infeasibility and lower others to the point of near necessity. Although treating political institutions solely as external incentive structures leads to a limited understanding of their overall impact on political decision-making, this approach—which can be frequently aligned with Public Choice approaches, via rational choice institutionalism[53]—has produced a good deal of useful scholarship with respect to institutional design.

A prime example of this perspective is Tsebelis's concept of "veto players." A veto player is defined as "an individual or collective actor whose agreement is required for a policy decision."[54] This theory suggests that the likelihood of achieving sufficient agreement to enact a change is reduced where there is an increase in the number of veto players in a system, a dissimilarity of policy positions among veto players, or an increase in the cohesion of a given veto player's constituent group. In short, the more actors whose assent is required for a regulatory change, the less likely that change becomes. The number of veto points is affected by institutional design (e.g., executive and legislative organization, the presence and form of federalism, and voting procedures),[55] as well as less formally by the presence of entrenched interests such as farmers' organizations in the agricultural policy sector (as discussed in Chapter 5) or business associations and labor unions on matters of immigration policy (as discussed in Chapter 6). As the number of veto players increases, so too does the likelihood that compensation or other forms of mitigation will be necessary to effect the desired change.

A more expansive conception of institutions sees them not only as constraining behavior and altering incentive structures, but also as providers of standard operating procedures, behavioral norms, and identities to those who function within them. Conceived of in this way, institutions shape the subjective maps and preferences of those interacting with them, providing internalized logics of appropriateness.[56] Institutions in this sense are seen as collections of rules and routines that define appropriate behavior.[57] Thus, although "a good deal of behavior is goal-oriented or strategic... the range of options canvassed by a strategic actor is likely to be circumscribed by a culturally-specific sense of appropriate action."[58] For example, although there may be an argument for adopting a "zero-growth" approach to addressing the challenge of climate change,[59] it is unlikely that policy analysts will seriously consider it: it does not resonate with fundamental Western precepts of government policymaking.[60] Moreover, even if it were advanced, the institutional norms of the bureaucracy and political establishment would not be receptive to it. As I discuss more fully in Chapter 8 on climate change policy, a zero-growth policy does not make sense given a basic set of background normative beliefs that include the promotion of economic growth as a central policy goal.

A more dynamic institutional approach suggests that change is at least partially the result of unintended outcomes and randomness, meaning that the results cannot be controlled by fiat or fully predicted.[61] In the most basic sense, it can be expressed as the assertion that "what happened at an earlier point in time will affect the possible outcomes of a sequence of events occurring at a later point in time."[62] Inherent in this approach is a rejection of the idea that social institutions, policies, and regulation are, at some level, directly reducible to individual behavior. As institutions grow they are likely to acquire a certain inertia, leading them to develop resistance to change independent of the logic of their initial formation. This phenomenon, often termed path dependence, is principally attributed to positive feedback mechanisms or increasing returns. In other words, initial steps in a particular direction have self-reinforcing properties.[63]

The challenges of institutional reform in developing countries, discussed in Chapter 9, provides ample evidence of the importance of historical context and enculturated interests and ideas in conditioning the viability and efficacy of institutional reforms in these countries.[64] If there is one concrete lesson that can be taken from attempts to foster development through the top-down imposition of "one size fits all" packages of institutional reforms it is that their effects are not constant across jurisdictions.[65] Moreover, such experiences suggest that the layering of institutions, particularly the imposition of formal change on top of a traditional structure, may have unintended and potentially perverse effects.[66]

C. PSYCHOLOGICAL EXPLANATIONS

Psychological approaches are premised on the existence of more or less hardwired mental processes and emphasize the impact of systematic biases, misperceptions, instincts, or affects.[67] Several insights of behavioral economics are particularly relevant in this regard.

For example, the endowment effect describes the predilection of individuals to value the things they have more highly than the things they do not.[68] Put differently, individuals tend to feel the loss of something they have more than not gaining something of equal value (loss aversion).[69] A key implication of this is that individuals are likely to attach greater importance to the loss in value of assets in their possession (at least nominally) as a result of a regulatory or policy change than the prospective opportunities for gain that might be closed off as the result of other public policies.[70]

The availability heuristic describes the tendency of individuals to base their estimates of probability and importance on particularly salient information they can readily call to mind (perhaps because of pesonal experiences). The problem with this proclivity is that memorable events are often unrepresentative. Relatedly, individuals also tend to improperly weight new information. One manifestation of this is a tendency to excessively privilege information that one first comes into contact with regarding a particular topic or issue, even if the reason that this "anchor" information was encountered first was arbitrary.[71] For example, individuals' prior attitudes toward climate change play a strong role in their evaluation of the credibility of scientific findings—those with value-based predispositions against global warming are substantially less likely to find compelling scientific evidence supporting its existence than do others, regardless of the source. These biases appear to play important roles in, inter alia, debates over climate change and the limited efficacy of policies and international negotiations to date, issues discussed more fully in Chapter 8.

Group dynamics also affect individual attitudes to current policy changes. Much social science literature finds that when people find themselves in groups of like-minded people who perhaps share a moderate predisposition to a particular view of an issue, they are likely to move to more extreme versions of this view through group interactions and reinforcement, often triggering information and reputation cascades.[72]

Perhaps the most troubling aspect of Public Choice theory is the assumption that self-interest can be generalized into particular sets of self-regarding goals for particular types of actors: politicians seek election or re-election and trade their legislative capacity for money or votes; business organizations seek to prevent regulation that would impose costs on their operations (e.g., caps on carbon emission) and motivate deregulation that would increase their profits (e.g., the removal of health and safety regulations); bureaucrats seek to increase their budgets, power, and prestige; and regulators are captives of the interests they purport to regulate. This understanding of behavior does not map well onto the real world of politics, however parsimonious it may be and however crisp its predictions.

Politicians may make concessions for electoral reasons, but they also take principled stands on some issues. Not all interest groups seek to advance the interests of only their members (e.g., Greenpeace or Human Rights Watch), nor are the interests they advance always material (e.g., the American Civil Liberties Union). Bureaucracies routinely manage (or are compelled) to reduce their budgets, eliminate services, and cut jobs. Regulators often discharge their regulatory responsibilities effectively. As Alan Jacobs has recently noted, politicians in electoral democracies can and do adopt policies that entail short-term costs in return for larger, long-run social gains (e.g., investments in infrastructure, education, research and development, environmental conservation). The controlling factor, he contends, is that they must be able to do so within the constraints of electoral safety while maintaining confidence on the part of policy elites and organized interest groups that the benefits will be of the scale and certainty necessary to justify the risks, and that there is sufficient institutional capacity to implement and sustain such policies.[73]

Experimental research also suggests that individuals are willing to make personal sacrifices in order to punish what they believe to be unfair or unjust behavior on the part of others. A notable example of this is the Ultimatum Game. One actor (A) is told to propose a division of an amount of money between herself and another actor (B). If B accepts the proposal, it is adopted and A and B receive payment accordingly. If B rejects the proposal, neither actor receives anything.[74] From a purely rational perspective, A ought to propose a division along the lines of 99 percent for herself and 1 percent for B: B has an incentive to accept the offer as he or she is made better off by it, if only by a marginal amount. Generally, however, this kind of offer is rejected, as are most offers below an 80–20 percent division. In fact, the average proposed division tends to be about 67–33 percent in favor of A. In a similar experiment, the Dictator Game, B has no opportunity to reject the proposal. Nevertheless, B tends to receive a substantial percentage (albeit less than in the Ultimatum Game). In short, "the evidence suggests that, for many people, self-interest maximization can be somewhat tempered by the affirmative desire to treat others fairly."[75]

D. IDEATIONAL EXPLANATIONS

Ideational claims are particularistic in that they rely on the consequences of prior contingent actions and trace the causes of action to some constellation of practices, norms, and ideas through which individuals interpret the world.[76] There are, however, limits. As Parsons notes, "people may invent a stunning range of beliefs and practices, but they do not quite do so in infinitely flexible ways."[77] Popular and elite beliefs about the appropriate ordering of society and role of the state play a pivotal, though not determinative, role in the shaping of attitudes toward particular policy changes and whether or not compensation or mitigation is appropriate.[78] These beliefs tend to remain relatively static,[79] and serve as an important foundation to which policy proposals must generally be tied, in one form or another, in order to gain popular acceptance.[80] However, the generality of these values and beliefs means that concrete policy recommendations require translation and simplification in order to appeal to individuals' senses of fairness and appropriateness. Linking policy proposals to core beliefs and values is not a precise exercise; in many circumstances multiple, potentially contradictory associations can be made through strategic framing and communication.[81]

Ideas about cause and effect—based on the recommendations of communities of experts,[82] the proposals of advocacy coalitions,[83] or bureaucratic analysis[84] — also have a substantial role to play in shaping the type of policy instruments that receive consideration, as well as their political feasibility. First, uncertainty may cause decision-makers to be unable to identify their allies or the strategies that will enable them to achieve their goals. Second, the inability of existing institutions to address emergent problems—or the perception that they may not be able to—may make those institutions unworkable and untrusted, leading to a search for new approaches, evaluative criteria, or policy venues. Thus, decision-makers have several incentives to consult experts under conditions of uncertainty: they can provide insight into the likely effects of given actions; they can shed light on the complex interactions of various issues and forces; they can help to define the interests of the state and of individual decision-makers. In politicized situations experts can assist decision-makers in advancing their preferred outcomes, although possibly in a modified form, by justifying or legitimating a desired policy by reference to "expert opinion." Advocacy coalitions or networks, be they domestic[85] or transnational,[86] are identifiable by the centrality of values or principled ideas as a common bond between members.[87] They can also be characterized as holding a belief in the ability of individuals to "make a difference," their creative use of information, and their employment of sophisticated and targeted political campaigning. These networks seek to change both policy outcomes and the terms and nature of debate. In doing so, they "'frame' issues to make them 'fit' with favorable institutional venues." Further, they "contribute to changing perceptions that both state and society actors may have of their interests, identities, and preferences, transforming their discursive positions, and ultimately to changing procedures, policies and behaviour."[88]

The effectiveness of these groups stems from their ability to construct cognitive frames that successfully link their preferred approach to existing values, ideas of fairness, and other underlying currents of political culture. To accomplish this, they employ some combination of four strategies. First, by generating and disseminating alternative information (increasingly through social media), leading to the construction of simple right-versus-wrong frames in order to persuade people or stimulate action. The information must be both timely and dramatic. Second, by invoking symbols and stories to enable actors, who may be quite removed from the actual events or issues in question, to make sense of the situation. Third, by calling upon more powerful actors to employ their influence or power in either material terms—linking the issue to money, goods, or prestige at the international level in order to persuade or coerce more powerful actors to act—or in moral terms, through the "mobilization of shame." Fourth, by holding more powerful actors publicly accountable to their commitments.[89]

Learning, defined as an evidence-based change of beliefs,[90] also has a role to play in determining the feasibility of policy changes. Bureaucrats and others are likely to learn from both their own experience and the experience of other jurisdictions—be they bad or good. Such analyses tend to focus on policy impact, although political outcomes (i.e., whether a given policy has been politically popular) may also matter.[91] This learning may occur in a plethora of ways, but the basic insight is that observations of the operation and effects of policies in jurisdictions or situations believed to be similar will shape the perceived feasibility of a given policy option.

The framing of policy proposals and solutions also conditions the political viability of a proposed policy change.[92] The ability of a programmatic idea to be framed as congruent with or supportive of central cultural values or public sentiments is, in many cases, an essential component of its adoption. "Every public policy problem," Baumgartner and Jones argue, "is usually understood, even by the politically sophisticated, in simplified and symbolic terms."[93] It is not uncommon, they suggest, for divergent opinions regarding policy solutions to be understandable predominantly in reference to two competing sets of policy images, which, followed to their respective conclusions, lead to irreconcilable policy preferences. Thus, "[p]rivate problems need to be linked to public causes in order to demand governmental attention. Argumentation and the construction of policy images play a role in this."[94] Success in doing so can be conceptualized as creating a form of intellectual path dependence, locking in one's preferred outcomes by framing the problem in such a way as to make it the "appropriate" solution.[95]

E. THE IMPLICATIONS OF ALTERNATIVE EXPLANATIONS OF POLITICAL BEHAVIOR FOR TRANSITION POLICIES IN THE POLITICAL PROCESS

For present purposes, the limitations of the Public Choice conception of the role of the individual are twofold: (1) individuals are not wholly self-interested, and (2) individuals are not fully rational. The ways in which individuals fail to fully conform to these ideal-types is shaped by both inherent cognitive limits and biases and the social and material context in which they develop and operate. Because individuals rely on heuristics, habits, and imperfect information to make decisions, those decisions will not always result in the desired outcome, from either the subjective perspective of the actor or from an "objective," social welfare–based perspective. Because individuals' normative values, such as notions of fairness and justice, are conceived of as general principles and may often be in competition with one another, the way in which those values are manifested in assessments of the fairness of policy proposals and the justice of (non) compensation or (non) mitigation will vary based on the way in which they are framed. These factors will affect the way in which the interests of particular groups, and the nature of the interests themselves, will be advanced in the political arena. Moreover, the heuristics and cognitive maps employed by individuals to understand and evaluate policy proposals will be systematically shaped by their institutional environments, as will their expectations and, at least to some extent, their preferences.

The boundedness of individual rationality means that although policy proposals may be more or less conducive to framing in a way that will attract support from publics or policymakers, in many instances it will be possible to present a given proposal in ways that resonate with different cognitive and normative beliefs. This means that communication and translation will play an important role in determining feasibility. So, too, will the visibility of an issue. Behind closed doors, justification beyond an implicit desire to extract rents may be unnecessary. But, as public awareness of an issue increases, so too does the importance of issue framing—of persuading attentive publics of the justness of one's preferred policy option.

What, then, are the practical applications of these insights to the transition cost mitigation issue? In situations where a government regulatory scheme is responsible for creating things of value, particularly where this has been done *intentionally* as in the case of public pension entitlements (discussed in Chapter 3), the long-standing mortgage interest tax deductibility provision in the United States (discussed in Chapter 4), trade protectionism (discussed in Chapter 5), or the creation of property-like milk production quotas (discussed in Chapter 6), moves to deregulate or otherwise lower the value of participants' investments, are the most likely to require compensation or mitigation for at least three reasons. First, individuals tend to attach greater importance to out-of-pocket losses than to prospective gains. Thus, those whose assets suffer a substantial decrease in net worth have a greater incentive, and are therefore more likely, to mobilize against policy change than those who are prevented from achieving gains of the same magnitude. Second, the need to compensate those who lose investments as a result of regulatory change is more plausibly framed and presented to the general public as an issue of fairness than the loss of opportunities to gain. In turn, this should increase public willingness to accept the cost burden of compensation or other forms of mitigation, reducing the likelihood of mobilization against such measures. Additionally, the longer a program has been in place, the more likely it will have come to form an integral part of beneficiaries' expectations and the more likely those individuals are to identify with one another and mobilize to defend what they perceive as their due.[96] As individuals live with(in) particular regulatory environments, they are not only more likely to adapt to these situations, but are also more likely to accept them as appropriate. This, in turn, is likely to engender a greater reliance on the policy. Individuals may also form identities based on their shared reliance or experiences, which might also be sufficient to overcome collective action problems. Indeed, this appears to have been the case in France where, as discussed in Chapter 3, widespread protests at the increase in retirement age contributed to the the downfall of the government and subsequent repeal of the measure. Third, a failure to provide some form of compensation or mitigation weakens the credibility of commitments made by governments and their agents to individuals or organizations, driving up future costs of shaping private sector behavior and the size of incentives (such as subsidies and tax breaks) necessary to induce specific desired private investments, given the risks involved.

It is also likely that the scale of a proposed policy change will shape whether and how compensation or mitigation ought to be provided. In general, the more foundational a policy change, the greater the relative impact of values and principles on the decision-making process. This is particularly true in situations of uncertainty where interests and causal relationships are unclear. In order to be successful in such circumstances, policy proposals must both resonate with core beliefs about fairness and ideas about the appropriate role of the state. In this process, experts can assist not only in providing solutions, but also in identifying problems and interests by drawing out cause-and-effect relationships and explaining the probable consequences of particular courses of action. In so doing, they can also provide political cover by creating narratives that present a given policy change as the only or most logical possible solution. Expert opinion, however, is far from a panacea for overcoming opposition to reforms. In the case of climate change, for example, the scientific community is as close to consensus as is reasonably possible that human activity is affecting the global climate in a way that will have severe future impacts on the environment in general, and particular subsets of civilization. Nevertheless, as outlined in Chapter 8, little is being done on the scale necessary to address these problems.

The framing of a given issue will also condition both elite and popular reactions to particular proposals. Although individuals' normative values are generally stable, the boundedness of their rationality means that the translation of those values into concrete policy prescriptions is an imprecise endeavor, one that is influenced by the sequence of exposure to information, the content of cognitive maps and heuristics provided by institutions, and the strategic construction and communication of norms, symbols, and narratives. Advocacy coalitions and networks may actively engage in attempts to reframe a given issue or even redefine the nature of the problem by disseminating information, or creating symbols and narratives that frame a change or proposal in a particular way. Additionally, because individuals are often willing to make sacrifices in the interests of fairness, opposition to a proposed change from those with a vested interest in maintaining the status quo may be lessened by convincing them that fairness does not entitle them to compensation or mitigation. Conversely, compensation or mitigation may be made more palatable on the same grounds. This, as Chapter 4 notes, is frequently the case during the negotiation of trade liberalization treaties. An additional example of the importance of framing is evident with respect to immigration policy (as discussed in Chapter 7): on the one hand, labor is not likely to be sympathetic to the liberalization of immigration on the basis of increasing the workforce, as this may cause downward pressure on wages and employment. However, restrictive immigration policies are less likely to gain popular support if liberalization can be framed as an issue of human rights, family reunification, and enhancing access to highly skilled labor that will generate positive employment spin-offs and higher levels of innovation.

The existence of organized interest groups and the possibility of conflict also suggests that the formal and informal organization of the political system and policy area at issue will also play an important role with regard to the provision of compensation or other mitigation strategies. In general, the greater the number of individuals or organizations who could potentially veto a given policy change, the more difficult change will be to implement without compensation or other forms of mitigation. As such, the allocation of authority and responsibility in a political system and the malleability of a given policy area will affect the ability of actors to shift policy venues and attract public attention to a given issue. Because few, if any, policy issues can be thought of as lying exclusively within the purview of a particular agency or ministry, active attempts to reframe an issue may lead to a change in the composition of a decision-making body or a change in decision-making venue. This, in turn, may bring in new veto players or eliminate others. At the same time, it can also increase the public visibility of an issue, making the justification for or against a proposed change (i.e., the manner in which it is framed) increasingly salient.

Finally, the arrangement and internal logics of institutions in a given polity are intimately connected with public and elite perceptions of the appropriate role of the state in a given area. These arrangements are contingent on historical decisions that establish particular institutional trajectories that affect the desirability of given policies insofar as they condition the capacity of politicians and bureaucracies to provide relevant information and effectively utilize particular policy instruments.

This suggests that in practice there are not universally desirable, not to mention desired, policy prescriptions. Rather, the desirability of a given policy will be conditioned by the attitudes and expectations of mass publics and elites as well as by the particular constellation of standard operating procedures and institutional capacities that make up the machinery of a given state apparatus. The importance of these considerations is exemplified by the challenges confronting recent attempts at institutional reform in developing countries (discussed in Chapter 9).

IV. Conclusion

Returning to my initial reservations about the existing literature on transition policies, I believe that there are several issues that limit the overall usefulness of this literature for dealing with whether and when to compensate regulatory losers or otherwise mitigate their losses. Perhaps foremost among these is the overemphasis on purportedly universal prescriptions. For example, Kaplow argues that the simultaneous consideration of risk and incentives leads to the conclusion that government transitional relief is generally undesirable. According to him, market mechanisms—most notably contractual arrangements, insurance, and diversification—permit private actors to make arrangements that provide an efficient trade-off between the benefits of risk spreading and the social costs that result from distorted incentives.[97] Not only is this proposition contestable in its own terms in many contexts, but it may very well create an environment in which long-run, welfare-enhancing policy changes are not made, as a result of an inability to overcome the opposition of negatively affected interests, substantially exacerbating the risk of policy paralysis.

I also believe that the focus on the US Constitution's Takings Clause and the related idea of explicit compensation, rather than implicit (and much more common) mitigation strategies such as grandfathering, exceptions, and delayed or phased implementation, has led scholarly debate in this area astray. In particular, it focuses attention on the courts as the ultimate arbiter of losses and the determination of "just compensation" (as opposed to other transition cost mitigation strategies). In so doing, it draws attention away from the political institutions tasked with developing and implementing policy decisions: institutions whose decisions—regarding not only transition strategies, but whether to implement a given change at all—play a much more important role in shaping policy. Moreover, judicial decision-making in this area tends to be an all-or-nothing affair, adding additional uncertainty to regulatory change and rendering the type of bargaining or compromises—"politicking"—that would result in a more tractable policy reform strategy impossible.

In order to anchor the foregoing discussion of approaches to transition costs in concrete policy contexts, in the balance of this book I briefly describe and critically assess transition policies in seven policy contexts: public pension reform, mortgage interest deductibility, trade liberalization, agricultural supply management, immigration policy, climate change, and institutional reform in developing countries. Although the contexts and challenges of each of these seven policy contexts differ widely, they share in common the centrality of transition costs as a potential impediment to generally socially desirable policy reforms. Only the first two are primarily domestic in their policy focus; the other five combine domestic and international policy issues, which is the way of the modern world. Based in part on these case studies, I conclude this book with some reflections on politically optimal transition policies.

{ 3 }

Public Pensions: Reconciling Fiscal Sustainability with Intergenerational Equity

I. Introduction

In May of 2010, the government of France announced that it would increase the eligibility age for public pension benefits. The minimum eligibility age would be increased by two years to 62, and eligibility for full benefits would come at 67 instead of 65. Employment minister Eric Woerth noted that similar reforms had been carried out in many European countries. Woerth said that, given the perilous state of French pension scheme finances, "there is no magical solution...working for longer is inevitable."[1]

Many French people very strongly disagreed with this assessment. Over the summer and fall of 2010, a series of general strikes protesting the reform gripped the country. More than a million people took to the streets, and 1400 were arrested.[2] France's largest oil port was blockaded for 24 days, creating widespread fuel shortages.[3] In a poll taken at the height of the strikes, 59 percent of French people stated that they wanted the protests to continue.[4] There was a determined opposition filibuster in the Senate, and the pension reform passed in October 2010 only after the government invoked emergency powers in the constitution.[5] Shortly after defeating the previous government in the 2012 election, President François Hollande moved to honor his election pledge and restore the eligibility ages to their previous levels.[6]

Why have many other wealthy countries increased benefit eligibility ages in their public pension programs? Is public outrage an inevitable consequence of such measures? What does public pension policy tell us about transition costs? This case study seeks to illuminate these questions by drawing on Alan Jacobs's recent notable book, *Governing for the Long Term*,[7] in addition to the analytical tools developed in Chapter 2 of this book.

This case study begins by describing the public pension sustainability problems that aging populations have created in many developed countries. Increasing the benefit eligibility age is one response to the sustainability problem, which has strong support in the literature reviewed below, and which has been adopted by over half of all OECD countries.[8] However, this reform imposes a number of different types of losses on all current contributors to a public pension scheme, and the total loss is greatest for those contributors who are closest to the pre-reform eligibility age. As France's experience suggests, pension reform can create enormous controversy and can even be derailed when its "losers" are not taken seriously enough. Nonetheless, many other countries have increased the eligibility age with limited opposition. The two transition strategies most frequently deployed are the *phase-in* of reforms and the *grandfathering* of existing benefit recipients.

Considered in light of the theories and concepts introduced in Chapter 2, grandfathering and phase-in appear to be pragamtically effective ways to facilitate a welfare-maximizing reform that may otherwise be politically impossible. Appropriately calibrated phase-in is also normatively sound, insofar as it can equalize the total losses experienced by contributors of different ages. Grandfathering is more difficult to justify in a principled fashion, as it may unfairly confine the burden of reform to younger contributors and unborn generations.

II. Public Pension Plans and the Sustainability Problem

Public pension plans, such as Social Security Retirement Benefits in the United States and the Canada Pension Plan, are supported by mandatory contributions or taxes, and pay benefits to individuals who have reached a certain age.[9] In most public pensions, the benefits are "defined," which means that they do not fluctuate with market returns unless they are amended by policymakers.[10] Public pensions are "pay-as-you-go" but are at present partially "funded."[11] This means that current contributions are used to pay benefits to current recipients, while any surplus is remitted to a reserve fund that is invested.[12] The reserve fund, including investment returns therefrom, is used to cover the shortfall between contributions and benefit obligations caused by demographic shifts in the proportions of contributors and recipients.

A sustainability problem occurs in a public pension plan when the projected benefit obligations of the plan exceed the projected contribution receipts and reserve funds. Most public pension plans in OECD countries have experienced a sustainability problem within the last 40 years, and several are presently experiencing one.[13] In the absence of reform or unexpected investment returns, a sustainability problem will eventually render a public pension plan unable to meet its benefit obligations.

The primary cause of these sustainability problems is a decreasing *old-age support ratio*.[14] This measure is the ratio of the number of people in a population who are considered to be of working age (generally 20–64) to the number of people who are eligible to receive retirement benefits.[15] In 1950, the OECD average was seven

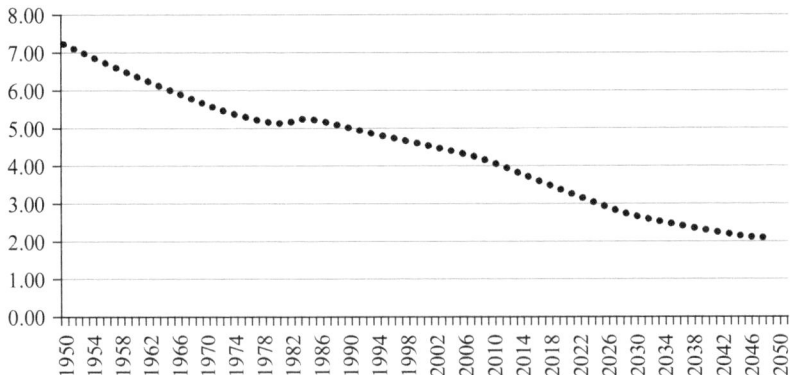

FIGURE 3.1 *Old-Age Support Ratios in OECD Countries: Historical and Projected Values, 1950–2050.*

Data from OECD Staff, Pensions at a Glance 2011: Retirement-Income Systems in Oecd and G20 Countries (New York: Organization for Economic Co-Operation and Development, 2011)

working people per eligible pension beneficiary; by 2047, it is projected that there will be only two workers for every pension-age person in these countries.[16]

The declining old-age support ratio is driven by two demographic phenomena. First, average lifespans at retirement age have increased dramatically. Since 1960, the average 65-year-old in an OECD country has gained almost five years in expected lifespan.[17] The United Nations predicts a further average lifespan increase of more than three years by 2050.[18] Because defined benefit public pensions pay a guaranteed stream of benefits for as long as the recipient lives, average lifespan has a direct impact on total plan obligations (Figure 3.1).[19]

The second major contributor to the sustainability problem is diminished fertility. The OECD fertility rate fell from 2.26 children per woman in the 1975–1980 period to 1.69 per woman in 2005–2010.[20] The problem has been exacerbated by this pattern of postwar baby boom followed by baby bust. While the "Boomer" generation is now starting to become eligible for benefits, members of the "Bust" generation are beginning their working and contributing lives. This demographic pattern spurred many countries to use the Boomers' contributions to create reserve funds after fertility started declining. However, these funds are in most cases insufficient to resolve the sustainability problem.[21]

III. Policy Responses to the Sustainability Problem

The public pension sustainability problem in wealthy countries has been obvious for several decades and has spawned a variety of responses across the OECD. In addition to their technical and economic consequences, public pension reform options have complex distributional effects.[22] Although increasing life expectancy and decreasing fertility have major benefits,[23] they also have a cost, which is most obviously reflected in the pension sustainability challenge. A key question facing contemporary policymakers is how this cost ought to be allocated among different sectors of the population. Closely related to this, Alan Jacobs has called attention to the *intertemporal* consequences of public pension reform.[24] Jacobs proposes that policy options be analyzed not only in terms of how they distribute resources among different groups in the near term, but also in terms of how they distribute resources between consumption possibilities in the short term and consumption possibilities in the long term. It will be shown below that policy choices in this sphere, and the transitional mechanisms that accompany them, have both redistributive and intertemporal consequences. First, however, it is necessary to identify the options available to a state confronting a public pension sustainability problem.

Reducing benefit payments is one possibility. Fourteen of the largest OECD countries have cut pension benefits, by an average of 20 percent, in order to increase sustainability.[25] Several of these have tied benefit levels to life expectancy, so that increases in average lifespan automatically produce reductions in benefit levels.[26] Another alternative is to increase revenues. For example, Canada increased its CPP contribution rate from 5.6 percent to 9.9 percent of earnings (up to a maximum insurable gross income of $50,100 per annum) over a five-year period beginning in 1997.[27] From a distributional point of view, reducing benefits divides the loss among current recipients and contributors, whereas increasing contributions places it entirely on contributors.[28] A third option is to increase the cap on income from which contributions are levied. This would have a redistributive effect—from high earners to middle and low earners—as well as placing the burden solely on contributors.

A more drastic response to the sustainability challenge is to transform public pension schemes into "individual accounts."[29] Under these reform proposals, some or all of the contributions currently collected and administered by the state would instead be directed into investable accounts, over which contributors would have some control.[30] This reform was adopted in Chile, and is the subject of ongoing debate in the United States. However, it has not gained much traction elsewhere insofar as it would mean abandoning or compromising the popular defined benefit guarantee. It would also potentially make retirement security depend on prudent individual choices and good luck in the stock market. Those whose investments do not succeed could be impoverished or dependent on other government benefits. Individual accounts may also involve higher total administration and investment fees than a state-run program.

The primary alternative, and in most respects more appropriate, means by which to improve pension plan sustainability is increasing the age at which one can receive full benefits. Half of the countries in the OECD are either currently increasing their "pensionable age" or have announced that they will do so.[31] Increasing the eligibility age has relatively strong support as an effective and fair way to improve sustainability. Unlike cutting benefits or increasing contributions, it has a double effect on sustainability, insofar as it both reduces plan obligations and increases revenues. Delaying eligibility increases labor force participation among older workers, in turn increasing contributions or tax revenues from these workers.[32] The sustainability benefits of the reform can therefore be quite dramatic. For example, the US General Accounting Office has shown that increasing the normal eligibility age from 67 to 71 years by 2065 would reduce by 70 percent the much-discussed Social Security funding shortfall in that country.[33] In the United Kingdom, increasing the pensionable age by only one year is projected to reduce payments by £62.6 billion, and increase revenues by £9.7 billion.[34]

The reform also has broader benefits, especially in comparison to the alternatives. A contribution rate increase is effectively a payroll tax, which suppresses wages and increases unemployment.[35] Historically, increasing the public pension eligibility age has had a positive effect on labor force participation by workers in their sixties, and there is no obvious reason to believe that this relationship would not hold for further increases.[36] Encouraging their continued labor force participation may contribute to overall economic growth.[37] Quality of life might also be improved as there is some evidence that many people tend to be healthier and happier when they continue working instead of retiring.[38]

Alan Jacobs's theorization of pension reform options helps explain the structure of the eligibility age increase. As noted above, he argues that policy reform options should be analyzed both in terms of their capacity to redistribute among groups and in terms of their capacity to redistribute across time periods. Jacobs, in passing, identifies eligibility age increases as a redistribution away from pension recipients toward pension contributors.[39] Although this characterization is not developed in his text, it follows logically from his analytical scheme. In a pure "pay-as-you-go" scheme an eligibility age increase immediately reduces contribution requirements. In a funded scheme, the reform enhances the reserve fund and thereby reduces the likelihood and magnitude of future contribution increases.

Of course, "recipients" and "contributors" are not totally independent categories. Most contributors to public pensions are individuals who will eventually become recipients. In a scheme funded from general revenues (such as Canada's Old Age Security means-tested pension supplement), many beneficiaries are taxpayers and therefore also contributors. However, Jacobs treats recipients and contributors as distinct groups, and doing so allows him to distinguish a "cross-sectional" redistribution between these groups from an intertemporal transfer. Moreover, most public pension plans will also receive contributions from employers and/or from corporate taxpayers, who will never be recipients.

The most innovative part of Jacobs's analysis is his identification of intertemporal transfers. An immediate eligibility age increase in a funded pension scheme, if unaccompanied by any transition mechanisms, is what Jacobs describes as a *policy investment*. His first criterion for a policy investment is that it "imposes a cost in the short term by restricting the current aggregate consumption opportunities of a society."[40] A two-year delay in pension eligibility without transition immediately deprives those celebrating their 65th birthdays of two years' worth of benefits.

Jacobs' second criterion for policy investments is that "those resources extracted from society in the short run must be directed to (or subject to) an identifiable mechanism for increasing long-term consumption possibilities."[41] Jacobs emphasizes that this criterion depends on the "structure" of the policy, and not on its consequences or the motives of the policymaker in adopting it.[42] Eligibility age increases qualify because they are structured to increase long-term consumption possibilites through "accumulation"—they cause additional funds to build up in the reserve fund that can be spent later on benefits, keeping contribution rates lower. Eligibility age increases can also increase long-term consumption possibilties through the "creation of capital goods,"[43] such as infrastructure, if the reserve fund is invested in the economy or loaned to the government for the creation of such goods. An immediate eligibility age increase therefore both redistributes from recipients to contributors, and accepts short-term costs to society in anticipation of long-run benefits to society.

Jacobs's analysis is descriptive rather than normative; "policy investment" is not intended to be an approbation of a particular policy option. However, increasing the eligibility age does seem to be relatively fair, especially if it is accompanied by other sustainability reforms ensuring that the necessary loss is spread fairly among the population. Given growing lifespans, *not* implementing this reform means funding a steadily increasing number of years of benefits for each recipient.[44] The eligibility age can be increased while holding constant each citizen's ratio of contributing-years to receiving-years,[45] and an even larger increase can be introduced while holding constant the absolute number of receiving years.[46]

Despite these advantages, increasing the eligibility age undeniably creates "losers," and many people who lose in their capacity as recipients are not compensated in their capacity as contributors. All current contributors lose their entitlement to the benefits that they would have received during the period between the pre-reform and post-reform eligibility ages. The monetary value of this loss is equal for all current and future contributors. Only current recipients are spared any loss (assuming that current recipients younger than the post-reform eligibility age are exempted from the effect of the reform).

However, especially for older contributors, forgoing years or months of benefits is not their only loss. They may also suffer reliance damages, if for example they increased their exposure to risky asset classes or made expensive retirement lifestyle commitments because they were counting on the benefits. Psychic losses may also be experienced, such as disappointment or a sense that the government has broken its promise. To borrow Frank Michelman's phrase, pension losses for older contributors and benefit recipients may involve "demoralization costs" in addition to their pocketbook impacts.[47] The extent of these intangible losses may depend in part on other characteristics of the pension plan, such as whether it was funded by employment contributions as opposed to general revenues and what percentage of pre-retirement income it promised to replace. Given the significant direct and indirect losses occasioned by increases in the eligibility age, it is not surprising that polls in Europe and Canada have found more than two-thirds of people opposed to this policy option.[48]

The reform may also be regressive, imposing greater losses on poorer citizens. Wealthier people are more likely to have employer-sponsored pensions and private savings. A delay in public pension eligibility therefore has a smaller impact on the total resources that wealthier people have available to finance retirement.[49] Income is also correlated with lifespan,[50] so the average poor person receives less lifetime value from a stream of defined benefits than the average rich person does. Cutting years from the projected period of benefits therefore has a proportionately larger impact on the lifetime total of benefits for poorer recipients.[51] Increasing the eligibility age from 65 to 67 is an 8 percent cut to the total benefits of a person who lives to age 90. The same eligibility age increase is a 13.3 percent cut to the total benefits of a person who lives to age 80. However, these regressive effects of increasing eligibility age can be mitigated if means-tested income support programs are available to complement the public pension scheme.

IV. Options for Dealing with the Losers

Dealing appropriately with losers is essential for governments seeking to delay public pension eligibility. As France's experience demonstrates, principled arguments are not necessarily sufficient to make change politically acceptable. Pension reform, however, is not necessarily so controversial. Canada introduced a very similar change to its Old Age Security pension scheme in March 2012, increasing eligibility ages by two years. Although opposed by opposition parties and some civil society groups, the Canadian reform did not produce any significant public resistance.[52] This was presumably not a surprise to the government, given that polling and a trial balloon speech by the prime minister indicated public receptiveness.[53] Although there are many differences between these two countries and the contexts in which they attempted the policy change, their choices of transition mechanisms may well have had consequences for public reaction.

One way to ease the transition is to directly compensate the losers. For example, each contributor to the plan could be issued a partial refund of his or her benefit contributions. If a two-year eligibility delay would reduce the total lifetime benefits by an average of 10 percent, then each contributor could be issued an immediate refund of 10 percent of his or her contributions to date. Although the expense of this strategy would obviously reduce the sustainability benefit of the reform, it would not totally eliminate it even if the refund were equal to the entire benefit loss for each contributor. This is because at least part of the effect on labor force participation and increased contribution revenue would be preserved.

Making the old-age income system more redistributive is a transition strategy that counteracts the regressive effect of eligibility-delay described above. For example, when Australia and the UK increased the eligibility age they also enhanced benefits for low-income seniors.[54] Canada is among the OECD countries that have managed to increase eligibility ages and keep overall public pension expenditures modest, while still attaining relatively low rates of old-age poverty.[55] The proportion of pre-retirement income that is replaced by the public pension scheme in Canada is close to 100 percent for low-income seniors, but approximately 40 percent for the average recipient, and even less for those with high incomes.[56] By contrast, the OECD average replacement rate is 60.6 percent for median income earners, and 72 percent for those who earned half of the average income.[57]

Another way to deal with the losers is to allow each of them to "structure" his or her loss, choosing between delayed benefits and reduced benefits. This transition strategy could allow the average age of first benefit receipt to be increased through incentives, without compelling any individual to delay receipt. Most OECD countries already allow plan members some choice in timing benefits, with a trade-off between monthly benefit amount and commencement date. For example, although 65 is the "normal" eligibility age for Canada's CPP, an eligible person is allowed to claim the benefits as early as age 60. Receiving benefits before age 65 means a reduced amount each month. Those who commence receipt at age 60 will eventually receive 36 percent less than those who commence at age 65, while a person who delays CPP receipt until his or her 70th birthday will receive a 42 percent bonus in monthly benefits.[58] Further freedom could be offered by allowing contributors to choose to delay receipt after age 70, with corresponding upward adjustments of the benefits.[59]

Because people have differing needs and place different weights on the time value of money, this transition strategy will in principle allow each person to structure the benefit flow in his or her preferred fashion, and thereby mitigate the loss created by the reform.[60] So long as the adjustments are actuarially neutral, the strategy has minimal cost to the state.[61] The drawback is that some people may make choices that are not in their long-run interest, for example failing ever to trigger the benefits, or triggering benefits at the earliest possible date and then falling into poverty after their other resources are exhausted. The latter risk may be particularly significant in pension plans such as Canada's that offer only modest income replacement rates for average earners. As the degree of freedom is increased, the "choice architecture" surrounding the benefit commencement decision becomes increasingly important. Under the "libertarian paternalist" approach espoused by Richard Thaler and Cass Sunstein, it might be appropriate for the state to "nudge" each citizen toward a later commencement date that will allow a benefit quantum sufficient to keep him or her out of poverty and minimize the moral hazard of early receipt (relying on the state to mitigate the consequences of subsequent indigence).[62]

The transition strategies most frequently deployed by OECD governments that have increased public pension benefit eligibility ages are *phase-in* and *grandfathering*. Phase-in applies multiple eligibility ages to different people based on their date of birth. In the case of Canada's Old Age Security (OAS) reform, the new age 67 eligibility will apply only to people born on February 1, 1962 or later. A person born in January 1962 will be eligible at age 66 and 11 months, a person born in April 1958 will be eligible at age 65 and 1 month, and so forth.[63] Grandfathering means preventing the reform from having any effect on the oldest group of current contributors. For example the US Social Security retirement benefit eligibility age was increased by two years in 1983, but the effect was delayed until 2003.[64]

Most if not all OECD countries increasing the eligibility age have deployed some combination of phase-in and grandfathering. The unusual French experience might reflect the fact that most other countries used more generous phase-in and grandfathering transition strategies, which muted resistance to the reform. France proposed to fully implement its reform by 2018, only six years after announcing it.[65] By contrast, the United States provided a 20-year grandfathering period followed by a 24-year phase-in period for the same two-year increase. The United Kingdom is in the process of introducing a three-year eligibility age increase over a time frame similar to that of the United States.[66]

If we return to Jacobs's analytical scheme, phase-in and grandfathering diminish the "temporal tradeoff toward the future" involved in the eligibility age increase. They reduce the short-term cost of the policy by eliminating the entire cost during the grandfathering period and reducing it during the subsequent phase-in period. However, they also weaken the "mechanism for increasing long-term consumption possiblities" because they reduce the sustainability benefit of the reform. The plan accumulates fewer resources than it would if the reform were implemented immediately, and the potential for capital accumulation is also reduced. Eligibility age increases always redistribute from recipients to contributors. However, if grandfathering and phase-in postpone their effect far enough into the future, they are no longer *policy investments* under Jacobs's definition, because both their costs and their benefits are long-run in nature.

To achieve the same sustainability benefit as the immediate eligibility age increase, a policymaker committed to phase-in and grandfathering must make a larger eventual transfer from recipients to contributors. For example, if the Hollande administration in France uses these strategies to mitigate opposition, but wishes to reap the same sustainability effect as the Sarkozy reform would have had, it will have to increase the eligibility age by more than two years. Conversely, a policymaker who is prepared to forgo or reduce the transition period can obtain the same sustainability effect with a smaller delay in eligibility (e.g., only a one-year increase instead of two).

V. Public Choice and Normative Analysis

Public Choice theory suggests that eligibility age increases accompanied by sufficient grandfathering and phase-in will be a politically preferred response to the sustainability challenge. This is partially because, unlike contribution refunds or means-tested income supports, these two transition strategies are "off-budget." However Public Choice theory's archetypal, re-election–seeking politicians would especially prize their ability to confine the losses to young people. An increase in the eligibility age accompanied by generous grandfathering and phase-in protects older contributors and leaves the loss to be born by younger and future contributors.

Why would political support–maximizing politicians want young people to bear the entire pension loss? Older citizens are highly influential in many wealthy democracies, in part because they are often well-organized and more likely to vote.[67] According to Public Choice theory, this should make politicians more attentive to their interests. Moreover, compared to younger contributors, older contributors suffer greater demoralization losses from downward adjustments to their pension wealth, because they are more immediately focused on these entitlements and attach more value to them. Those old enough to be already receiving the benefits are likely to be even more sensitive to any loss and less well able to adopt adaptive strategies.

Conversely, the average younger person attaches relatively low value to pension benefits, which are many decades in the future. Thus, not only are pension-related losses felt less acutely by younger citizens, but their lower probability of voting means that any loss they do experience is less likely to lead to the loss of a vote for the governing party. The political support maximization thesis therefore predicts that, if a pension sustainability problem forces policymakers to impose losses on some group of citizens, they will impose it on the youngest possible group.

Public Choice theory also helps to explain why alternative sustainability reforms are more politically risky. A benefit cut would impose a highly salient loss on older people, who are politically influential.[68] An immediate eligibility age increase unaccompanied by grandfathering and phase-in would also impose a loss on older contributors, who are relatively likely to vote and who are likely to be paying attention to their pension entitlements. A contribution rate increase is politically problematic for two reasons. First, unlike in the case of the eligibility age increase, there is no good pretext for confining its costs to younger voters. Second, because this cost entails a payroll tax increase and has an immediate pocketbook impact, it is more salient to younger people than a loss in their pension benefit eligibility. An eligibility age hike with lengthy phase-in and grandfathering avoids all these problems: it confines the loss to young people who are politically less influential and less well-organized, and who in any case are not yet much concerned about their eventual pension entitlements.

However, as this book argues, these cynical calculations do not entirely account either for public policy decisions or for citizens' reactions to them. Jacobs argues that, although electoral considerations are important, they are not determinative in explaining decisions to make policy investments.[69] He also contends that policymakers will make temporal trade-offs in favor of the future if and only if (1) it is electorally safe, (2) they perceive that the long-run benefits will exceed the short-run costs, and (3) they have the institutional capacity to make the investment, despite opposition from organized groups.[70] It was argued above that increasing grandfathering and phase-in means reducing the policy investment character of an eligibility age increase. One can therefore hypothesize from

Jacobs's argument that the extent to which different states that have increased the eligibility age have used these transition mechanisms will reflect the extent to which they enjoyed the three circumstances that *Governing for the Long Term* identifies.

Another departure from Public Choice identified by Chapter 2 of this book is behavioral research which suggests that the perceived fairness of a proposal influences a person's attitude toward it, and not merely that person's narrowly defined self-interest.[71] Some polls suggest that current recipients are just as likely to oppose increases in the eligibility age as current contributors are, even though they have nothing to lose.[72] The success of the reform in question might be attributable, at least in part, to its perceived fairness.

Is this perception accurate? There is a strong case that phase-in is in fact fair, according to utilitarian and social contract theories. As noted above, the non-monetary losses and demoralization costs associated with the eligibility age delay are greater for older contributors. Behind a Rawlsian veil of ignorance, few would want 64-year-olds to face a sudden and unheralded two-year delay in benefit eligibility.

Phase-in can help equalize the total losses experienced by contributors of different ages. As noted above, total losses from public pension eligibility delay include not only the loss of benefit payments for a period of time, but also indirect losses such as reliance losses and psychic harm. These indirect losses are greater for older contributors, but phase-in counteracts this distributional inequity by reducing the direct benefit loss for older contributors. An appropriately calibrated phase-in is therefore not merely a pretext for passing the entire loss to the politically less influential younger generations.

However, the normative case for grandfathering is much weaker. Grandfathering means that the oldest contributors experience no loss whatsoever, leaving it to be borne in its entirety by younger contributors and future contributors. Although a 34-year-old unquestionably experiences less total loss from a month of eligibility delay than a 64-year-old, the loss experienced by the younger contributor is real and non-negligible. If the 34-year-old must suffer a two-year benefit delay, then there is no principled reason a 55- or even a 64-year-old should not share some part of the loss, even if in the latter case the appropriate delay is only a matter of weeks.

VI. Conclusion

Each politician walks with an angel (or Saint Francis of Assisi) on one shoulder, and a devil (or Machiavelli) on the other (reflecting competing strands in most of our individual value systems). The angel calls her to make welfare-maximizing decisions in the public interest, and to spread any necessary pain fairly among the population. The devil speaks the language of Public Choice, encouraging her to pander to powerful voters and organized interest groups at the expense of the weak and the unorganized.

If this politician is confronted with a public pension sustainability problem, both the devil and the angel will encourage her to phase-in an eligibility age increase. The angel notes that this option imposes a smaller total loss on society than the alternatives do, and spreads the total loss more equally among contributors. The devil observes that this approach spares her the wrath of current benefit recipients.

It is only the devil, however, who counsels complete grandfathering. Our leader will be sorely tempted to excuse older contributors from any part of the loss, because they may well punish her at the polls if she does otherwise. However, we should hope that she resists this temptation and espouses gradual phase-in, starting immediately, accompanied by a modest benefit cut for both current and future recipients. This is a challenging stategy for an enlightened leader, but it is the only politically feasible path to at least rough justice.

{ 4 }

Reforming the US Home Mortgage Interest Deduction

I. Introduction

All governmental policy changes that impose costs and confer benefits can be thought of as subsidies and taxes, regardless of whether they are administered through the tax system.[1] Where there is a "winner" created by a rule change, the government has granted a subsidy. Where there are "losers" whose prior investments are devalued by the change, the government has imposed a tax. This also applies to changes in the tax law itself. However, the "losers" in tax law transitions may be particularly hobbled in calling attention to their plight. A subsidy financed or otherwise implemented through the tax code often distributes the costs of the subsidy over a large number of taxpayers, causing an increase in the price of government. However, the immediate consequences of a particular subsidy are often impossible for individual taxpayers to discern or are so small as to be unlikely to provoke strenuous objection.

This chapter examines a particular provision of the tax law in the United States that is notorious for producing winners (and, less noticeably, losers). The so-called mortgage interest deduction (MID) allows many taxpayers to reduce their taxable incomes by the amount of home mortgage interest that they pay each year.[2] A particular taxpayer's tax savings from the MID can be calculated by multiplying the amount of mortgage interest claimed as a deduction by the taxpayer's marginal tax rate. Higher-income taxpayers benefit more from this policy than lower-income taxpayers, both because high incomes generally predict larger mortgages, and because the progressive rate schedule ensures that higher-income taxpayers face higher marginal tax rates.

From a simplistic perspective, the MID can be seen as reducing taxpayers' effective costs of borrowing to buy a home, such that equilibrium consumption of owner-occupied housing will increase as more taxpayers access tax-subsidized debt financing. But this is only a short-run effect. In the longer run, the subsidy may increase demand for owner-occupied housing and the credit to buy such housing. All else being equal, increased demand will push up the equilibrium price of houses and interest rates for home loans. This in turn may encourage housing suppliers (i.e., builders) and lenders to enter the market. The overall effect on price will depend on elasticities and the shape of supply and demand curves for housing and home loans, but it is certainly possible that where supply of homes or capital to build homes is fairly inelastic, increased prices due to the subsidy may be accompanied by very little in the way of increased quantity of homeownership. This dynamic story is generally consistent with evidence that the MID quickly became capitalized in house prices, has not dramatically affected rates of homeownership, and has caused modest increases in interest rates for home mortgages.

The MID is just one in a series of individual income tax items that receive the subsidy of income tax deductibility under current law. But the MID is one of the most costly to the federal government. Forgone revenue from allowing taxpayers to deduct their mortgage interest was among the top three US "tax expenditures" (policy subsidies executed through the tax code) affecting individuals.[3] The Joint Committee on Taxation estimated that, for 2012, the MID represented a tax expenditure of approximately $68.5 billion.[4]

The MID has been widely criticized as inequitable, inefficient, and ineffective.[5] In fact, a recent survey conducted by the National Tax Association of its members (who include tax economists, tax lawyers, and tax policy analysts) revealed that only 23 percent believe that mortgage interest should be deductible.[6] However, because the subsidy affects an asset—a home—that, in many instances, comprises a large proportion of an individual or family's wealth, proposals to eliminate or phase out the MID have engendered strong opposition from homeowners. Moreover, as a result of the importance of housing to the macroeconomy, there is a vocal and well-organized constituency of housing-related professionals (realtors, home builders, suppliers, and others)[7] who are quick to denounce steps toward curtailing the MID as a betrayal of the American Dream.[8] According to Roberta Mann, the real estate industry made contributions to Congress in 2008 totaling $135.9 million, ranking fourth among industries behind lawyers, retirees, and investment firms.[9] Thus, the prospect of removing the subsidy has much in common with other policy transitions, such as trade liberalization or the phase-out of dairy supply management (discussed in Chapters 5 and 6 of this book).

II. How Does the MID Work?

A. THE ELECTION TO ITEMIZE

The MID cannot be understood except in relation to an idiosyncratic feature of the US income tax system, which offers taxpayers a choice regarding how to calculate their personal income taxes owed. Each filer can calculate her taxable income by subtracting from her adjusted gross income the default "standard deduction"[10] or by electing to "itemize" her deductible expenses.[11] Generally, taxpayers elect to itemize their expenses if the total dollar value of their itemized deductions exceeds the value of the standard deduction.[12] Under current law,[13] the MID is one of a list of itemizable expenses that also includes the deduction for (non-federal) taxes paid,[14] casualty or theft losses,[15] gambling losses,[16] charitable donations,[17] medical expenses (above a certain threshold of adjusted gross income),[18] impairment-related work expenses,[19] and certain "miscellaneous itemized deductions" that can be claimed only if they exceed, in the aggregate, more than 2 percent of the taxpayer's adjusted gross income.[20]

Therefore, a taxpayer can benefit from the MID if and only if she chooses to itemize her expenses. For a single taxpayer in 2012, this means that her mortgage interest paid plus other itemizable expenses must total more than $5950 (the amount of the standard deduction). A subsequent subpart will explore in more detail the distributional effects of the benefits of MID. But because only approximately one out of every three taxpayers itemizes,[21] the direct consequences of the subsidy are less straightforward than if every taxpayer's mortgage interest expenses were deductible.

B. THE MECHANICS OF THE MID

For the taxpayer who elects to itemize and pays interest on a residential mortgage, the MID applies to "qualified residence interest."[22] This is defined to mean "any interest which is paid or accrued during the taxable year on—(i) acquisition indebtedness with respect to any qualified residence of the taxpayer, or (ii) home equity indebtedness with respect to any qualified residence of the taxpayer."[23] A "qualified residence" includes both the principal residence of the taxpayer as well as one "other residence of the taxpayer which is selected by the taxpayer for purposes of this subsection for the taxable year and which is used by the taxpayer as a residence..."[24]

Unlike miscellaneous itemized deductions that are subject to the 2 percent floor, there is no floor on the amount of mortgage interest that the taxpayer may itemize—even small amounts can be deducted. However, there is a cap—acquisition indebtedness is deductible only to the extent that the acquisition loan principal is less than $1 million, and home equity indebtedness is deductible only to the extent that the home equity loan principal is less than $100,000. Nonetheless, the Internal Revenue Service has held that where a taxpayer's total acquisition indebtedness exceeds $1.1 million, it is permissible to deduct interest on up to $1.1 million as qualified residence interest.[25] Thus, for all practical purposes, the cap on deductible interest incurred in acquiring, constructing, or substantially improving a qualified residence is $1.1 million. Finally, the total amount of debt that may be treated as acquisition indebtedness may not exceed the cost of the residence (including the cost of any improvements).[26]

C. THE MID IN THE CONTEXT OF OTHER TAX TREATMENT OF HOUSING

The MID is far from being the only tax-based government subsidy to promote homeownership: others include the exclusion of up to $500,000 of capital gain on the sale of principal residences (imposing a revenue cost of $15 billion in 2010), the deduction for property taxes (another $15 billion in forgone revenue in 2010), and other temporary measures to assist first-time homebuyers or homeowners facing foreclosure.[27]

Importantly, the MID subsidizes the cost of borrowing for buying a home precisely because of another expense that is *not* taxable. The Code does not require homeowners to include the imputed income they realize from "renting" their dwellings to themselves, even though in an analogous arm's length transaction, a renter would pay after-tax dollars to a landlord, who would include such payments in his taxable income while deducting depreciation associated with the property and interest payments on debt used to acquire the property. If imputed rental income was included in a homeowner's taxable income, allowing a deduction for mortgage interest (as well as depreciation) would be neutral in regard to subsidizing homeownership: the homeowner would be treated equivalently to a landlord who rents property at arm's length. But the status quo, in which imputed rent is excluded from taxable income but mortgage interest is deductible, renders the MID a substantial subsidy for homeownership.[28]

III. History of the Deductibility of Home Mortgage Interest

A. ORIGINS OF THE MID

From the time that the US income tax was adopted in 1913, the concept of itemization as we know it today has been present.[29] It reflects the notion that the proper tax base should track the earnings of the individual or family net of expenses incurred to produce those earnings, but should also take into account adjustments for circumstances that reduce taxpayers' ability to pay taxes. The 1913 income tax statute stated categorically that "personal, living or family expenses" fell outside of the boundaries of a deductible business expense.[30] However, it enumerated a series of non-business expenses that were considered exceptions to this general rule because they reduced taxpayers' ability to pay taxes: consumer interest payments, casualty losses not otherwise compensated for, bad debts, and actual taxes paid, among others, could be deducted.[31] Thus, at the dawn of the income tax, *all* interest expenses on consumer debt—including but not limited to mortgage interest—were permissible deductions from gross income.

Despite this "catchall tax provision for personal interest expenses,"[32] few mortgage holders were able to take advantage of the deduction until the 1940s.[33] In 1913, only 2 percent of households exceeded the "zero-bracket" exemption amounts. During World War I, this percentage rose to 15 percent, but only in the early 1940s did wartime revenue demands lead policymakers to decrease exemption amounts enough that the majority of households became subject to the income tax. Moreover, an increasingly progressive rate structure—top marginal rates hovered over 90 percent until the 1960s—inflated the value of claiming deductions.[34] To illustrate, a taxpayer who faced a marginal tax rate of 94 percent would reduce her tax liability by $94 if she was able to claim $100 of tax-deductible expenses.

At approximately the same time that the income tax went from being a "class tax" to a "mass tax,"[35] Congress adopted the standard deduction in 1944 as a simplification measure.[36] Instead of itemizing a complicated list of deductible expenses, taxpayers could choose to take the standard deduction. The standard deduction was initially set at a level that led only about 20 percent of taxpayers to elect to itemize (because, presumably, their deductible expenses exceeded the value of the standard deduction). However, the percentage of itemizers climbed to 29 percent in 1955, 40 percent in 1960, and increased further to 48 percent in 1970.[37] This increase in the proportion of taxpayers who itemized accompanied booming growth in homeownership, much of which was financed by mortgages that had become easier to obtain on an insured basis due to New Deal agencies such as the Federal Housing Administration.[38] According to Ventry's history of the MID, during the postwar period:

> [T]he personal interest deduction had been rising faster than any other itemized deduction, driven in large part by skyrocketing mortgage payments. The MID was now on the radar of experts and politicians, a growing number of whom formed a postwar tax-policymaking consensus that sought tax reform alongside tax cuts. Eliminating tax subsidies like the MID could pay for significant rate reduction, as much as 30 percent across the board.... Thus, a long-term strategy emerged among reformers—many of whom later worked in the Treasury Department during the 1960s—aimed at undermining housing tax subsidies: (1) raise the standard deduction as a way to extend comparable tax savings to nonitemizing taxpayers and to erode public support for the itemized subsidies, and (2) develop an annual accounting of all "tax expenditure" items that deviated from a comprehensive base so that policymakers could reevaluate them on an annual basis. Restating tax programs in traditional budget language, reformers thought, could help identify the inefficient, "upside-down" subsidies.[39]

Only the first of the two prongs of tax reformers' long-term strategy was destined for success—the second, tax expenditure accounting, appeared to do little to sway voters' views about tax priorities. Congress raised the standard deduction as part of a 1969 tax reform, and raised it again in the mid-1970s, such that by 1980 only about 25 percent of taxpayers were itemizers and benefited at all from the deductibility of mortgage interest.[40] Despite the fact that these beneficiaries were largely affluent taxpayers, support for the subsidy grew as price inflation eroded the value of the standard deduction while increasing nominal mortgage interest, causing more taxpayers to itemize. In 1985, immediately before the passage of the Tax Reform Act of 1986 (the "TRA86"), almost 40 percent of taxpayers itemized.[41]

B. THE POLITICS LEADING TO THE CODIFICATION OF THE MID

Advocates of government support for owner-occupied housing, including the MID, argue that there are positive externalities from homeownership that the market does not internalize. As a result, it is argued, the level of homeownership would otherwise be lower than optimal, and government policy that succeeds in increasing homeownership will increase social welfare. Leaving aside for a moment the issue of whether the MID does in fact increase homeownership rates, these positive externalities provide the foundation for proponents of housing subsidies.

President Reagan made comprehensive tax reform a prominent part of his agenda in his second term.[42] Anticipating an attack on the housing subsidies, including the MID, the housing industry responded by playing up their economic importance.[43] In 1984, facing an impending midterm election, President Reagan capitulated to pressure from the housing industry and instructed his Treasury Department to craft a base-broadening, rate-lowering reform proposal while still preserving "that part of the American dream which the home mortgage interest deduction symbolizes."[44] I take particular note of this phrasing as an excellent example of strategic framing on the part of a political leader. By attaching this policy choice directly to the protection of a core cultural value—the independence and affluence associated with homeownership—it becomes much more difficult for its opponents to attack.

The sweeping changes of TRA86 succeeded in dramatically reducing tax rates and broadening the overall tax base. However, mortgage interest was duly excluded from this newly broadened base, and new Code section 163(h)(1) enshrined the MID in its own right even as other consumer interest was excluded from deductibility.[45] But, as Ventry points out, the victory of the housing industry was mitigated by the structural changes in the tax code.[46] The standard deduction was raised, such that after passage of the reform, the percentage of taxpayers itemizing their deductions decreased to 33 percent from almost 40 percent. Further, because marginal tax rates were decreased, the value of the deduction to taxpayers was proportionally diminished. The MID was "effectively worthless" for households with incomes below $42,500 ($80,000 in 2009 dollars).[47]

IV. The Policy Case Against the MID

A government subsidy for owning a home may be justified to the extent that there are (positive) externalities to society from homeownership and persuasive evidence that the particular subsidy program increases the level of homeownership.[48] However, commentators have argued that there are also negative externalities from homeownership, which might offset the positive externalities or militate in favor of a tax on ownership. Overall, scholars agree that the MID is a poorly targeted and ineffective policy instrument for allowing taxpayers to internalize any net positive externalities that may exist from homeownership. Moreover, it is highly inequitable. This Section briefly summarizes these arguments.

A. JUSTIFICATIONS FOR SUBSIDIZING HOMEOWNERSHIP

i. Positive Externalities from Consuming More or Better Housing

Glaeser and Shapiro identify three main positive externalities that plausibly stem from the quantity or quality of housing consumption: safety (consumption of more or better housing reduces risks of fire and disease), aesthetic considerations (consumption of more or better housing allows taxpayers to benefit more from making their houses look more attractive), and benefits to children (consumption of more or better housing might specifically benefit children).[49] If any of these externalities were compelling, there could be a case for subsidizing homeownership, although not necessarily through the mechanism of the MID.

Glaeser and Shapiro dismiss the first concern—safety externalities—due to the prevalence of well-enforced fire and safety codes except among the poorest in society. Moreover, MID does not benefit the poor facing insecure or unsafe housing because they are disproportionately unlikely to itemize or to own rather than rent housing.[50]

To measure the second—aesthetic externalities—Glaeser and Shapiro test whether high-income people are willing to pay more for "homes in places where other homes are nicer," using a hedonistic regression approach.[51] They find that there may be some measurable externalities, but they conclude that the MID is a poorly designed means for helping taxpayers internalize these externalities—the subsidy is far too high based on the externality estimates that the authors generate.[52] Moreover, given the diversity of tastes among taxpayers, local zoning, land use, and building codes are likely far better tools to regulate such issues.

Finally, there may be positive externalities to the consumption of more or better housing from an intergenerational perspective. Housing subsidies may induce families to choose an optimal quantity and quality of housing taking into account children's preferences and need for space to grow, relative to what they would choose absent a subsidy. Certainly, children are likely to be happier when there is more space for a family, but it is difficult if not impossible to quantify the appropriate subsidy level that would induce optimal choices. Here again, the MID appears to be poorly targeted as a tool to help families internalize this type of intergenerational externality: the poorest families in society, who might suffer most from crowding, typically do not benefit at all from the MID.[53]

ii. Positive Externalities in Choice of Renting versus Owning a Home

The second margin of substitution that the MID affects is between renting and owning a home. If there are positive externalities from homeownership relative to renting, encouraging ownership among renters may increase social welfare. However, if there are negative externalities from owning relative to renting, a subsidy for homeownership will reduce welfare.

The economics literature identifies two main positive externalities and a negative externality of owning as compared to renting. First, because homeowners are less transient and their substantial asset is connected to the well-being of their local community, they are likely to be more invested in improving their locality (through, e.g., volunteering for organizations, voting, and other kinds of civic participation) than a similarly situated renter.[54] Economists have found evidence that homeowners invest more social capital in their neighborhoods and have higher levels of political awareness and participation.[55] Second, there may be aesthetic externalities similar to those generated by consuming more or better housing—owners may be more likely to maintain and beautify their homes than renters in conjunction with landlords.[56] Indeed, Glaeser and Shapiro cite strong evidence that homeowners invest more resources in gardening and maintenance.[57]

However, there also may be downsides to neighborhood attachments. In particular, homeownership may reduce labor force mobility due to the high transaction costs of buying and selling a home.[58] In more extreme cases, homeownership may cause homeowners to become caught in areas of high unemployment. This occurs when housing prices fall and owners cannot afford to move until they sell their home. In the presence of such negative externalities, a subsidy such as the MID would exacerbate rather than ameliorate the problem.

B. JUSTIFICATIONS FOR NOT SUBSIDIZING HOMEOWNERSHIP—NEGATIVE EXTERNALITIES

In addition, as examined by Voith, there may be negative externalities from subsidizing housing consumption.[59] In particular, housing subsidies may induce people to leave small city rental apartments to consume larger homes in the suburbs. This exodus from the city might itself impose negative externalities on cities and the people who remain there as well as entailing more negative externalities from more commuting.[60] Further, a tax code that subsidizes housing for the rich relative to the poor will, in equilibrium, increase economic segregation as well as exacerbate racial segregation because income differences are often correlated with race.[61] If economically and racially integrated neighborhoods are important for a harmonious society, housing subsidies may impede such outcomes.[62]

C. THE MID IS INEFFECTIVE IN ADDRESSING EXTERNALITIES

Even if the existence of the above-mentioned externalities of owning a home were conclusively established to be on balance positive (i.e., after taking into account negative externalities), one more step is necessary: the subsidy chosen by the government as the policy instrument to support owner-occupied housing must succeed in increasing rates of homeownership relative to the non-subsidized status quo. However, there is a consensus among scholars that the current policy, the MID, fails to achieve its ostensible goal of increasing homeownership.[63]

Glaeser and Shapiro test the efficacy of the MID in increasing homeownership in three different ways using time series data: first, by exploiting variation across the value of the MID due to changes in inflation rates; second, by observing the connection (or lack thereof) between increased rates of itemization and increased homeownership; and, third, by exploiting variation across states in the magnitude of the subsidy from the MID (i.e., whether it is deductible for state income tax purposes). They conclude that "over the past 40 years, the inflation rate and the share of people who itemize both have had major ups and downs. The homeownership rate has been extraordinarily flat, and the immobility of the homeownership rate serves as evidence for the weak connection between the home mortgage interest deduction and the level of homeownership."[64] Similarly, they find "there is essentially no relationship" between the homeownership rate and the magnitude of the subsidy after taking into account state income tax deductibility.[65] In addition, a series of cross-country studies have concluded that the US's homeownership rate is no higher than that in other developed countries such as Canada and Australia, which do not offer a tax subsidy for mortgage interest.[66]

One piece of the explanation of why the MID does not increase homeownership is that taxpayers may inaccurately assess the impact of the MID on their after-tax cost of housing (i.e., the MID may not be fully "salient" for taxpayers). The MID, although fairly straightforward as far as tax provisions go, is confusing to a substantial segment of taxpayers. Goldin and Listokin present survey evidence that many taxpayers misapprehend the applicability of the MID.[67] They observe that itemizers often incorrectly believe that the MID does not apply to them, while almost equal numbers of non-itemizers incorrectly think that the MID provides them with a tax subsidy when it does not. Moreover, for those taxpayers who believe the MID benefits them when it does not, budgeting errors may result—taxpayers may think their taxes will be lower than they are in reality.[68] These results suggest that there may be additional costs to taxpayers that stem from the MID at the same time that they reduce its efficacy in increasing homeownership—complexity costs and budgeting mistakes. In one respect, then, perhaps the policy would work better if a simple and relatively cheap policy option were employed: information provision.

D. THE MID IS INEFFICIENT AND INEQUITABLE

i. Efficiency Critiques of the MID

a. Modest Distortion of Home Prices

It is well-established that the expected tax benefits from the MID are capitalized into home prices,[69] increasing prices by as much as 10 percent.[70]

As Shaviro observes, this capitalization of the MID in house-prices is problematic not in any inherent sense but because some borrowers face credit market constraints and cannot simply borrow more to cover the increased cost of a house.[71] Particularly for first-time homebuyers and others with limited credit (such as the young or those without assets other than their future expected labor earnings), the house price inflation caused by the MID may perversely cause them to be unable to finance the purchase of a home.[72]

Separate but related to this is the argument that the MID may distort investment choices. To the extent that the MID changes the price of owning a home relative to renting a home, this may skew individuals' portfolio choices toward overinvestment in a single asset (residential real estate) to the detriment of overall portfolio diversification, including business assets.[73] Unless this distortion can be shown to correct a preexisting externality, it can cause individuals to depart from first-best efficient allocations. A consensus factor in the US financial crisis of 2008 is that housing overinvestment caused under-diversified portfolios.[74] And, as noted above, the MID may also exacerbate a key negative externality of homeownership—decreased labor mobility.

b. Distortion of Mortgage Debt Interest Rates

According to scholars who specialize in housing economics, most econometric analyses of the effect of the MID on house prices and taxpayers' decisions to rent or buy housing generally treat the gross interest rate on home mortgages (i.e., before the tax subsidy) as independent of the subsidy created by the MID.[75] Andrew Hanson points out that this is equivalent to assuming that the economic incidence of the MID subsidy falls entirely on borrowers—but do borrowers really benefit from the MID to the exclusion of lenders?[76] Hanson tests this assumption by examining whether the availability of the MID affects the interest rate charged by lenders on home purchase loans.[77] He estimates that, on average, "between 9 and 17 percent of the subsidy created by the MID is offset by lenders charging a higher interest rate than they would in the absence of the MID."[78]

These findings suggest that, because mortgage lenders capture some of the surplus from the MID, the subsidy is distorting the effective mortgage interest rates faced by borrowers *less* than would otherwise be the case. But because the distortion results in a transfer to lenders, the repeal of the MID would negatively affect this additional group of "winners." This is particularly important as the financial sector has been notoriously successful (at least in popular discourse) at achieving its regulatory goals.

c. Distortion of the Allocation of Homes Among Taxpayers

Holding constant the size of a given mortgage across taxpayers, the value of the MID to an individual taxpayer depends first on the taxpayer's decision to itemize his deductible expenses and, second, on an individual taxpayer's marginal tax rate. As a result, the MID introduces distortions in the allocation of housing among itemizers versus non-itemizers and those facing higher versus lower marginal tax rates.[79] And because lower-income taxpayers are more likely to struggle to finance a home, this allocation will not assist, and will likely disadvantage, those who may be more deserving of housing assistance from a distributive justice standpoint.[80]

ii. Equity Critique of the MID

The MID is inequitable as among taxpayers of different income classes. First, it applies only to taxpayers whose itemized deductions exceed the standard deduction—by construction, these itemizing taxpayers are likely to have higher incomes (and multiple properties) than non-itemizers. Second, because the value of the MID is linked to the taxpayer's marginal tax rate, higher-income taxpayers facing steeper marginal tax rates will benefit more from the subsidy. As Ventry writes, "[the MID] also provided increasingly larger subsidies to wealthier taxpayers—larger because their value corresponded to marginal tax rates and because there was no limit on the value of deductions a taxpayer with sufficient income could enjoy. In other words, they produced an 'upside-down result utterly at variance with usual expenditure policies' that if restated as direct expenditures would appear inequitable and inefficient."[81]

Poterba and Sinai use 2004 data to estimate the equity impacts of the MID and find clear evidence of income regressivity, as well as trends by age cohort:

> Higher-income households enjoy larger tax subsidies than poorer households, with the average subsidy approximately doubling for each income category. For example, households earning between $75,000 and $125,000 receive less than 60 percent of the average subsidy ($5,862) of households earning between $125,000 and $250,000 ($10,704). In general, within income category, the average subsidy rises with age. However, in some income categories, the subsidy falls for the oldest households.[82]

The following table, produced by the bipartisan Joint Committee on Taxation, illustrates the regressive nature of the MID—the lion's share (about 70 percent) of the value of the subsidy accrues to taxpayers earning more than $100,000.[83]

Crucially, even among homeowners, nearly half do not receive the benefit of the MID. Those with itemizable deductions, including mortgage interest, that total less than the standard deduction do not itemize and thus are not assisted by the MID. This group is comprised predominantly of lower-to-moderate–income taxpayers who have more modest interest payments on their home mortgages.[84]

V. Reform Options

For the equity and efficiency reasons discussed above, there is a strong case that the MID should be repealed in its entirety. Less clear are the outlines of a path

Distribution by Income Class of the Tax Expenditure for the Home Mortgage Interest Deduction at 2009 Rates and 2009 Income Levels

Income Class[1]	Tax Expenditure for Home Mortgage Interest Deduction		
	Returns (thousands)	Amount ($ millions.)	Average Per Return in Dollars
Below $10,000	(2)	(3)	---
$10,000 to $20,000	311	88	283
$20,000 to $30,000	1,000	521	521
$30,000 to $40,000	2,023	1,292	639
$40,000 to $50,000	2,923	2,329	797
$50,000 to $75,000	7,603	9,332	1,227
$75,000 to $100,000	6,754	10,066	1,490
$100,000 to $200,000	10,594	30,261	2,856
$200,000 and over	3,424	22,768	6,650
Total	34,632	76,656	2,213

1. Excludes individuals who are dependents of other taxpayers and taxpayers with negative income.

The income concept used to place tax returns into classes is adjusted gross income ("AGI") plus: (a) tax-exempt interest, (b) employer contributions for health plans and life insurance, (c) employer share of FICA tax, (d) workers' compensation, (e) nontaxable Social Security benefits, (f) insurance value of Medicare benefits, (g) alternative minimum tax preference items, and (h) excluded income of U.S. citizens living abroad.

2. Fewer than 500 returns.

3. Positive tax expenditure of less than $500,000.

Note: Details may not add to totals due to rounding.

Source: Joint Committee on Taxation, "Present Law, Data and Analysis Relating to Tax Incentives for Homeownership,". September 30, 2011, JCX-50-11, page 28 (available at https://www.jct.gov/publications.html?func=startdown&id=4366).

through "the places in between" the status quo and full repeal. Should the losers from the policy change be compensated or their losses otherwise mitigated? What is the least-cost transition strategy, in economic terms, in terms of minimizing Michelman's demoralization costs, and with respect to political feasibility?

A. AFFECTED CONSTITUENCIES

To puzzle through the political and economic issues at stake in reforming the MID, it is helpful to note Tullock's transitional gains trap.[85] In particular, his analysis of the manner in which government subsidies become "stranded" as their value is capitalized in assets prompts the following question: which constituencies have been impacted by the MID's capitalization in house prices? And which have been impacted by its distortion of choices concerning homeownership?

There are two key groups whose interests need to be considered in a transition: (1) homeowners, and (2) construction/realty-related firms. Among the homeowners there appear to be two subgroups that are differentially affected: the cohort of homeowners that currently benefits from the MID (i.e., those who pay interest on their mortgages and deduct those interest payments when they itemize their tax returns) and the broader category of homeowners who do not directly benefit from mortgage deductibility but whose house prices reflect the capitalized value of the MID.

Although it is reasonable to assume that all of these constituencies will demand transition assistance in the event of a reform, there are two mitigating factors. First, many homeowners currently paying deductible interest on mortgages will be able to mitigate the costs of eliminating the MID by using other assets to retire some or all of their mortgage debt. In particular, Gervais and Pandy find that "households would alter their balance sheets if mortgage interest were no longer deductible," and thus that the cost to households of repealing the MID is only one- to two-thirds as high as conventional estimates.[86] Second, because the MID is less than fully salient even to those taxpayers who benefit from it, the political ramifications (i.e., mobilized opposition and electoral backlash) of its repeal may be mitigated.[87]

B. CURRENT DEVELOPMENTS AND THE AVAILABILITY OF INSURANCE

As has been prominently featured in recent news coverage regarding deficit reduction and policy responses to the "fiscal cliff" in the United States, there are myriad proposals being offered to reform the MID. Because the debate is very much still in progress, this subsection outlines several options for reform, with a brief discussion of their transition issues. However, the drama, urgency, and most of all the uncertainty surrounding US tax policy at the present time may be a variant of the "cataclysmic shocks...that call for drastic and immediate policy responses."[88] To the extent that housing firms and homeowners could once claim to have a reliance interest in the continued deductibility of mortgage interest, it is arguable that their reasonable reliance interests have been attenuated by the possibility of dramatic tax hikes and sharp reductions in tax expenditures, including the MID.[89] In short, the political perturbations surrounding the fiscal cliff may have caused some repositioning of traditional adversaries of change. Rather than fighting tooth and nail to stymie a common-sense, shared-pain plan to terminate the MID, current beneficiaries may be more disposed to tacitly accept gradual reforms (especially in a period of historically low interest rates).

Shaviro notes that the risks of policy changes affecting the MID are difficult to diversify for taxpayers who are not in the wealthiest segment of society: "the ownership of a home often conflicts with what one might consider optimal asset diversification...in principle, people would be willing to pay some positive amount of insurance, at least against the transition risk of an adverse policy change."[90] There does not appear to be insurance available to homeowners that would protect them, at least partially, against the losses from a repeal of the MID, in part because of the highly correlated nature of the risks in question. And, in the event that they lack other assets that could be used to retire their mortgage debt once the subsidy is no longer available, self-insuring against repeal of the MID may be challenging,[91] or even impossible for those individuals on the margins who, without the MID, would have remained renters. In the current situation, however, it is possible that existing policies aimed at preventing foreclosures would act as de facto mitigation.

C. CLASSES OF STRATEGIES FOR REFORMING THE MID

Below are a series of strategies for moving away from the MID as we know it today. With the exception of the first option, all of the reforms can be phased in or coupled with other reforms that eliminate the MID over time. Morrow argues that a gradual approach is recommended regardless of the political environment because it will minimize the risk of costly housing market dislocations, such as a sudden fall in prices or a jump in foreclosures.[92]

i. Cold Turkey: Cancel the MID Overnight

Although such a drastic move might have been unthinkable a few years ago, and would have aroused public uproar, the popular press is replete with reports that the MID is in jeopardy, particularly as low mortgage interest rates reduce the (relative) value of the subsidy.[93] To the extent that these reports are credible, it may be the case that housing prices have adjusted to account for the risk that the subsidy will be cancelled. However, given the political clout of housing and building-related industry players, outright repeal of the MID is unlikely as a successful opening salvo in the showdown between tax-raisers and expenditure-reducers in Washington.

ii. Replace the MID with a Credit

As discussed above, the equity profile of the MID speaks for itself. There is little policy justification for keeping in place an expensive subsidy that disproportionately benefits the least needy taxpayers. For instance, the deficit reduction commission headed by Erskine Bowles and Alan Simpson, as well as a growing number of commentators and scholars, have proposed replacing the MID with a housing tax credit.[94] The Bowles Simpson variant would replace the MID with a nonrefundable 12 percent credit, capped at $500,000 principal amount and limited to one home.

Other proposals have suggested something similar to the first-time homebuyers' credit (FTHBC) that was initially passed by Congress in 2008.[95] Because the credit was refundable (i.e., even if the taxpayer owed no taxes, she would still get cash from the credit amount) and was available only to taxpayers under a certain income threshold, it was disproportionately used by lower-income taxpayers.[96] Like the FTHBC, a credit that replaced the MID could be passed with a sunset provision to prevent it from becoming a permanent feature of the tax code and engendering the kinds of transition difficulties of the MID. Replacing the MID with a sun-setting credit (refundable or otherwise) as a transition strategy toward the full repeal of housing subsidies might temper opposition from the building and housing industry.

iii. Grandfathering

Shaviro notes that grandfathering, or a repeal of the MID on a prospective basis combined with allowing incumbent homeowners to take advantage of the MID while it is phased out for new homeowners, may be justified by the lack of ability of lower-income taxpayers to diversify their asset portfolio. There are many variants on how grandfathering the subsidy could work: it could apply unconditionally for the life of the home, expire once the current owner transferred the property, or be tied to the particular mortgage loans in place at the time of the repeal.[97] However, implementing such policies may involve nontrivial administrative and enforcement costs. Moreover, grandfathering can be legitimately portrayed as unfair because it places most of the burden of reform on future generations.

iv. Capping the Deductibility of the MID (and Other Itemized Deductions)

The status quo MID incorporates a cap on the loan principal amount on which interest can be deducted, but at $1.1 million (comprising acquisition indebtedness plus home equity indebtedness) the cap is very high and therefore limited in its impact. However, capping the MID as a transition strategy or more permanently to limit its costs is an approach that has clear merits as well as many different permutations.

There are many other proposals for effectively capping the MID, often by limiting the overall "basket" of total itemized deductions. Some prominent proposals include:

- Instituting an annual flat-dollar cap on all individual itemized income tax deductions, including the MID. This could be significant from an equity standpoint if the cap were low enough, but, as Daniel Shaviro points out, such an approach is unlikely to be optimal from a tax design perspective—it is akin to "slopping together a bucket list of disparate items" that may not make any sense to directly trade off with one another.[98]
- Continuing to allow the MID for itemizing taxpayers, but instituting a limit on all itemized deductions that would cap their value at that which would accrue to a taxpayer in a certain marginal tax bracket. For itemizing taxpayers facing lower tax brackets, the cap would not be binding. But for higher-income taxpayers who face marginal rates higher than, for example, 28 percent, the 28 percent bracket would be substituted (i.e., a taxpayer with $10,000 of deductions who has a marginal tax rate of 35 percent would be able to deduct only $2800 instead of $3500). This has some of the same design drawbacks as a flat-dollar cap.
- Capping an individual's total tax savings from itemization and other provisions so that it cannot exceed a maximum percentage of income. Martin Feldstein has proposed limiting the value of deductions, credits

and exclusions to 2 percent of adjusted gross income.[100] This has the benefit of putting a firm limit on the extent to which *all* reductions to tax can cut into the tax base. But, as with the proposal to cap the broader basket of all itemized deductions, it is likely to encounter opposition from a variety of constituencies.

v. Phaseouts of the MID Over Time

Phasing out the MID over an extended period of time combines some of the attributes of a cap (i.e., the MID would be capped at different levels until it was fully eliminated) with the end result of removing the subsidy completely by the end of the transition period. The phaseout could be structured in many different ways—a series of declining caps could take effect at different times, with high-income/high-deduction taxpayers being affected earlier than lower-income/lower-deduction taxpayers. Another approach that has the merit of simplicity and shared pain is simply phasing out the MID by reducing over time the percentage of mortgage interest that could be deducted from income. For example, in year one, taxpayers could deduct 90 percent of their mortgage interest payments from their adjusted gross income; in year two, 80 percent, and so on over 10 years.

In the lead-up to the fiscal cliff negotiations, many different kinds of limits on the MID and itemized deductions in general were discussed by politicians and policy analysts.[101] In fact, the American Taxpayer Relief Act of 2012 that was signed by President Obama on January 1, 2013, reduced the quantum of itemized deductions that individuals with income of more than $250,000 (or $300,000 for married taxpayers filing joint returns) can claim on their tax returns. For singles with incomes over $250,000 and couples with incomes over $300,000, itemized deductions will be reduced by 3 cents for every dollar of their income above the threshold.[102] However, this so-called itemized deduction "phaseout" has the effect of increasing marginal tax rates for those earning over the threshold, which concomitantly increases the value of claiming additional deductions. In the example used by Len Burman, a taxpayer over the cap who considers earning an additional $10,000 would "lose $300 of itemized deductions (3% of $10,000), so his taxable income (AGI minus deductions) would increase by $10,300, not $10,000. Again, assuming he is in the [new] 39.6% bracket, his additional tax would be $4,079 (39.6% of $10,300), so his effective tax rate is 40.8%, not 39.6%."[103] As a result, the taxpayer's benefit from itemizing deductions such as mortgage interest increases, rather than decreases. Writes Burman, "[it] is really a sneaky way to raise marginal income tax rates."[104] Moreover, as with all phased policy changes, the greater the phasing period, the more likely possible repeal in the face of increasing mobilization becomes.

vi. Raising the Standard Deduction

Raising the standard deduction was a strategy that policymakers pursued as part of TRA86—although the MID was codified, its applicability was limited because fewer taxpayers found it beneficial to itemize. Although it seems natural that using the standard deduction to restrict the number of taxpayers who have the opportunity to benefit from the MID would undermine political support for it, the salience survey evidence noted above may indicate otherwise.[105] Widespread taxpayer misperceptions about how the MID works could frustrate the strategy of using an increased standard deduction to wean taxpayers off the MID and would offset some or all of the revenue-raising effects of abolishing the MID.

VI. Conclusion

As the above discussion has illustrated, the MID is a subsidy that, like other tax subsidies in different national or regional contexts, would generate losers if it were withdrawn. However, there is a strong case for dismantling it. If the underlying policy objective of the MID is to increase rates of homeownership and thereby to capture the positive externalities that homeownership may confer on society in general and neighborhoods in particular, the MID is poorly designed. At the same time, the subsidy imposes additional negative externalities on the housing market. Its regressive "upside down" profile, whereby its benefit increases in income as a taxpayer's marginal tax rate rises, prevents it from providing an incentive to precisely the cohort of lower-income taxpayers likely to face the most challenges in buying a home. Furthermore, by distorting taxpayers' choices of the quality and quantity of housing to consume, whether to own or rent, and how large a loan to take relative to the house's value, the MID has led to inefficiencies in the residential housing market. In particular, there is evidence that the MID subsidy has been largely capitalized in the value of home prices—because some taxpayers can benefit richly from the subsidy, overall house prices have increased.

Therefore, the MID presents paradigmatic policy transition problems—the provision not only benefits taxpayers who itemize their deductible mortgage interest payments, but all homeowners, regardless of whether they itemize, would be harmed if the subsidy was withdrawn and house prices dropped. Further, there is a concentrated and highly organized cadre of housing industry-related firms that have made it their mission to block the MID's repeal.

In considering proposals about how to manage some of the "losers" from a policy transition away from the MID, policymakers should focus first and foremost on those who are directly impacted by the subsidy—homeowners. To the extent that there is transition relief offered to homeowners, presumably the secondary impact on housing and building-related firms will be dampened along with the political ramifications of their opposition. Starting with the directly affected homeowners, therefore, is there a case for transition relief?

I believe that there is. Even though there has been much discussion in policy circles about repealing the MID, many believe that the housing market is still fragile, and households' budgets are tightly stretched. Canceling the MID overnight would create serious budget problems for those taxpayers who rely on the reduction in taxes from the MID to cover their living costs. And as the cold-turkey repeal reverberates in falling house prices, the possibility that over-leveraged taxpayers would be forced to pay non–tax-deductible interest on home loans that are now "underwater" (where the outstanding loan amount exceeds the property's value) could ignite another wave of foreclosures.

To avoid such economically detrimental results, any transition strategy should help taxpayers with current mortgages meet their budget constraints at least in the short term as they make adjustments, and support an orderly adjustment in house prices. To the extent that the MID subsidy is substantially capitalized in house prices, withdrawing it over time could prevent a sudden, steep drop in prices and as a result may be superior to canceling it overnight, despite the ever-present risk that subsequent legislative action could reverse course and reinstitute the MID.

As a result, the ideal candidate for reform is one that can be implemented gradually. I recommend phasing out the MID over a span of 10 years during which the percentage of deductible mortgage payments would slowly decrease. In particular, I suggest backloading the bulk of the reductions over the transition period: in each of the first three years of the transition, decrease the amount of deductible mortgage interest payments by 5 percent. In each of the next four years, decrease the deductible amount by 10 percent. Finally, in each of the last three years of the transition, decrease the deductible amount by 15 percent. To the extent that individuals tend to excessively discount the cost of events that are expected to occur more distantly in the future (relative to those that are expected to occur sooner, via hyperbolic discounting), delaying the larger annual decreases until later in the transition schedule might help weaken political resistance to the reform.[106]

The approach of phasing-out of the MID is attractive for two key reasons. First, it has the merit of simplicity—there would be no complicated calculation of the cap (or reduction in amount that could be itemized, as under the current law). Taxpayers would be able to easily understand the manner in which the MID was being phased-out (or at least not do worse than their flawed understanding of the status quo) and could adjust their budgets accordingly. Second, because it proportionally decreases the benefit from the subsidy, and the subsidy itself is regressive, the repeal through a phaseout is progressive. Higher income taxpayers reducing their deductions by 10 percent will, of course, face higher marginal tax rates on the income that is included. The fact that the pain from the transition "undoes" to some extent the historical regressiveness of the MID is likely to be an important political selling point.

One qualification to this proposal that might be worth considering, even if largely politically symbolic, would be to preserve the mortgage interest deduction for first-time home buyers, with houschold income below some middle-class income cutoff, but phased out over a 10-year period as proposed above, so that it is a time-limited, income-tested exception to the general phaseout of the deduction, signifying continuing political support for the American Dream of home ownership (although most qualifying families may prefer to elect the standard deduction).

Why not grandfathering? It shares the benefit of phasing out the subsidy over time, but it introduces additional distortions, which are undesirable. In particular, there are so-called "lock-in" problems. If the mortgage subsidy is tied to a particular property, owner, or mortgage loan that was outstanding on the date of adoption, such a policy would deter otherwise-efficient transfers of ownership or refinancing of mortgages. In particular, homeowners who are considering moving for purposes of finding new or better work would be adversely affected if such a move would deprive them of the grandfathered MID, thereby distorting the larger market for labor. Although phasing-out of the subsidy over a decade would not eliminate transition costs for losers, spreading them out and allowing time for re-optimization of arrangements seems certain to dominate a cold-turkey-type reform or a capitulation to keeping some level of MID subsidy in effect despite the clear policy rationale for eliminating it.

This chapter has examined a very specific subsidy for residential housing that is effected through a provision of the US income tax code. Very few other countries have analogous provisions that allow mortgage interest payments to be deductible. However, the tax codes of almost every country embody subsidies for one type of behavior over another. The list is long and varied, but all tax subsidies have a similar effect—the cost of the subsidy is capitalized in prices of the affected assets, and taxpayers adjust their investment and consumption choices to reflect the price wedge between the tax-favored activity and non–tax-favored activities. The case made here for moving away from distortive tax subsidies can be applied readily to other national contexts where tax subsidies are at issue.

{ 5 }

Trade Liberalization: Gradualism, Reciprocity, Reversibility

I. Introduction

Few arguments are so widely accepted by economists as the case for free trade.[1] However, policies designed to promote it will not involve an equal distribution of benefits, and will impose costs on some sectors of the economy. This case study seeks to explore the adjustment costs associated with the transition to free trade, and explain how governments can use policy instruments to facilitate this adjustment. In doing so, I draw on and update my earlier work on trade and transitions.[2]

From the perspective of neoclassical economics, trade restrictions have little to commend them, theoretically or empirically. By restricting the available contract-opportunity set, trade barriers force societies to forgo mutual gains from exchange and specialization. As Adam Smith recognized long ago in *The Wealth of Nations* (1776),[3] the degree of specialization (or the division of labor) possible is limited only by the extent of the market. According to Smith, just as a tailor should not try to make his own shoes, and a shoemaker should not try to make his own suits, but buy shoes and suits from one another, and a family should not try to produce goods and services to meet all their own needs, so neither should a country seek to meet all its own needs. Important refinements by David Ricardo, in 1817, led to the theory of comparative advantage, where a country should produce and export goods when it enjoyed a comparative advantage and import goods when other countries enjoyed a comparative advantage. As a matter of neoclassical economic theory, the gains to domestic consumers from foreign trade are almost always greater than the gains to domestic producers from purely domestic trade. The reason is that, when domestic prices are higher than foreign prices, there is a transfer of resources from domestic consumers to domestic producers (arguably creating matching decreases and increases in welfare); *in addition,* some domestic consumers are priced out of the market by the higher prices and forced to allocate their resources to less-preferred consumption choices, resulting in a net social loss.[4]

In practice, the cost to consumers for each job saved by trade protection typically far exceeds the average compensation per worker in the industry affected.[5] To cite some examples from past episodes of protectionism, protecting the US specialty steel industry cost Americans US$1 million per year for each job preserved when the average annual compensation for those jobs was less than US$60,000. Consumers of automobiles in the United States paid US$160,000 per year for each job saved through protection when the annual compensation in the industry was less than one-quarter of this amount.[6] In Canada, the statistics are similar. Consumers of footwear were "taxed" through trade protection between C$53,668 and C$69,460 per job saved when the annual compensation for a worker in the industry was C$7,145; consumers of textiles and clothing paid C$40,600 to C$50,982 per year for each job saved when average earnings were $10,000; and consumers of automobiles paid C$179,000 to C$226,394 per year for each job saved when the average compensation in the industry was C$29,000 to C$35,000.[7]

These statistics make apparent the significant gains to be had from liberalizing trade. Richardson argues, however, that, in evaluating such gains, any dynamic analysis must take account of two kinds of social costs: dislocation costs and adjustment costs.[8] *Dislocation costs* entail the output of goods or services sacrificed from any unemployment, temporary or otherwise, of labor and other resources caused by trade liberalization. Wage and input price rigidities mean that, at least in the short run, markets do not clear instantaneously in response to changes in the terms of trade, and resources are likely to be rendered idle. *Adjustment costs* entail resources sacrificed to retrain labor, retool machines, refurbish factories, redevelop land, and relocate the factors of production that trade liberalization causes to be redeployed intra- or intersectorally.

II. Measuring Adjustment Costs

The magnitude of adjustment costs is largely a reflection of the ease with which resources are reallocated in response to trade liberalization.[9] This transition relies on well-functioning credit and labor markets, as adjustment to liberalization often requires firms to make large capital investments and attract labor into different sectors of the economy. As some factor markets operate more smoothly than others, adjustment costs are often unevenly distributed and concentrated in some sectors. Francois et al. point out that adjustment costs also depend on the speed at which firms in contracting sectors are able to release the factors of production.[10] Correspondingly, the minimization of adjustment costs "requires a careful balance between the speed at which factors are released, and the speed at which they can be re-employed."[11]

Although transition costs can be significant for some groups,[12] the majority of studies find that the benefits of liberalization outweigh the corresponding dislocation and adjustment costs.[13] The two most prominent early research papers on the subject found adjustment costs to be negligible, comprising less than 5 percent of the total gains from trade liberalization.[14] Subsequent research has found that adjustment costs may be much higher (in the range of 30–80 percent of total gains), but generally concludes that the costs associated with the transition to trade liberalization are smaller than the total benefits.[15] In the case of developing countries, it is also often argued that because of low levels of education; poor physical infrastructure; weakly developed financial, credit, and insurance markets; and inadequate or nonexistent social safety nets, adjustment costs in moving to a fully open international trade regime are likely to prove much more severe than those facing developed countries embarking upon a similar strategy of trade liberalization (and hence justify special dispensations).[16]

Richardson argues that dislocation and adjustment costs "can be fatal to the economic welfare case for trade liberalization." Similarly, Davidson and Matuz argue that adjustment costs can outweigh gains from liberalization in nations with sluggish labor markets.[17] Although there are reasons for skepticism about such assertions,[18] it is clear that the dislocation and adjustment costs associated with trade liberalization may be significant. There are also important political economy considerations, as politicians may need to support adjustment cost policies in order to garner the requisite political support for the adoption of liberalization policies. Moreover, there are normative grounds for supporting such policies (as I discuss below). Thus, even assuming that trade liberalization increases social welfare on balance, how governments should deal with adjustment costs in the context of trade liberalization raises important policy issues.

III. History of Adjustment Cost Policies

The concern with adjustment costs caused by changes in trade patterns or policies has long antecedents.[19] The General Agreement on Tariffs and Trade (GATT), from its inception in 1947, has provided for safeguard relief (Article XIX) through the temporary reinstatement of previous tariff concessions if foreign imports are causing severe disruption to a domestic industry.[20]

Interest in national adjustment assistance policies sharply intensified in the 1970s for a number of reasons: the two oil price shocks and accompanying recessions, the rise of Japan and other newly industrializing countries as major international trading powers, and further trade liberalization as envisaged by the Tokyo Round of GATT tariff reductions and codes restricting the use of various nontariff barriers to trade. In an environment of economic stagnation and increased import competition, many governments in Western industrialized countries sought strategies that would, in various degrees, restore international competitiveness to established industries through rationalization or modernization, achieve international competitiveness in new "growth" industries, and ease exit costs for capital and labor in industries whose comparative advantage was perceived as permanently lost. Alternatively, industrialized countries adopted defensive policies (such as industrial subsidies) designed to protect domestic industries from the effects of international competition. These concerns persisted into the 1980s and early 1990s, intensified by deep, worldwide recessions in the early years of both decades.

Further trade liberalization has occurred as a result of a proliferating number of regional trade pacts, including the Canada-US Free Trade Agreement, the North American Free Trade Agreement (NAFTA), Europe 1992, and the Australian-New Zealand Closer Economic Cooperation Treaty, as well as the Uruguay Round of multilateral negotiations that culminated in 1993; economic liberalization in the Soviet bloc, as well as China, India, and other developing countries; and the globalization of capital markets. All of these developments have increased the speed of the capital reallocation process and the volatility of exchange rates, suggesting that many countries continue to confront significant adjustment pressures and the correlative challenge of choosing appropriate adjustment policy responses to those pressures.

IV. Normative Rationales for and Against Intervention

Various normative perspectives may call for the adoption of public policies to address the transition costs associated with trade liberalization.

A. ECONOMIC EFFICIENCY

As the analysis above suggests, an efficiency perspective strongly supports trade liberalization. A separate question, however, is whether efficiency considerations also suggest that government should intervene on behalf of those who suffer private dislocation and adjustment costs.[21] There are efficiency arguments both favoring and opposing such assistance.

Compensation for losses resulting from trade liberalization, whether because of a decline in the value of industry-specific capital (human or otherwise) may create inefficient incentives. As discussed in Chapter 2. Kaplow argues that if individuals or firms anticipate compensation for losses suffered from a change in government policy, they have little incentive to act in ways to mitigate these losses.[22] Thus, even if firms anticipate that trade liberalization will have harmful effects on their business, they may continue to make industry-specific investments (and individuals may continue to make investments in industry-specific human capital), if they expect that they will be compensated for them. Anticipation of compensation creates inefficient investment incentives.

On the other hand, compensation or mitigation strategies may prove necessary to avoid derailing trade liberalization through the intense lobbying efforts of freer trade's losers. Because of the relatively diffuse benefits of freer trade for consumers generally and the relatively focused adverse effects on firm owners and workers,

Public Choice theory suggests that intense lobbying by focused anti–free-trade interest groups may jeopardize trade liberalization. Promising compensation or mitigation to those harmed by trade liberalization may act as a "bribe" that smoothes the political transition to a more efficient trade regime. In other words, inefficient investment incentives engendered by compensation or mitigation may have to be tolerated in pursuit of efficient liberalization.

A common form of intervention, as I discuss below, is to compensate workers through subsidized retraining schemes or income support. Although the considerations of inefficient investment incentives and efficient "bribery" pertain to these programs, other idiosyncratic considerations also apply. In terms of economic efficiency alone, it may seem unclear why government ought to compensate trade-dislocated workers. There are, however, inherent limits to the efficient, private, ex ante allocation of the risk of job loss from trade liberalization. Making sound predictions about the nature and extent of this risk is very difficult. As a consequence, although worker self-insurance through personal savings undoubtedly exists, such savings are likely to be too high or too low, given lack of good information about risk. Moreover, private insurance markets simply do not exist. Their absence cannot be explained by the presence of basic public unemployment insurance in most industrial democracies as it is unclear why a private market for supplemental benefits does not exist, as public insurance benefits cover only a portion of income loss and, in some countries, for only relatively short periods.[23]

One possible explanation for the absence of private insurance is the severe moral hazard problems involved. Full insurance of the risk of dislocation due to trade liberalization would likely lead some workers and firms to take greater risks or to underinvest in precautions (such as skills diversification) against the risks.[24]

A somewhat different economic efficiency rationale for adjustment policies stems from the real danger that, absent government intervention, trade-induced worker dislocation may result in an erosion of human capital. Workers who lose their jobs due to freer trade or other structural changes may, out of desperation and in the absence of retraining assistance, seek employment at lower wage levels and in occupations of lower skill and labor productivity. Empirical evidence suggests that a significant percentage of dislocated workers end up in lower-wage, lower-skill occupations and, in fact, never regain the earnings levels of their previous employment. Worse still, a protracted period of unemployment may also entail physical and mental illness, family breakup, alcoholism, and drug use, which, in addition to creating added costs for various social safety nets, are almost certain to reduce both the productive capacity of workers (as well as those of their families more generally) and the chances that they will return to the workplace, leading instead to dependence on the social welfare system.

All of these factors are likely to be aggravated by the problem of sour grapes[25] or adaptive preferences: the longer workers are unemployed or underemployed, the less likely they are to believe in their own inherent capabilities and hence actively to seek better opportunities.[26] In sum, the human effects of dislocation on workers and their families may well lead to long-term suboptimal development of workers' capacities, absent positive adjustment measures.

Although workers affected by trade liberalization may have private incentives to retrain, liquidity problems may imply that workers may find it difficult to finance retraining. This challenge supports subsidized retraining from an efficiency perspective only if capital markets have some imperfection that hinders efficient investment in human capital. The difficulty in providing security for loans against human capital, for example, may limit the ability of workers to seek private financing for retraining.

B. DISTRIBUTIVE JUSTICE

Two paradigms that I have invoked throughout this book are utilitarianism and Rawlsian distributive justice. Utilitarianism does not distinguish between the pecuniary and nonpecuniary costs of adjustment—both are sources of individual disutility and should be weighed against the gains in utility to other members of the community from trade liberalization in arriving at a determination of whether average utility (not simply income) has been increased.[27] The private and psychological costs of change may be substantial.[28] This fact may militate against freer trade generally, but it may also have implications for compensation or mitigation. Utilitarians will require consideration of both psychological and pecuniary costs of change when determining adequate compensation for adjustment costs. Additionally, utilitarians may call for compensation for the harm inflicted on relatively disadvantaged members of society, such as unskilled workers. The logic behind this is that even if an equal distribution of loss is assumed, the impact of a $1 loss may have a larger impact, in terms of experienced utility, on a low wage individual than on a high wage individual.

A Rawlsian distributive justice perspective argues that, behind the hypothetical veil of ignorance where the social contract is constructed and where our individual lots in life and endowments are not known, everyone agrees that society should pursue no collective policy that does not improve the lot of the least advantaged. In other words, we would all agree to a form of social insurance against the risk of finding ourselves in this plight. Rawls's theory is not indifferent, however, to concerns of aggregate social welfare; he is prepared to accept the idea that distributive policies that benefit the least advantaged ought to be achieved at minimum necessary costs to other groups or to society in general.[29] Thus, the Rawlsian perspective may call for compensation to those adversely affected by trade liberalization, particularly if they are among the most disadvantaged members of society to begin with (such as low-paid factory workers).

C. COMMUNITARIANISM

The communitarian perspective may suggest policies that diverge considerably from those driven by utilitarian or social contract frameworks. First, although the latter permit conceptualizing the psychological costs of change as real costs that may merit compensation, communitarians see the exit option—even when accompanied by compensation—as unjustified if it involves severing the bonds to extended family, neighborhood or community, and workplace colleagues. Loss of a significant part of one's human identity may simply not be compensable through redistributive policies. Policies that enhance the stay option may be preferred if they can keep intact the attachments that, according to communitarians, make life worth living. Thus, communitarian considerations clearly have implications for the formulation of adjustment policies. For example, a justifiable policy mix to address social losses experienced by a community followed by a decline in a local industry from trade liberalization may involve relocation assistance to younger workers, retraining for other sectors in the same community or region for middle-aged employees, and an early retirement package for older workers.

To economists, of course, policies that actually retard the speed of a market-driven reallocation of labor and capital are less justifiable than those that are merely compensatory. But in a morally pluralistic society, paying off the losers is not enough; the values they hold dear may have a legitimate place in the policy process. This point is well put by Calabresi:

> A decision which recognizes the values on the losing side as real and significant tends to keep us from becoming callous with respect to the moralisms and beliefs that lose out.... [I]t tells the losers that, though they lost, they and their values do carry weight and are recognized in our society, even when they don't win out.[30]

V. Political Considerations

Trade policy is particularly vulnerable to capture by special interest groups. This phenomenon was noted as early as 1776, when Adam Smith wrote that businessmen often collude to subvert the national interest in freer trade.[31] Public Choice theory suggests that the losses from trade liberalization are often concentrated on large and politically influential domestic producers, whereas the benefits from free trade are often thinly spread across other segments of the economy, including especially final consumers. Accordingly, vulnerable domestic industries may have a strong incentive to devote extensive resources to opposition to trade liberalization policies, although export-oriented industries may be an important political counterweight.[32] However, the extent of protection is not uniform, and the demands of special interest groups vary widely across industries and countries as does their power to achieve them. A substantial body of literature attempts to explain the emergence of powerful special interest groups, and the relationship between these groups and protectionism. Generally, the empirical research on the subject finds (perhaps surprisingly) little relationship between firm size, industry concentration, and the extent of protectionist measures (for example, agriculture is often a heavily protected sector).[33]

Baldwin points out that if uncertainty and imperfect information are introduced into the Public Choice model, risk averse individuals may prefer protectionist policies.[34] This may reflect endowment effects (discussed in Chapter 2), and there is some empirical support for the proposition that, in the presence of uncertainty and incomplete insurance markets due to imperfect information, protectionism may reduce both variability in input prices and fluctuations in income,[35] while some economists suggest that national protectionism is often adopted as a result of the well-known free-rider problem among diffuse potential beneficiaries of free trade.[36]

Another branch of the literature on the politics of trade liberalization attempts to explain the emergence of international trade agreements, as opposed to unilateral trade liberalization. Irwin, Mavroidis, and Sykes articulate three possible explanations for the emergence of the GATT: economic theory, commitment theory, and foreign policy.[37]

Economic theories of multilateral trade agreements tend to assume that governments seek to increase national income, but are sometimes deterred from this goal for political reasons, such as raising campaign funds or maintaining the support necessary to gain re-election.[38] Correspondingly, governments may seek to enter into international trade agreements if this is more likely to improve the terms-of-trade for the country, thereby increasing national income.[39] However, if countries act independently, they may not be able to achieve an efficient outcome. When one country unilaterally reduces trade barriers, other countries may have an incentive to maintain trade barriers against the tariff-reducing country.[40]

However, terms-of-trade theory has been regarded with some skepticism.[41] Indeed, Paul Krugman argues that it plays a negligible role in actual trade negotiations,[42] and the statements made by national representatives during the opening of the 1944 Geneva conference on trade provide little support for the hypothesis.[43] Additionally, empirical research suggests that countries are not motivated to enter into trade agreements because of declining terms of trade (declining export prices relative to import prices), but rather declining levels of trade overall.[44]

Commitment theorists contend that due to the existence of powerful lobby groups, governments are often unable to pursue welfare-maximizing policies. Commitments made under free trade agreements permit governments to claim that their hands are tied in the face of pressure from domestic lobby groups.[45] However, there is a large body of literature devoted to disputing the basic premises of commitment theory. Some authors argue that, when the government is facing domestic lobby group pressure, it is unclear why it feels a need to make international commitments.[46] Others point to the fact that GATT commitments are often not perceived as entirely credible, and many provisions within the GATT framework permit deviation from the commitments in the face of domestic pressures.[47]

It is also possible that foreign policy motivates free-trade negotiations. Generally, proponents of this line of argument suggest that the principal purpose of the GATT is to establish mechanisms for dispute resolution, and to introduce a sense of order into international politics.[48] One version of the foreign policy theory of trade agreements is the concept of hegemonic-stability, which suggests that a single dominant actor in international politics will establish and sustain stable international economic conditions.[49] Additionally, conflict theorists suggest that international trade is recognized as a mechanism for preventing the outbreak of war, as economic interdependence may align national interests.[50] There is a large body of empirical literature devoted to estimating the relationship between trade and conflict. Generally, these studies suggest that international economic integration inhibits conflict.[51]

There are many additional explanations for the emergence of international trade agreements. Some commentators argue that the postwar proliferation of free trade agreements was a result of shifting preferences among voters.[52] The state of the national economy may affect a government's ability to enter into free trade negotiations. While some argue that recessions increase the demand for protectionism,[53] others propose that economic downturns give policymakers more freedom to overturn existing protectionist policies.[54] Exemplifying the concept of "focussing events", Rodrik suggests that the debt crisis in the United States in the 1980s significantly weakened the powerful interests that benefited from protection, permitting governments to pursue free trade policies.[55] Further, increased public attention to an issue such as this may well lead policymakers to consult with "experts" in search of viable policy options (as well as insulation from related fallout). In this case, the consultation of economists would have led to a relatively uniform answer: free trade.

VI. Policy Instruments

Potential public policy responses to the costs of adjustment to trade liberalization fall into four major classes: gradualism, reciprocity, reversibility, and labor market policies. The first three categories of adjustment policies are a reflection of the fact that the form of the implementation of trade liberalization may mitigate some of the potential adjustment costs.[56] Multilateral and bilateral trade agreements typically include provisions to mitigate adjustment costs. These policy tools include gradual transition periods, reciprocal concessions by trading partners, and safeguard measures that allow for the temporary reinstatement of protectionist measures in the event of severe disruption to domestic industries. Gradualism and reciprocity can be thought of as ex ante policies designed to alleviate the transition costs associated with trade liberalization, and can have similar effects as outright protectionist measures. Reversibility, on the other hand, is an ex post policy that temporarily reinstates trade restrictions. Labor market policies are implemented as ex post assistance to workers affected by trade liberalization.

A. GRADUALISM

First, as has been the case with most major multilateral and regional initiatives in recent decades, trade liberalization involving tariff or subsidy reductions (or quota expansion) can follow a gentle phaseout trajectory—such as a 10-year time frame for implementation.[57] Such policies attenuate adjustment costs by providing for an adjustment process that is temporally dispersed rather than lumpy. For the same reason, they also delay the benefits from trade liberalization. Economists generally doubt that this policy is likely to enhance economic welfare,[58] and tend to see economic Darwinism (like Kaplow) as the best recipe for efficient adjustment. Indeed, delaying the removal of trade barriers necessarily postpones the realization of the full gains from trade liberalization. Similarly, economists may argue that not all adjustment costs are time-dependent. If the timing of the transition will not alter the size of the adjustment cost, immediate liberalization may be desirable, as it will permit the country to begin to reap the benefits from freer trade immediately. Additionally, if adjustment costs are such that it is best to adjust slowly, economic theory suggests that workers and firms will choose to do so.[59] For example, individual worker adjustment costs may depend on the number of people who decide to switch industries during the transition time period. In this situation, workers may choose to remain in their current jobs until labor market bottlenecks subside.[60]

However, the phasing-out of trade restrictions may be considered an appropriate policy for reducing the private costs of rapid adjustment, due to the prevention of negative spillover effects of the sudden shrinkage of large domestic industries. Bacchetta and Jansen argue that trade liberalization may be followed by mass layoffs and, correspondingly, congestion in labor markets.[61] In addition to these economic considerations, mass layoffs, particularly those that are geographically concentrated, can have devestating effects on commmunities as a whole. Consider, for example, the trajectory of Flint, Michigan (or Detroit) over the past 20 years. In his simulation of this phenomenon, Mussa found that trade reform triggers mass layoffs because of the presence of minimum wages.[62] He confirmed that gradual liberalization would lead to gradual adjustment, with a lower cost to the economy as a whole. Implementing trade liberalization policies gradually may prevent labor market congestion and therefore reduce transition costs associated with liberalization.

Governments often announce the future implementation of trade liberalization policies well in advance, in order to give firms and workers time to prepare for the transition.[63] This may be particularly important for countries with highly protected or subsidized industries or government-owned monopolies. Indeed, many firms may not survive if they are required to go through the process of privatization and exposure to foreign markets simultaneously. For example, Pastor demonstrates that the gradual implementation of trade liberalization in Spain permitted the Spanish banking sector to become competitive through domestic deregulation, before being exposed to foreign competition.[64]

B. RECIPROCITY

Although classical economic trade theory asserts that unilateral trade liberalization will yield a net benefit for the liberalizing country, most free trade agreements are made conditional on reciprocal concessions by trading partners.[65] Indeed, Paul Krugman noted that "if economists ruled the world, there would be no need for a World Trade Organization, [...] the economist's case for free trade is essentially a unilateral case,"[66] although it should be noted that Bagwell and Staiger argue that reciprocity may be an efficient mechanism for resolving terms-of-trade beggar-thy-neighbor prisoners' dilemmas among major trading powers (despite Krugman's scepticism).[67]

Despite wide recognition of the theoretical support for unilateral trade liberalization, countries rarely agree to open their markets to foreign competition without a reciprocal agreement from trading partners to liberalize foreign access to their own economies. Reciprocity provides a liberalizing country some assurance that adjustment costs caused by greater import penetration can be partially offset by increased access to export markets into which displaced resources can be redeployed over time.[68]

In practice, reciprocity conditions play an important role in generating the necessary political incentives in favor of implementing trade liberalization policies. The support of export-oriented producer interests may often be needed in order to countervail the lobbying efforts of import-sensitive industries likely to be uncompetitive in an open economy.[69] Reciprocity agreements thus can alleviate the transition costs associated with greater import penetration, and may be necessitated by political economy factors.

C. REVERSIBILITY

Provision can be made for temporary reinstatement of trade protection measures if liberalization threatens serious disruption to a domestic industry and its workforce. Whereas gradualism and reciprocity provisions permit governments to address expected transition costs ex ante, safeguard regimes allow for an ex post reaction to unanticipated costs and disruptive events, such as import surges.

Reversibility measures can include both quantitative restrictions and tariff increases, and there are a variety of provisions within the GATT/WTO framework that permit safeguard mechanisms. The emergency safeguard provision in the GATT (Article XIX) is most clearly targeted at temporary adjustment problems.[70] Additionally, during the Uruguay Round, a new multilateral Agreement on Safeguards was negotiated. Countries must establish that an increase in imports was an "unforeseen development" that is determined to have caused "serious injury" to domestic producers.[71] This increase in imports must have been "recent enough, sudden enough, sharp enough and significant enough, both quantitatively and qualitatively, to cause or threaten to cause serious injury."[72]

Some proponents of safeguard measures argue that safeguard regimes permit domestic industries that have lost their ability to compete internationally to restructure and regain their competitiveness. Davidson and Matusz show that temporary tariffs can be helpful if a country experiences a temporary trade shock.[73] They argue that some negative trade shocks can push the country into an undesirable equilibria, and thus a policy that slows adjustment is desirable. In this situation, safeguard provisions may attenuate the adjustment costs incurred by investors, dependent communities, and workers.

Other authors, such as Alan Sykes, argue that safeguard regimes reduce the political risks inherent in ex ante trade liberalization agreements, and thus enhance the likelihood that political agents will be willing to undertake such agreements.[74] Indeed, proponents of safeguard measures often argue that, due to the unknown extent of transition costs associated with trade liberalization, governments would be reluctant to commit to trade liberalization without some form of safety valve.

The extent of support for opt-out or safeguard provisions varies widely among commentators. Rodrik, in his critique of the existing safeguards regime, would permit trade restrictions and the suspension of trade agreement obligations for a broad array of economic and social purposes, such as "distributional concerns, conflicts with domestic norms and social arrangements, prevention of the erosion of domestic regulations, or developmental priorities."[75] However, given this expansive range of opt-outs, initial trade liberalization agreements may lack credibility, thus discouraging the negotiation of such commitments in the first place. Sykes advocates a more moderate approach to safeguard reform.[76] Rather than expanding the list of appropriate circumstances for countries to renege on their treaty obligations, he suggests that the current criteria should be interpreted more permissively.[77] Indeed, he argues that the current safeguard regime has become essentially impossible to comply with, creating strong incentives for countries to resort to arrangements such as voluntary export restriction agreements or other trade remedies (such as antidumping measures).[78]

There are also fairness rationales for safeguard mechanisms, as evidence suggests that the adverse impacts of liberalization disproportionately affect low-paid, low-skilled, immobile workers. As noted above, an extensive body of empirical literature suggests that the impact of protectionist policies (such as the safeguard regimes) entail costs for domestic consumers that are "several orders of magnitude greater than the value of jobs preserved, at least as measured by wage levels in the industry in question."[79] However, the unequal distribution of costs and benefits suggests that safeguards may sometimes be warranted.

Although reversibility provisions can reduce unexpected and inequitable adjustment costs, an excessively expansive approach to reversibility regimes is likely to erode the significance of treaty obligations. Reversibility clauses must strike a delicate balance between maintaining the credibility of treaty obligations and still affording appropriate and adequate opportunities to reduce transition costs ex post.

D. LABOR MARKET ADJUSTMENT POLICIES

The case for active labor market adjustment policies is substantially more compelling than for an expansive opt-out regime.[80] Under conditions of close to full employment, we have little reason to be concerned about the dislocation effects of trade liberalization. The market, in effect, will soon reabsorb the dislocated workers (although proponents of a number of ethical perspectives may find it appropriate for government to bear some of the transition costs these workers face).

If, more realistically, we assume that re-employment is likely to be far from automatic, then the question arises as to what measures are required to facilitate it. The process of adjustment is complex. At one level, the problem may be understood as the time lag between a worker's being displaced from one job and finding another that is an adequate replacement. From this perspective, passive policies such as provision of temporary income support and search, job counseling, and relocation assistance seem to address the problem.

However, the fact that employment is being created primarily in sectors other than those where jobs are being lost raises serious questions about the adequacy of the unemployment insurance model. It may be necessary to go further and provide retraining of workers for new types of employment within the economy. This point is well expressed in the Canadian de Grandpré report, which contrasts the active, or "trampoline" approach (which emphasizes training and retraining) with the passive unemployment insurance model (the "safety net" approach). The report suggests:

> The "trampoline" approach seeks to prepare Canadian workers to prosper in a world of increasing technological change and international competition, in which Canada must use its access to the larger North American market to achieve greater economies of scale and higher productivity.[81]

Although the use of the "trampoline" and "safety net" metaphors encourages a more active approach toward labor policies, the comparative experience with labor market policies in various industrialized countries yields a very mixed record. Overall, the literature generally suggests that a well-designed combination of passive and active labor market policies is most effective at reducing the adjustment burden resulting from trade liberalization policies.[82] In the following section, passive and active labor policies will be reviewed, as well as those labor market policies explicitly aimed at alleviating *trade* adjustment costs.

i. Passive Policies: The Safety Net

Passive labor market policies help minimize the losses incurred by affected workers, and generally include both job security regulation and income support. In developed countries, passive worker benefit schemes comprise the majority of assistance for displaced workers. Most high-income countries provide unemployment benefits, but very few developing countries have an unemployment insurance scheme.[83]

Job security legislation provides workers some security in their job, and protection against arbitrary firing and wage reductions. However, because the gains from trade often necessitate some shift of workers between industries, policy should not impede this shift through excessively stringent job security legislation. Preferably, this legislation would maintain incentives to move jobs while providing some basic level of job security.[84] Unemployment benefits can help cover some of the costs incurred by displaced workers. However, empirical evidence suggests that workers often earn much less in their subsequent jobs, due to their lack of skills in other industries.[85]

Canada, the United Kingdom, France, the United States, and Australia have historically tended to favor a safety net approach rather than proactive labor market policies, while countries such as Germany and Sweden have tended to favor the latter.[86] However, in recent decades there has been an increasing emphasis on active labor market policies (ALMPs). This shift was, in part, prompted by recommendations in a series of OECD reports in the 1980s and 1990s.[87]

ii. Active Policies: The Trampoline

By helping trade-displaced workers reintegrate into the workforce, ALMPs can enhance the adaptive capacity of labor markets while mitigating the costs imposed on job losers. The experience in different OECD countries suggests that active programs work best if they are fully integrated with income support schemes and if they are tailored to the different needs of different job seekers.[88]

Existing ALMPs can be divided into four broad types: job search assistance, short-term classroom training, on-the-job training (which is, in many ways, equivalent to subsidized employment), and long-term remedial training. Evaluating the net impact of ALMPs is methodologically complex. It involves taking into account, in addition to direct costs and benefits, deadweight losses (participants who would have found employment without the program), substitution losses (participants who find jobs that would have been filled by nonparticipants), and displacement losses (participants who displace currently employed non-participants).

There is an extensive literature that attempts to evaluate active labor market programs, both in terms of their effect on individual workers, and the net effects on the national economy. Boone and von Ours, in their analysis of 20 OECD countries, find that ALMPs differ dramatically in effectiveness.[89] The studies generally suggest that the effectiveness of a policy varies based on the specific design of the ALMP.[90]

In what follows, I outline the relevance of job search assistance, short-term classroom training, and on-the-job training programs.

a. Job-Search Assistance

In both Canada and the United States, government-administered job-posting and placement programs help individuals find jobs for which they are qualified. In some cases, these programs have roughly the same success rates as the job-training programs referred to below, and at much lower cost.[91] A majority of the empirical studies of job assistance programs have found that they generate positive outcomes,[92] although some find that the programs may make little difference.[93] Evidence also suggests that they may be more effective when combined with heightened monitoring of job-search behavior.[94]

Some job-search assistance programs take the form of re-employment bonuses. These cash payments are given to recipients who find a job quickly, and are able to keep it for a certain period of time. Japan and Korea have such a system in place, and, recently, several US states have begun to experiment with the system with a significant level of success.[95]

The efficacy of such measures is a function of the type of unemployment problem at hand. For structural unemployment resulting from trade liberalization, mere job-search assistance cannot be effective because it does not address the basic problem: even with full information about the employment market, individuals without the requisite skills will remain unemployed. For frictional unemployment, however, this strategy is appropriate; all that is required is to provide adequate information to allow qualified workers and employers to discover one another.

b. Classroom Training

There is a large literature devoted to the evaluation of various training programs. The conclusions of these studies have varied widely, and by no means overwhelmingly support more funding for such programs. A meta-analysis by Card, Kluve, and Weber found that classroom and on-the-job training programs are more likely to yield favorable medium-term than short-term results.[96] Heckle LaLonde, and Smith found that short-term training programs increase the probability of re-employment but have only a modestly positive impact on earnings.[97] Martin found similar results: of all the program types, job training was one of the programs most likely to have a positive impact on employment rates.[98]

In Canada, although both classroom and on-the-job training have enjoyed only moderate success, the latter has been relatively more effective in improving an individual's chances of employability.[99] Many classroom-retraining programs have been too short to impart a significant new set of skills.

In Europe, classroom training is more often coupled with on-the-job training than in North America.[100] Although Sweden's classroom training programs are often cited as examples of effective labor market training, they have recently come under more critical scrutiny.[101] Researchers have found that those individuals who acquire practical, on-the-job training in the Swedish program are more successful than those who receive classroom instruction alone, although both programs have modest effects.[102]

c. On-the-Job Training

On-the-job training or subsidized employment is already part of government job-training strategy in both Canada and the United States. Certain problems are evident in the systems that give rise to concerns about its adequacy as a response to trade dislocation. First, most programs have been structured without the possibility of flexible adjustments to reflect changing labor market demands. Leaving the choice of skills acquired up to the individual worker would be a more efficient method of allocation. Another significant problem with current policies is that firms have strong incentives to spend little on training or simply do away with it altogether and exploit the opportunity to hire unskilled workers (whom they may have hired in any event) at little or no cost to themselves. Wage subsidy programs are often plagued by high deadweight, substitution, and displacement losses. Public employment programs tend to be temporary make-work programs with marginal effects on future employability.[103]

iii. Trade-Specific Adjustment Programs

Adjustment programs specifically targeted at trade-displaced workers are controversial. Unlike the aforementioned general schemes, trade-specific programs need to identify which workers in particular were displaced as a result of trade liberalization. This is an extremely difficult task, and many of the criticisms concerning trade-specific programs are concerned with their inability to accurately identify those workers displaced due to trade liberalization.[104]

Experience with trade-specific labor market policies has been mixed. For example, the US Trade Expansion Act of 1962 and the Trade Act of 1974 sought to provide adjustment assistance to workers dislocated by import competition. The 1962 Act had very strict eligibility criteria—requiring, for example, that imports were demonstrably a more important factor than all others combined in causing injury and that tariff concessions and injury must have occurred simultaneously—and it was largely unsuccessful as an instrument of assistance. From 1962 to 1974, only 54,000 workers were certified for assistance, which involved total expenditures of US$85 million.[105] Adjustment assistance grew substantially after the passage of the 1974 act, under which the level of benefits was increased and the eligibility criteria were greatly relaxed. Subsequent amendments to the Act expanded its breadth, and Congress has approved additional funding for the Trade Adjustment Assistance (TAA) program with nearly every new free trade agreement.[106] In 2007, the United States spent approximately $855.1 million on the TAA program, and over 150,000 displaced workers received benefits. The program expanded dramatically with the enactment of the American Recovery and Reinvestment Act of 2009.

Despite broad support for the program among policymakers, recent empirical evidence suggests that the TAA program does not have a positive impact on the employment outcomes of the average participant.[107] However, there is some empirical support for the skills-training component of the TAA. Although the income support, job search assistance, and relocation payments and other TAA benefits may not help workers find new, well-paying employment, skills training does tend to improve employment outcomes for these workers. Participation in TAA-funded training opportunities increased the likelihood of new employment by 10–12 percentage points, and reduced earning losses by 8–10 percentage points.[108]

This evidence is not damning to trade-related worker adjustment assistance programs *as such*. Rather, it suggests that policies should be designed to ensure that priority is placed on job losses that are likely to be permanent and that eligibility criteria are not tilted in favor of sectors represented by powerful lobby groups. These points reinforce the conclusion that assistance programs must be targeted carefully at their intended beneficiaries.

In many sectors undergoing major restructuring (steel and textiles, for example), it is often unclear which jobs lost are due to trade effects and which are due to technological change or declining demand. Even if causes and effects can be disentangled, is it normatively defensible to offer differential treatment to workers in the same industry who are displaced for different reasons? The logic of targeting or disaggregating adjustment assistance is that workers displaced by trade liberalization may be more likely to require retraining than those who lose their jobs due to cyclical downturns or the bankruptcy of a particular firm, because trade-induced dislocation may reflect a need to restructure permanently an entire industry or sector in response to increased import competition. Moreover, pragmatically, political pressure against social-welfare–increasing trade liberalization may be less when assistance is offered to workers than when it is not.

iv. Other Policies

There are a wide variety of other domestic policies that can help to reduce adjustment costs associated with trade liberalization. For example, stable macroeconomic conditions, adequate infrastructure, and well-functioning labor and capital markets can alleviate adjustment costs.[109] Indeed, Bacchetta and Jansen demonstrate that adjustment costs are significantly higher when firms face credit constraints due to inefficiently functioning credit markets.[110]

Additionally, many countries have used industrial subsidies to cope with the cost of adjusting to liberalization. In many industrialized countries since the early 1970s, sectors such as shipbuilding, coal, steel, textiles, clothing and footwear, and, in some cases, automobiles have experienced substantial competitive pressures from imports.[111] Countries under import pressure have often resorted to various kinds of industrial subsidies apart from trade restrictions. In general, these subsidy policies have not been effective in avoiding the ultimate need for adjustment or in moderating its severity. Pure output-related subsidies have been the least effective in that they flatly deny the need for adjustment; although they maintain employment in an industry, it can be sustained only if the subsidies are endless (and often increasing). These policies clearly manifest Kaplow's moral hazard concerns with compensation for transition costs.[112]

Other forms of industrial subsidies have been designed to facilitate the modernization of obsolete capital. Proponents argue that state assistance to facilitate capital modernization may be necessary to make a distressed industry internationally competitive again. However, obsolete plants are often the result, not the cause, of the loss of international competitiveness. Firms that are able to cover only variable costs are constrained to allow their fixed assets to run down, and correspondingly, long-term capacity. If new fixed assets could garner an adequate return, private capital markets presumably would provide the funds required for the investment.

VII. Conclusion

This case study has reviewed rationales and instruments for intervention in response to economic dislocation caused by changes in trade policy. As economies adjust to trade liberalization, some sectors of the economy will incur losses. Although the benefits generated by trade liberalization will generally offset these losses, this case study emphasizes the importance of policies commonly used to mitigate adjustment costs.

Throughout the postwar period of trade liberalization, industrialized countries have resorted to a variety of policy instruments to mitigate the adjustment costs associated with freer trade. Indeed, the international experience with trade negotiations has demonstrated that policies of gradualism, reciprocity, and reversibility are politically indispensable to a trade liberalization strategy. Although these policies can, at least temporarily, reduce the gains from trade liberalization, their existence is critical to the political feasibility of trade liberalization agreements.

In contrast, industrial subsidies are neither politically indispensable nor theoretically defensible. Subsidies deny the need for adjustment, and prevent a nation from benefiting from trade liberalization. Such policies cannot be thought of as an ex ante or ex post mechanism to alleviate adjustment costs. Instead, they act as a barrier to the adjustment process itself.

Some labor market policies have successfully reduced unemployment and wage-loss associated with trade liberalization. However, labor market policies differ widely in terms of their effectiveness, and are highly sensitive to design issues, although active labor market policies that emphasize classroom and on-the-job retraining for job opportunities elsewhere in the economy tend to be more effective than passive time-limited income support policies. Trade-targeted labor market policies are especially controversial. It is extremely difficult to identify with confidence trade-related job displacement, relative to other causes of displacement. Additionally, fairness concerns are raised by the preferential treatment of workers displaced as a result of trade liberalization relative to workers displaced for other reasons.

{ 6 }

Agricultural Supply Management: Unraveling the Transitional Gains Trap

I. Introduction

Agricultural protectionism is a long-standing policy in many developed countries. It has often taken the form of domestic and export subsidies, restrictions on imports, and guaranteed pricing schemes. Sometimes agricultural subsidies are explicit; in other cases they are implicit, as in supply management programs. The degree of protectionism varies widely among Organisation for Economic Co-operation and Development (OECD) countries. For example, estimated producer support as a percentage of gross farm receipts (Producer Support Estimate or PSE) in Australia and New Zealand is relatively low (3 percent and 0.5 percent, respectively); in the United States, Canada, and the European Union (EU) it is 8.5 percent, 16 percent, and 22 percent, respectively; while in countries such as Norway and Japan producer support is near or over 50 percent of farm receipts. The PSE of the OECD as a whole is roughly 20 percent.[1]

The instruments of agricultural protection in these countries are varied as well.[2] The EU's Common Agricultural Policy (CAP) has traditionally guaranteed minimum prices for sales within the European Union, protected through variable import levies, guaranteed sales (i.e., government purchase of oversupply), and rebates on export sales below EU prices. Canada maintains marketing and production restrictions on poultry, eggs, and milk through guaranteed prices, import tariffs, and domestic quotas. Supply restrictions reduce the problems of overproduction and displacement of foreign producers in third-country markets that have tended to result from the CAP. The United States employs price support measures coupled with production restrictions, and certain forms of export subsidies, among other measures. Japan's extensive agricultural protection programs employ a range of instruments including price stabilization, supply management, import quotas, and extremely high tariffs.[3]

In each case, the rents or subsidies provided by agricultural protectionism tend to become capitalized in farm investments, such as land or quotas. These investments may then lose value when a government reduces its support for the particular industry. Farm groups threatened by such changes will often have strong financial incentives to oppose reductions in support, and may be aided in opposition efforts by a concentrated interest group advantage, public sympathy for farmers, concerns about food security and foreign dependence, ignorance among consumers or taxpayers, and institutional features of local political systems, such as the disproportionate weight accorded to rural electorates and a high number of "veto players"[4] (as discussed in Chapter 2). The presence of these factors increases the likelihood that compensation or other forms of transition cost mitigation will be necessary in order to implement reforms that are in the general public interest.

These dynamics are starkly illustrated in the example of the dairy industry in Canada, the largest of the country's three supply-managed farm sectors. Rich government-mandated rents under the program have been capitalized in quota values, creating an asset class valued at $28 billion[5] in total that would have no value following the dismantling of the program—a problem characterized by Gordon Tullock as a "transitional gains trap."[6] Thus far, most dairy farmers have fiercely and predictably opposed reform. Any government wishing to remove the program faces two main difficulties—building support for reform by convincing the public or other interest groups that the status quo is not to their benefit (and that it is worth their effort to change it), and overcoming the formidable opposition to reform, most likely through a carefully tailored plan of compensation and transition cost mitigation.

This chapter seeks lessons from Canada's experience with dairy supply management, as well as the successes of Australia and New Zealand, which might be applied globally to supply management and other agricultural protection programs, as well as to transition policy generally. Many of the considerations discussed below would similarly apply, with variations for local features, to programs such as the European Union's CAP and heavily protected farm sectors in the United States. I believe that many of the lessons to be learned from this case study could also be fruitfully applied to other policy contexts, especially where a transitional gains trap makes reform difficult (as with mortgage interest tax deductibility, discussed in Chapter 4).

II. Dairy Supply Management in Canada

A. THE STRUCTURE OF CANADA'S DAIRY SUPPLY MANAGEMENT SCHEME

The supply management scheme for dairy in Canada is often said to rest on three "pillars."[7] The first pillar is setting standard prices to be paid for milk. This is done by federal and provincial government boards. Milk to be sold as a fluid (milk and cream) is priced by provincial boards, while "industrial milk" to be processed into butter, cheese, and yogurt is priced by the Canadian Dairy Commission (CDC). Price-setting boards at both levels take into account farmers' average production costs, which creates a disincentive to control costs or to innovate, as efficient production methods would reduce farmers' income.[8] Soaring quota prices are thought to be prima facie evidence that production costs have been systematically overestimated at both levels.[9] The other key factor at the CDC level is the Commissioners' own judgment of what constitutes a "fair return" for farmers.[10] The resulting price is "highly controlled and stable, and dramatically higher than returns found in peer industries."[11] Moreover, there is "no requirement to consider the level of processor or consumer prices."[12] CDC Commissioners tend to be dairy farmers and lobbyists and thus tend to take a one-sided view of "fairness."[13] Similarly, a provincial board may actually be the provincial dairy lobby itself, as in the case of Quebec (a classic case of regulatory "capture").[14]

The second pillar is setting milk production levels. To produce milk for sale, farmers must hold quotas, which represent their share of the national allowed production total.[15] Quota amounts are distributed to the provinces according to a complex set of factors, including population size and history of dairy farming, rather than according to comparative advantage.[16] Quebec (37 percent), Ontario (32 percent) and Alberta (9 percent) have the largest shares of the national production quota.[17] Individual quotas are tradable on provincial exchanges. The monopoly profits on dairy production are capitalized in the quotas and drive up their value. At the same time, high quota values also put upward pressure on the milk price, as dairy farmers lobby for richer profits to help them pay off debts incurred in buying quotas. The result of this "quota-price treadmill"[18] is that the value of quotas has soared: in 2007–2008 the average value of quota for the milk production of one cow was $28,000, up from $16,000 only 10 years before.[19] An Ontario milk producer could sell a quota in 2009 for three times what it would have cost to purchase that quota in 1995.[20] In response to this rise, Quebec and Ontario have instituted quota value caps at $25,000 (although these may be largely offset by appreciation in land values). High quota values both present significant barriers to entry to the industry and galvanize support among holders of quotas for continuation of the supply management scheme. In 2009 a typical Canadian dairy farm held $2 million in quotas and, as noted above, the entire value of dairy quotas was estimated at $28 billion.[21] Such numbers make unattractive the prospect of eliminating supply management by buying out quotas.[22] At the same time, concerns about fairness, negative externalities pertaining to farmers' dislocation, and the possibility of public backlash in response to a policy perceived as "destroying a way of life" make compensation or mitigation of some type a virtual necessity.

The third pillar of the scheme is limiting imports, so as to preserve the above-normal profits of domestic farmers. The level of tariffs required to keep imports out helps illustrate how far above world prices Canadian dairy prices are.

In 2011, the tariff on imports above minimum access levels was: for butter, 298 percent; for cheese, 245 percent; for yogurt, 237 percent.[23] These tariffs are an anomaly in Canadian trade policy. The average of Canada's most favored nation tariffs across all industries in 2002 was 6 percent and the average for agricultural products was 21.7 percent.[24]

B. THE EFFECTS OF CANADA'S DAIRY SCHEME

It is often argued that the economic costs of agricultural protection outweigh its benefits.[25] Higher dairy prices not only transfer consumer income to farmers, they also cause a deadweight loss by pricing marginal (often low-income) consumers out of the market for some dairy products.[26] Some of the costs and inequitable results of Canada's dairy supply management scheme, which support the case for reform, are briefly canvassed in this section.

Consumers bear most of the costs of this scheme, as it forces them to pay higher prices than would be available in a free market. "Rather than subsidize farmers directly with money collected in taxes from citizens, the government lets producers raise prices by giving them monopoly privileges."[27] The price-setting boards have boosted milk prices faster than inflation in recent years.[28] More important, the level of retail prices for dairy products is far above what it would be in a free market. The OECD calculates that the value of gross government-mandated transfers from Canadian consumers to dairy producers in 2010 was $3.6 billion (all figures CAD unless otherwise noted).[29] This transfer accounts for 60.5 percent of gross dairy farm receipts.[30] In its consumer effect, this massive wealth transfer is no different from a grocery tax on dairy products of roughly 150 percent. The OECD and other analysts have concluded that Canada's supply management system has caused dairy prices to be "much higher than those prevailing on world markets."[31] Comparable price data for consumer prices can be difficult to find. However, studies have found that the Canadian retail price of a pound of butter in 2009 was 60 percent, or $1.50 (CAD), higher than in Australia, where there is no government support for dairy production, and 31 percent, or 94 cents, higher than in the United States,[32] where there is some support, but much less than in Canada.[33] In 2012 whole milk in Canada cost more than twice the price in the United States.[34]

Moreover, the above-market pricing mandated by supply management has a regressive effect—it affects the poorest Canadians the most, as they spend a larger share of their budgets on food. "This regressive effect is the opposite of what would result if farmers in supply-managed sectors instead benefited from government payments financed by general taxation, since tax liabilities vary directly with the ability to pay."[35] The $3.6 billion in consumer price support to dairy farmers in 2011 cost $105 per Canadian, or $420 for a family of four.[36] This is a serious burden for families of modest means.

The harm is greater given the often positive effects of dairy on nutrition. In Canada, a liter of milk costs more than double the price of a liter of cola.[37] Supply management has "made the cost of basic nutrition more expensive for the poor."[38] Dairy and baked goods have "been the greatest contributors to the surge in food inflation in recent years."[39] As the milk price has steadily risen over the years,[40] dairy consumption in 2009 fell to a level not seen since 1975.[41] Health Canada recommends that adults consume two cups of milk (or alternative) each day—and that youths aged 9–18 consume between three and four cups.[42] Dairy provides key nutrients such as calcium and can improve bone health, especially in children.[43] Supply management's above-market pricing makes it costly for the poorest Canadians to meet the minimum requirements of a healthy diet for their families. One commentator notes that Canada's poorest households "appear to have been abandoned in this matter by the usual groups which defend low-income citizens."[44]

At the same time, the farmers benefiting from these rents are some of the richest people in the country. In 2009 the average dairy farmer had a net worth of over $2.5 million,[45] much of this being quota value. According to one study, the top 5 percent of Canadians had a net worth above $1.2 million in 2005.[46] Dairy farmers had an average net worth above $2 million that year.[47] Another study shows that the average net income of dairy farmers in 2007 put them comfortably in the top 10 percent of Canadian earners.[48] Moreover, the gap between rich dairy farmers and other Canadians may be growing: the richest 10 percent of Canadians account for 41 percent of all pre-tax income, the largest share since World War II.[49]

Nor are the rents from supply management distributed evenly. Ontario and Quebec together receive 69 percent of the benefit of this rich program. Together they represent 62 percent of the Canadian population. In particular, although Quebec had only 23 percent of the population of Canada in 2011,[50] it had 37 percent of the dairy cows.[51] This distribution may be significant given that dairy supply management alone accounts for nearly half of Canada's total agricultural price support.[52] Moreover, dairy farms made up only 6.4 percent of all Canadian farms at the last Census of Canadian Agriculture.[53] Dairy farms are also among those operating on the largest scale, with 57.3 percent earning gross receipts above $250,000.[54] There is, furthermore, "no evidence that [dairy farmers'] situation is fundamentally different" from that of other farmers.[55] Dairy supply management alone has caused Canada's overall level of agricultural protection to resemble the European Union's more than the more modest US level.[56]

High dairy tariffs undermine Canada's claim to be a supporter of free trade and harm Canada's international trade agenda.[57] During the Doha Round of WTO negotiations in 2004, Canadian Trade Minister Jim Peterson told journalists that Canada was alone in supporting supply management: "it was one against 146. We had absolutely no allies at the negotiating table."[58] Supporting supply management has hobbled the country's trade agenda in recent years[59] and it continues to do so: supply management will be a "major stumbling block" in talks toward the potentially major Trans-Pacific Partnership (TPP) trade deal that could account for 54 percent of global GDP,[60] and it will likely define the extent of increased access to the EU market for Canada's non–supply-managed farmers under the prospective bilateral Comprehensive Economic and Trade Agreement.[61] Under a recently signed tentative accord, quotas on EU cheese imports will be significantly raised (in return for increased access to the EU market for Canadian meat exports), eliciting predictable protests and demands for compensation by the Canadian dairy industry. However, "[e]xport opportunities are critical for the growth of most Canadian agriculture and agri-food industries."[62] Canada's stubbornness on dairy seriously hinders the ability of export-oriented farmers and businesses to prosper. Further, the harm to dairy farmers themselves, in the form of opportunity costs, should not be discounted. Since a 2002 WTO decision found the scheme to be an export subsidy,[63] supply management has effectively confined dairy farmers to a declining domestic market,[64] while farmers in deregulated markets such as New Zealand have made broad export gains.[65]

C. THE POLITICS OF DAIRY—THE NECESSITY OF COMPENSATION

In light of its harms, dairy supply management in Canada has had remarkable staying power. At the beginning of the 1960s dairy producers had been organized in cooperatives for several decades, but external factors, such as depressed prices and the loss of the UK export market after the United Kingdom joined the European Union, were buffeting the industry.[66] Through the 1960s producers organized into a strong political pressure group, and incrementally succeeded in bringing about a nationally managed dairy supply scheme by the early 1970s. The system remains essentially unchanged today.[67] Scores of studies documenting the harmful economic effects of dairy supply management do not seem to have weakened its political support.[68] This section outlines the key reasons it has survived, and why eliminating the scheme would be politically difficult.

i. Public Choice Theory

As discussed in Chapter 2 of this book, a fundamental insight of Public Choice theory is that concentrated interest groups are likely to have a disproportionately large effect on public policy.[69] This is particularly likely when the costs of a particular policy are spread across a diffuse body of citizens. Small groups with a strong incentive to seek a particular policy will often have more success in organizing and, in turn, greater political success than large groups with weak incentives to oppose it. This is, in fact, a basic premise of economic theories of group behavior.[70] It has been argued that this is "why farmers in rich countries... are dramatically politically successful."[71] Indeed, Canada's roughly 13,000 milk producers[72] (down from 145,000 when the current scheme was instituted in 1971) have a strong incentive to organize and lobby for continued wealth transfers from consumers, while dairy consumers, the majority of the Canadian populace, each have little individual incentive to fight back, and suffer from collective action problems in organizing.[73] Supply management in 2010 raised the cost of living by about $420 for each family of four.[74] These costs are substantial, but Canadians' lack of information about the costs of supply management contributes to public apathy with respect to its continued existence. And the cost per consumer is dwarfed by the benefit per dairy farm owner. The average dairy farmer gained roughly $277,000 from supply management price support in 2010.[75] In light of consumer apathy, politicians have "[found] it in their best interests (i.e., maximizing the likelihood of re-election) to please the milk producers and to ignore the plight of consumers."[76] Processors, grocers, restaurateurs, and other concentrated interest groups who may oppose supply management have had little success in lobbying against it.[77] The lack of information among consumers (exacerbated by the opaqueness of the regime) and the inability of consumer and other groups to effectively mobilize in opposition has meant that the political benefits from policy change in this area continue to be outweighed by the costs of antagonizing small but well-organized dairy farmers' groups. Indeed, as recently as 2005 the Canadian Parliament unanimously passed a motion in support of supply management programs.[78]

ii. Public Sympathy

Public sympathy for farmers plays a role in preserving the status quo. Three rationales are often offered for differential treatment of the agricultural sector generally.[79] First, it is argued that in times of national emergency it would benefit a country to have a strong domestic food production industry for survival's sake. This consideration at best supports the notion of a dairy industry, rather than specifically a supply-managed one. Second, it is argued that agricultural products suffer from exceptional price volatility.[80] However, a study commissioned by the International Dairy Foods Association, a US dairy processor group, concluded that "milk supply control programs... have not reduced price volatility," and noted that the milk price collapsed in 2008–2009 in all countries studied "whether they had active supply control policies or not."[81] Third, supply management benefits from vague popular notions that might be called communitarianism.[82] The idea is "that keeping land and people in farming is a social good in itself"[83] and that agricultural price supports help to do so. Because of communitarian ideas, Canadian farmers "enjoy an undercurrent of sympathy among urban voters which confers political power on them quite out of proportion to their numbers."[84] Claims that supply management meets the practical goals implicit in such communitarian values are doubtful,[85] but as an emotional response, communitarian support for supply management is powerful. Indeed, this is something that dairy farmers' associations have actively cultivated via advertising campaigns. Additionally, some consumers may support agricultural protectionism because they project their own job insecurities onto agriculture as "a symbolic declining industry."[86] Finally, regarding dairy in particular, some consumers believe that the removal of supply management would pressure dairy farmers to increase productivity and reduce investment in the health of their cows.[87] Such health fears might be met more effectively and at far lower cost with targeted regulation and oversight.

iii. Political Geography

It is often assumed that the distribution of dairy farms is a key factor in ensuring political support for supply management.[88] Even after the Fair Representation Act[89] comes into force in 2015, adding seats in Parliament for underrepresented, largely suburban regions, rural ridings are likely to maintain a disproportionate influence in provincial and federal legislatures. The concentration of dairy farmers across rural southern Ontario and southern Quebec[90] in "marginal ridings with political clout" is thought to give them strong political influence.[91] The attempt of Eugene Whelan, federal agriculture minister, to rein in dairy price supports in the 1970s led to what was, at the time, the largest ever protest on Parliament Hill. Further, the "producer-provincial-federal agreements" and interrelated federal and provincial legislation on which the system is based would entail at least bi-level cooperation (i.e., an increased number of veto-players) in reform efforts—a further complication, reflecting the complex politics of Canadian federalism.[92]

iv. Transitional Gains Trap

Finally, the supply management system is stuck in a transitional gains trap.[93] Extraordinary profits garnered under the supply management system have been capitalized in quota prices, pushing farmers to lobby bureaucrats to set the milk prices ever higher to recoup their initial outlay. Farmers who received quotas for free or bought them cheaply many years ago received the benefit of the transitional gains, but if the system is dismantled it will be today's producers who will lose money invested in quotas. Banks that have taken quotas as collateral for loans may also be exposed to large losses and are likely to act as a nontrivial source of opposition to uncompensated reform.

III. Overcoming Challenges to Reform

With such forces lined up against advocates of an efficient dairy policy, it is easy to see why a reform-minded government might hesitate to take on the dairy industry. The political benefits from reform would largely depend on convincing an uninformed, apathetic, or even oppositional dairy-consuming public that reform is in their interests, and would in any case be mostly dispersed, while the political costs would be concentrated on a powerful rural interest group. This analysis suggests that there are two key challenges for a government minded to dismantle an entrenched, rich agricultural support program such as Canada's dairy supply management. First, the public must be persuaded that the current supply management scheme is contrary to the public welfare, and that the issue is sufficiently serious as to warrant political attention. In other words, the issue must be made sufficiently salient and must be appropriately framed. Second, opposition to reform from farmers' groups and their sympathizers will need to be mitigated by way of a carefully tailored program of compensation and transition cost mitigation. The following sections deal with these challenges in turn.

A. PERSUADING THE PUBLIC

Many commentators have analyzed the structure, politics, and effects of Canada's dairy supply management system.[94] Some have offered policy ideas for reform, including a proposal by William Robson and Colin Busby to slowly increase the number of quotas, to ease the farmers into a free market system.[95] However, as I have previously argued, "ideas need a congenial political context if they are to take root...ideas without supportive and salient political interests are doomed to political oblivion."[96] The costs of supply management, as they arise from a technically complex, off-budget and low-profile support program, are largely hidden from public view and are therefore less likely to be a concern for voters.[97] A key obstacle for a reform-minded government, and one that has received comparatively little attention from commentators,[98] is the twin challenge of convincing voters that the status quo is not in the public interest and of building a coalition of interest groups that might support a reform effort.

Public sentiment respecting any reform proposal to reduce or remove dairy price supports is likely to play a key part in the success or failure of its implementation. Already the realm of public information is seen by stakeholders as a key battleground in the fight over the future of supply management programs in Canada.[99] The fact that the average Canadian knows little or nothing about supply management[100] has helped the policy survive. For example, a vague notion that supply management helps to preserve family farms (there is no evidence that is does[101]), coupled with a lack of information about the costs it imposes on families of modest means, may make many consumers unlikely to consider supply management a problem, let alone one that deserves prominent political attention.

In addition, a government considering proposing reform might be wise to court interest groups that could be persuaded to support the effort. Groups that purchase milk or dairy products, such as restaurant, grocery, grocery distributor, food manufacturer, and consumer groups, largely oppose milk price hikes and may support reform.[102] Dairy processors pay high farm-gate prices for milk but "are fierce competitors in the marketplace and often support opposing policy alternatives."[103] Finally, farms that are export-dependent (91.6 percent of all Canadian farms[104]) suffer from diminished market access in foreign countries, as Canada's high dairy tariffs make other countries reluctant to grant market access for Canadian exports such as beef and grains.[105] Export-oriented farmers might be a particularly powerful ally, but it is not clear whether farmers' groups would be willing to publicly back the retraction of government support for other farmers.[106]

Framing efforts are likely to be crucial to creating the political context needed for reform. Voters' economic considerations and their sense of fairness are likely targets for competing framing efforts that would accompany any reform effort in this area. Recent research suggests that on the topic of agricultural protectionism, framing may be particularly influential.[107] Dissemination of information on the costs of a current agricultural program by a broad and credible coalition of interests can make its reform less politically costly, as voters armed with relevant information can put pressure on all parties to reform negotiations, such as producer groups, bureaucrats, and other levels of government. The mass media may play an important role in framing efforts. Although politicians are often thought to be responsive to what is reported in the mass media,[108] agricultural policy seems usually not to be newsworthy. However, mass media reporting tends to be targeted to large groups, such as consumers.[109] Assuming broad interest in the issue, the mass media may provide information that is relevant to their interests.[110] Persuading the public that dairy sector reform is likely to improve the lives of Canadians and reduce inequalities in Canadian society is likely to be an important step in putting pressure on relevant parties to engage in candid discussions about how to achieve reform.

B. POLICY OPTIONS FOR COMPENSATION AND MITIGATING OPPOSITION TO REFORM

From a social welfare perspective, a careful removal of the supply management system would be beneficial. From a political perspective, shrewd framing may help create a congenial political context for reform. In both New Zealand and Australia, countries that eliminated price supports for dairy farmers, many farmers were in favor of reform prior to implementation.[111] These favorable conditions do not exist in Canada. Given the power of the Canadian dairy lobby, its vehement opposition to reform, and the $28 billion price tag of a full compensation program (about double the current federal budget deficit), dairy deregulation in Canada will be controversial and face significant opposition. Even assuming broad public support for reform, significant compensation will probably have to be offered to make it politically feasible.

i. Minor Reform

Minor reforms could reduce some of the costs of supply management programs, and in many cases may be more politically feasible than wholesale reform. In the case of Canada's dairy sector, institutional features of supply management help to entrench its farmer-first outcomes. Options for reform include increased participation in decision-making by non-farmer stakeholders (or the creation of truly independent regulatory agencies), revisions to price-setting formulas and board mandates to reflect consumer and processor interests in a lower price and to encourage farm efficiency (for example, by benchmarking price increases to the costs of the most efficient producers), and reforms to increase transparency and accountability.[112] Similarly, barriers to interprovincial trade and external tariffs could be reduced. Aggressive tariff reduction might even prompt some dairy farmers to advocate the removal of production quotas, preferring to expand their operations to better compete with imports.[113] In addition to putting downward pressure on milk prices, such reforms might cool the blazing markets for quotas, reducing the costs of a future compensated dismantling. Ideally, no compensation should be called for to enact such reforms, as they merely recognize that dairy policy is not all about farmers.

ii. Options for Dismantling Supply Management

The high social and economic costs of dairy supply management in Canada, explored above, make dismantling the system the best option. Australia's experience in dismantling its own dairy supply management system in 2000 offers several lessons for Canadian policymakers. In a study of the Australian experience, David Harris describes some key parameters of dismantling and compensation schemes. Under a *full impact approach*, dismantling is done overnight. The government predicts the impact on producer returns and the amount of assistance payments needed.[114] Under a *phased approach*, transition to a free market would happen gradually, with some continued supply control and implicit taxation of consumers in the interim.[115] Harris argues that the full impact approach is superior because, when coupled with explicit transition assistance, it speeds the adjustment to free market competition. "[F]armers receive immediate market signals on the full extent of the change in enterprise returns," and can either use payments to boost farm productivity or to transition to different industries.[116] Explicit assistance is also more flexible, allowing policymakers to target farmers who need it most.

Policymakers in Australia chose the full impact approach, announcing the end to all price support mechanisms nine months before overnight implementation on July 1, 2000.[117] A federal assistance package worth $2 billion (AUD) was to be made available if all states ended regulation on the same day, encouraging a coordinated approach.[118] The funding was fully paid for by a 10-year consumer tax of 11 cents on every liter of fluid milk sold.[119] In spite of the tax, consumer prices on milk fell significantly within a year and dropped 18–29 percent within six years.[120] The Australian Consumer and Competition Commission monitored the competitive practices of processors and retailers to ensure that savings were passed on to consumers.[121] Fears about the capacity of farmers to adjust to deregulation were "overly pessimistic": farmers were highly responsive and most successfully adjusted to new market conditions.[122]

Canada's dairy farmers, unlike Australia's, are nearly unified in opposition to change, and the cost of compensation would be far higher. This makes a phased approach the more likely option. A phased approach would be (1) more likely to assuage producer fears of an inability to compete in a free market, (2) less contentious to taxpayers and consumers than full compensation provided by a subsidy or a high "milk tax," and (3) more attractive to cash-strapped governments than a subsidized quota buy-back program or other direct forms of assistance. Robson and Busby propose a regular auction of new quotas over a period of 20 years: "An auction of 0.4 percent of today's total quota—about 1.2 million kg of butterfat—that rises to 15 million kg of butterfat by 2029 should ensure gradually declining, above-market returns."[123] The price-setting formulas would be abandoned and prices would slowly drop toward world market prices due to gradually diminishing supply restriction. Tariffs would be kept at high enough levels to maintain domestic prices. According to their model, the value of current quotas would drop immediately on adoption of the plan by about half, due to "access to only 20 years of protected markets and decreasing returns to quotas."[124] This phased approach would partially address the problem of compensating dairy farmers for the loss of $28 billion in quota values. It would provide implicit assistance of about $11.3 billion to dairy farmers, while farmers who wished to exit immediately could recoup an estimated half their quota value on the market.[125] Further, the sale of new quotas might generate roughly $300 million in revenue.[126] However, this proposal, in which half of quota value is wiped out immediately, would be highly unattractive to dairy farmers without more, as would similar proposals for a phaseout of import tariffs. As Stanbury argues: "it seems likely that a lobby group sufficiently strong to stop a sudden dismantling... would also be strong enough to prevent its members from being strangled slowly."[127] Such phased deregulation proposals also suffer from uncertainty as a future government could backtrack on the commitment to dismantle the system (the problem of time inconsistency).

iii. Options for Compensation and Transition Assistance Policies

Further transition assistance could help to mitigate these difficulties. It could also be targeted to achieve government objectives such as maintaining rural employment, helping farmers with smaller operations or more debt to transition, and providing capital for productivity-enhancing investments or for transitions to other industries.[128] In the absence of a particularly congenial, exogenously determined political context for reform, offers of substantial further assistance may play a crucial role in mitigating opposition to reform from farmers and those who might view dismantling as an expropriation of quota. A number of funding sources could be considered.

First, a consumer milk tax would provide a way of passing the costs of reform on to its main beneficiaries. For example, a tax on consumer fluid milk of 11 cents (CAD) per liter, like Australia's, would generate roughly $299 million per year at recent consumption levels,[129] or around $6 billion over the 20-year life of Robson and Busby's quota auction program.[130] A reduction in milk prices might in turn increase demand and result in further revenues from such a tax. A milk tax would unfortunately continue the unfairness toward consumers caused by supply management. Harm to low-income consumers could be mitigated by a tax credit, while other consumers would still benefit as prices fall—perhaps immediately—more than offsetting the additional tax.[131]

A second option, also premised on charging the beneficiaries of reform for its costs, would be to fund transition payments partially through a small time-limited export tax implemented in the context of a new trade agreement. Canada's reluctance to reduce tariffs protecting its supply-managed industries has often been a stumbling block in trade talks. But exporters in other Canadian industries might benefit greatly from increased export opportunities through a major trade deal such as the TPP. Canada could agree to reduce dairy tariffs in the context of the TPP, while also levying an export tax on products for which the deal could provide greatly expanded export opportunities.[132] The tax would apply to increased exports over the pre-TPP volume of such exports, and would amount to a small fraction of tariff cuts so as not to undermine the benefit of increased export opportunities. The tax would fund deregulation-related transition payments and thus redistribute a limited portion of the gains from the winners under a new trade deal to the losers. Furthermore, commitments made to trading partners in a trade treaty could make the political commitment to a phased removal of supply management more credible.

Third, funding transition payments or ongoing subsidies from the general pool of government revenue would provide a transparent, politically accountable way of spreading the costs of a transition program to the broader public.[133] With each budget, governments would be pressured to reconsider the importance of direct agricultural subsidies relative to that of other public expenditures. However, this option is unlikely to be attractive to cash-strapped governments in lean economic times, and farmers are unlikely to consider the long-term political commitment to on-budget transition payments to be credible.

IV. Normative Considerations Regarding Compensation and Transition Programs

I have argued herein that significant compensation may be necessary in order to eliminate an existing scheme of agricultural price support that on most criteria is detrimental to the public welfare. The normative theories explored in Chapter 2 of this book provide some ways of thinking about whether the losers from such a reform should be compensated and, if so, whether it should be in full or in part. Moreover, the normative positions voters take in a public battle over the future of supply management will likely have a substantial impact on the success of reform, although there is no assurance that the normative arguments advanced will be logically consistent or based on full information.

If, as I have argued, the costs of Canada's dairy supply management scheme outweigh its benefits, then a dismantling of the program would be considered efficient, assuming the added costs of dismantling the program and administering any compensation programs did not negate the net benefit. Whether efficiency concerns would militate in favor of compensation actually to be paid by the winners to the losers in the policy change (thereby making some better off and none worse off) in line with the dictates of Pareto efficiency is a normatively contestable matter. However, in the eyes of the broader public, a dismantling of supply management with no compensation is likely to be viewed as an abuse of a small, targeted constituency, and as equivalent to an uncompensated expropriation of physical property, especially given the government-created nature of the assets to be taken away. Uncompensated dismantling would likely give rise to serious "disaffection costs"— including anxiety and anger among farmers at being "singled out as the victims of uncompensated losses," and sympathy aroused in other citizens.[134] The optimal level of compensation from an efficiency perspective, taking into account these political considerations, might be considered to be that amount of money required to reduce opposition to reform to the point at which reform is possible, and no more.

A communitarian perspective may militate in favor of reform and compensation policies likely to inflict as little harm as possible on the communities in which the losers from a policy change reside. To address such concerns, separate transition payment programs dedicated to mitigating costs to the community arising from "the potential effect of lower farm incomes, farmer retirements and plant closures on employment in regional economies," such as Australia's Dairy Regional Adjustment Program, which provided partial funding to business investment, infrastructure, and retraining projects, might be considered.[135]

V. Conclusion

The concentration of political factors that has maintained dairy supply management in Canada, in spite of its high economic and social costs, remains formidable. This chapter has explored ways in which a reform-minded government might meet the challenge posed by these political obstacles, and tackle reform now, rather than waiting (perhaps forlornly) for a "critical juncture" to change the political arithmetic dramatically. My own preference would be to "lock-in" substantial increases in tariff rate quotas and reductions in out-of-quota tariffs in major international trade negotiations, such as the prospective Trans-Pacific Partnership Agreement. This increases the credibility of the commitments and enlists as future defenders of the commitments export-oriented industries who benefit from reciprocal concessions in these negotiations. These concessions on Canada's part might be phased in over, for example, a 10-year period. Over this period, the value of quotas would progressively decline as imports engross an increasing market share. If a suggestion by Barichello, Cranfield, and Meilke were adopted,[136] farmers would be compensated at the end of this period (or on earlier sale) for any diminution in the book value (acquisition cost) of these quotas (in constant dollars), in effect depriving many of them of most of the dramatic capital gains in quota values over the past 20 years. Although some farmers may reasonably argue that they have incurred reliance costs on the basis of the market value of their quotas, there is a limit to the justification for requiring consumers and taxpayers to pay twice ("coming and going") for the benefits of a scheme that dairy farmers have enjoyed since the early 1970s (farmers who acquired quotas earlier have enjoyed these benefits longer). This basis for compensation would probably reduce the total compensation bill by more than half of the current market value of quotas. This bill could then be partially financed by a modest 10-year dairy product tax on consumers, a modest 10-year export tax on expanded sales of firms benefiting from reciprocal concessions obtained in forthcoming trade negotiations, and the balance from general government revenues. This mix of transition strategies may facilitate the efficient restructuring of the Canadian dairy industry and enable it over time to become competitive in domestic and export markets (as in the case of the Canadian wine industry, which was successfully restructured after the Canada-US Free Trade Agreement (1988) liberalized trade in wine, partly with assistance from provincial governments in identifying new varieties of wines and product niches more suitable to Canada's climatic conditions).[137]

The politically entrenched agricultural program discussed in this chapter has many corollaries across the developed world, and thus many of the lessons one takes from this case study may apply, with variations for local features, to other entrenched agricultural support programs. It is not suggested that the prescriptions for reform explored here, including public persuasion and substantial targeted compensation payments, will be simply executed or necessarily successful. But the high costs of programs such as Canada's dairy supply management justify the effort. If such programs are to be reformed, policy choices should be attuned to political barriers such as public apathy, transitional gains traps, and special interest group advantages. The role for compensation and related transition cost mitigation strategies in the face of such barriers is likely to be critical.

{ 7 }

Liberalizing Immigration Policy: The Gains and Strains of Accommodating More and Diverse Newcomers

I. Introduction[1]

Classical free trade theory assumed that goods could often be readily traded across national borders but that the factors of production employed to produce those goods (land, capital, and labor) were fixed and immobile. In the contemporary world, largely due to technological changes, this has become dramatically untrue of capital, and much less true of labor. There are currently 192 million people, including 16 million refugees, living outside their countries of birth. Today, approximately one out of every 35 persons in the world is a migrant.[2] However, the frequent political resistance from actual or perceived losers to international mobility of goods, services, and capital is often dramatically intensified in the case of the international mobility of people and is reflected in restrictive immigration policies in many countries—restrictions that are minimally coordinated or constrained by international rules (in contrast to the international trading system, discussed in Chapter 5).[3]

Historically, business and employer interests have favored relatively permissive immigration policies in order to relieve shortages or bottlenecks in the supply of skilled or unskilled labor and to discipline wage demands, often favoring more pliant and dependent temporary workers (especially when they are legally tied to one employer). Labor unions and employee interests have tended to favor more restrictive immigration policies that are tightly constrained by the prevailing state of domestic labor markets and that severely limit the admission of temporary workers. Ethnic groups, comprising previous immigrants at one or more stages removed, have tended to favor generous family reunification policies and to be less concerned with the economic effects of immigration. Taxpayers (an admittedly amorphous group) have tended to be concerned with the effects of fiscally induced immigration on the sustainability of social programs, while "nativists" (again an admittedly amorphous category) have been concerned about the loss of social homogeneity and community solidarity from permissive immigration policies. Refugee claimants have attracted the support of limited domestic constituencies—church, human rights and civil society groups, and ethnic and religious groups that share affinities with the refugees.

In contrast to various concerns underlying political resistance to permissive immigration policies, in the mid-1980s Hamilton and Whalley[4] estimated that the elimination of all global restrictions on labor mobility could result in a net doubling of worldwide annual GNP. More recent and less sanguine assumptions result in estimated gains that are still highly significant from the perspective of global economic welfare and far exceed the gains from further trade liberalization.[5] Substantial liberalization of immigration policy would also engender a dramatically fairer distribution of world income.[6] Studies also find that substantial liberalization of movement of temporary workers would also generate substantial increases in global welfare and fairer distribution of world income.[7]

These figures raise important positive and normative puzzles that are of increasing importance in so-called knowledge-based economies in a globalizing world where specialized human capital and agglomeration economies are often a major source of comparative advantage.

II. Stylized Facts About Immigration Policies in Receiving Countries

Although the details of immigration policies in major destination countries such as the United States, Canada, and Australia vary widely, they typically entail three primary classes of immigrants: a family class, an independent or economic class, and a refugee class (often supplemented with temporary worker and investor classes). Generally speaking, each of these classes is subject to a quota limiting the number of immigrants who are admissible under the rubric of the relevant class in any given year (although inland refugee claimants are at least theoretically evaluated against the criteria set out in the 1951 UN Convention Relating to the Status of Refugees—the Geneva Convention—irrespective of any quota). In the United States, family sponsorship accounts for a substantially higher percentage of immigrants than independent immigrants, relative to Canada and Australia. Canada and Australia apply elaborate points systems for determining the admissibility of independent immigrants, designed with the objective of admitting those with a high probability of effective economic integration. The United States applies more loosely defined priority criteria to this category of immigrant. All three countries provide for short-term visas for tourists, students, and temporary workers. In the United States, illegal immigration is a major phenomenon (accounting for up to 400,000 immigrants a year in the past, but currently declining, compared to about 800,000–1 million legal immigrants). An estimated total of 11 million illegal or undocumented immigrants reside in the United States.[8]

Apart from Australia, Canada, and the United States, the other primary immigrant-receiving area is the European Union. The countries of the European Union do not (as of yet) have one officially agreed upon and collectively administered immigration policy relating to citizens of third-party countries, but they do have a very liberal policy for the internal movement of people.[9] Title IV of the EC Treaty, established in international law by the Treaty of Amsterdam as of May 1, 1999, provides for, inter alia, the free movement of all persons—citizens and noncitizens—within the European Union, and tighter control of external borders.

III. Normative Critiques of Prevailing Immigration Policies

The barriers to the international movement of people—for the skilled and unskilled, from developed and developing countries of origin alike—stem primarily from restrictive immigration policies in developed countries. Aggregate average income in the wealthiest 20 countries is more than 37 times greater than the average income in the world's 20 poorest countries.[10] With economic disparities so great, the deleterious effects on prospective immigrants from poor countries of the restrictive immigration policies of the developed nations are clear. Many workers in developing countries harbor a strongly held desire to emigrate to countries in which they can make productive contributions that are less likely to be made (for lack of effective institutions, complementary human capital, infrastructure, and financial resources) in their countries of origin.[11] The extent to which immigration policies that keep the highly skilled and the relatively unskilled alike from migrating freely are normatively justifiable varies dramatically from the perspectives of economic welfare, communitarianism, and liberalism.

A. ECONOMIC PERSPECTIVES[12]

With a set of assumptions that only tenuously approximate reality, neoclassical economic theory suggests that an optimal immigration policy would be not to have one at all.[13] That is, neoclassical economic theory suggests that borders should be open as any constraint on the operation of the international labor market (e.g., closed or only semi-open borders) will generate distortions in economic decision-making and impose welfare costs globally in terms of forgone production and, consequently, unrealized welfare gains. This suggests that prevailing restrictive immigration policy regimes are deeply misguided. Given the complexity of the issues involved, however, placing much importance on this initial appeal to the conclusions of neoclassical economic theory is premature.

In general, immigration policies are evaluated economically in two competing ways (although others are conceivable). The first entails the use of a global welfare function that weighs equally the welfare of all persons, wherever they may reside. The second is to use a narrower, or nationalistic welfare function in which only the effects on "insiders"—not including those in the country of origin or the immigrants themselves—are considered. Immigration policies are currently debated and designed within nation states, and it is clear that countries are concerned about the welfare of "insiders" to a greater extent than the welfare of "outsiders."[14]

There is now a substantial body of empirical evidence surrounding the economic impacts of immigration. However, there are still many issues that are far from satisfactorily resolved, because of the sheer complexity of the causes and effects of immigration. First, immigration policies differ functionally among developed countries so that empirical evidence drawn from one country cannot yield conclusive answers as to the effects of immigration in another country. Second, the nature of immigrant cohorts to a given country has not been static over time, reflecting shifts in "pull" and "push" factors, as well as changes in immigration policies within countries, making any attempt to draw general conclusions about the desirability of increasing immigration flows even within a given country problematic. Finally, immigrant cohorts to most developed countries have been and continue to be highly heterogeneous—refugees and asylees, family-sponsored immigrants, independent immigrants, temporary immigrants, and illegal immigrants are often considered together by economists in attempting to evaluate empirically the welfare effects of immigration. It would not be surprising if each subset (and indeed subsets of each subset) of immigrants had separate and differing welfare effects for recipient countries.

With these significant cautions in mind, however, the stylized facts and available empirical economic evidence suggest that immigration has been of net benefit to the vast majority of the residents of destination countries, the only possible losers being native workers or prior immigrants with very low skill levels.[15] The data are peculiarly at odds with prevailing public attitudes as revealed by various surveys over the past decade regarding the economic desirability of immigration.[16] The surveys generally show that a majority of residents in developed countries would prefer that current immigration levels be reduced, or at the very most maintained, but certainly not increased. The survey results reflect two broad classes of economic concerns: that increased numbers of immigrants will have adverse labor market effects, and that they will increase the fiscal burden borne by natives, yielding two major classes of domestic losers: workers and taxpayers.[17]

i. Labor Market Effects in Host Countries

Recent studies of the effects of immigration on labor markets have generally demonstrated that increased numbers of immigrants have played little observable role in reducing wages or in increasing unemployment.[18] After conducting a thorough review of the empirical evidence in the literature, the US National Academy of Sciences[19] concluded that "the weight of the empirical evidence suggests that the impact of immigration on the wages of competing native workers is small." These findings are superficially puzzling given the accepted labor economics account of the expected effects of greater labor market competition. The conventional analysis suggests that by increasing the supply of labor, ceteris paribus, wages will decrease among similarly endowed and situated workers. However, the ceteris paribus proviso is an important one. It requires immigrants to increase the supply of labor in domestic labor markets without contemporaneously increasing the demand for labor. However, an offsetting increase in the demand for labor is in fact quite plausible, as immigrants are consumers of goods and services, and the increased demand for and provision of goods and services inevitably associated with their presence ought to result in a corresponding increase in labor demand by domestic suppliers of goods and services.[20] Moreover, much recent evidence suggests that immigrants, including many unskilled immigrants, are mostly complements to rather than substitutes for domestic workers.

Research has found that immigrants with advanced degrees boost employment for US natives. For example, from 2000 to 2007 an additional 100 foreign-born workers with advanced degrees from US universities in science, technology, engineering, and mathematics (STEM) are associated with an additional 262 jobs among US natives. An additional 100 H-1B skilled temporary workers result in an additional 183 jobs among US natives. An additional 100 H-2B less skilled temporary workers have been found (perhaps surprisingly) to result in 464 jobs for US natives.[21] Other research finds that over the period 1994–2007, immigration raised the wages of US-born workers, including workers with less than a college education, modestly relative to foreign-born workers, and that any negative effects were mostly experienced by earlier immigrants.[22] Wadhwa[23] reports that a 2011 study found that first-generation immigrants or their children had founder roles in more than 40 percent of Fortune 500 companies, and a recent survey finds that more than half of Silicon Valley start-ups had one or more immigrants as a key founder (although this number has declined in recent years).[24]

ii. Fiscal Effects in Host Countries

The other common economic fear harbored by many members of the public with respect to increased immigration is that immigrants are likely to impose a collective cost upon the public sector's finances by burdening the welfare state with disproportionate claims for, inter alia, welfare payments, umemployment insurance, food stamps, subsidized public education, publicly provided or subsidized healthcare, public housing, and public pensions.

However, the most comprehensive study on the fiscal impact of immigration in the United States, produced by the National Research Council (NRC), suggests that each immigrant and his or her descendants will on average generate a net fiscal benefit of $80,000 for natives of the United States in net present value terms in 1996 dollars.[25] Highly skilled immigrants and their descendants generate a greater fiscal surplus ($198,000 each) than do lower-skilled immigrants ($51,000 each), but notably in each case there is a surplus.[26] A 2007 cost estimate by the Congressional Budget Office found that a path to legalization for illegal immigrants in the United States (estimated to be about 11 million) would increase federal revenues by $48 billion but would only incur $23 billion of increased costs from public services, producing a surplus of $25 billon for government coffers.[27]

A recent comparative analysis of the fiscal effects of immigration across OECD countries finds that these effects (positive or negative) are generally small.[28]

Thus, the preponderance of available empirical evidence suggests that immigrants have little impact upon labor market outcomes for natives, and that many immigrants generate a net fiscal surplus and rarely any significant fiscal loss. Nevertheless, it is important to emphasize that these findings apply only to the economic effects of immigration at roughly prevailing levels. Although even a considerable increase in the number of immigrants may continue to be welfare enhancing in net terms, at some threshold rate of immigration—perhaps an order of magnitude higher than now prevailing—it is reasonable to expect that negative congestion externalities and adverse labor market or fiscal effects may cause the current net benefit to become a net domestic welfare loss.

Indeed, Borjas's work on the United States[29] and Reitz's on Canada[30] report empirical findings that over the past two decades the economic performance of recent immigrants in terms of employment and earnings has declined significantly relative both to prior generations of immigrants and to the native-born. Although the educational qualifications of recent immigrants tend to be higher than those of prior generations of immigrants, they have increased less rapidly than the educational qualifications of the native-born. Moreover, in knowledge-based economies where specialized educational credentials and work experience carry an increasing premium, rigidities or protectionism in domestic educational and professional institutions in evaluating and recognizing foreign credentials and work experience (and providing effective "bridging" or skills- upgrading programs), and difficulties faced by domestic employers in evaluating foreign credentials and work experience, increasingly penalize skilled immigrants. These findings suggest the need to take concerns over fiscally induced immigration seriously, while at the same time seeking to mitigate inefficient domestic labor market rigidities.

iii. Implications for Existing Immigration Policies

Adopting an economic perspective on existing immigration policies, basic health, criminality, and national security checks are a standard feature of immigration policies in most developed countries and are likely to be considered valid categories of restraints on immigration by most economists from both a domestic and in some cases a global welfare perspective, in terms of reducing the social externalities from immigration.

However, current policies in many countries requiring that employers first ensure that no domestic workers are qualified for the job, or demanding that an employer demonstrate that the employment of the foreign worker at issue would not harm domestic workers, are difficult to justify economically, even if they are easily explained in political terms. If an employer has extended its recruitment drive to encompass foreign labor markets and is willing to absorb the additional transaction costs associated with sponsorship of a foreign worker, then this commitment should be considered to be prima facie evidence that equally qualified workers are not available domestically. Such labor certification conditions often prevent employers from hiring the most qualified candidates, due to the availability of a marginally qualified domestic candidate. Such restrictions promote mediocrity and inefficiency, especially with respect to more highly skilled human capital.

For economic or independent migrants, immigration policies in developed countries sometimes entail passing points tests (as in Canada and Australia) that depend on, inter alia, demonstrating language proficiency, possessing significant training and work experience, working in an occupation experiencing high demand, having relatives who are residents or citizens, and being of a demographically attractive age for the destination country. The available evidence suggests that point system restrictions may be justified from a narrow domestic economic perspective, although this is not uncontroversial.[31]

For family-sponsored immigrants under prevailing immigration policies in many developed countries it is often sufficient for entry to have as a sponsor an immediate family member who is already a citizen or permanent resident of the destination country. From a narrow domestic economic perspective, it may seem prima facie that having close relatives in the destination country would likely be irrelevant to subsequent economic performance and that, as a consequence, there should be no importance placed on the presence of relatives in the destination country. However, if the sponsor's welfare is included in the social welfare function, then the arrival of a close relative has an immediate and significantly positive welfare effect on the destination country. In addition, the presence of immediate family members will likely play an important role in labor market outcomes for most immigrants. Having immediate family in the country will aid labor market participants by providing a nucleus of social capital that can be used to make the economic social and cultural transition to a new country. This in turn is likely to increase the monetary remittances to relatives left behind in the country of origin. For these reasons, family-sponsored immigration may also be desirable from a global economic perspective, although it is difficult to assess definitively the cogency of this conclusion.

From the perspective of economic welfare, many illegal immigrants are also beneficial for their host economies. Many illegal immigrants work at jobs that natives do not want to do at prevailing wage levels—that is, positions that pay remuneration at rates below natives' reservation wage. In addition, illegal immigrants are almost certainly net contributors fiscally because they generate considerable tax revenues for host governments through property taxes, sales taxes, and mandatorily withheld income taxes, while remaining ineligible for most social programs. Moreover, they have little incentive to try to receive benefits from most social programs for fear of being discovered and returned to their country of origin. The monetary cost of the social services that illegal immigrants do use, such as emergency medical care or public education, almost certainly does not offset the tax contribution illegal immigrants make. From a global perspective, illegal immigration is also welfare enhancing. The illegal immigrants themselves obviously consider themselves better off, or else they would simply return as legitimate citizens to their countries of origin, relieved of the stigma associated with their illegal status, and would not incur the costs and risks of illegal migration.

B. NON-ECONOMIC PERSPECTIVES

Philosophically, the primary issue that needs to be addressed is the extent to which a nation and its citizens have a moral duty to admit (or the prerogative not to admit) outsiders. The ultimate resolution of this issue depends crucially upon the relative significance attached to liberal and communitarian ideals—the belief in the equal moral worth of individuals versus the belief in the freedom of a collection of persons to govern themselves free from the claims of those outside the group.[32] For many political theorists, taking liberty seriously is to a considerable extent irreconcilable with asserting the legitimacy of the exclusion of outsiders.[33] A strict adherence to the dictates of liberalism demands a recognition that the welfare of outsiders is as valuable as the welfare of insiders. As such, liberal values require strong justification for any restrictions on immigration.[34] A privileging of community over liberty, on the other hand, suggests that the interests of insiders are more important than the interests of outsiders, and that the nation-state, in the interests of insiders, can freely dictate any restrictions on immigration that it may consider desirable.

i. Communitarianism

Historically, countries have often sought to limit immigration to those who are culturally similar to natives or, what amounts to much the same thing, privilege for admission those who are culturally or ethnically similar to insiders. The national origins quota system, the core of US immigration policy from 1924 to 1965, privileged Europeans for admission to the country based on the fact that individuals of European origin made up the bulk of the US population at the time of the 1920 census. The German Aussiedler policy, which grants immediate citizenship (subject to certain quota restrictions) to any ethnic German who can prove German descent, pass a German language test, and demonstrate familiarity with German culture, is another example of ethnically driven immigration policies. Australia and Canada also have historical legacies replete with racially discriminatory approaches to immigration policy.[35]

Australia, Canada, and the United States do not currently have immigration policies that explicitly account for the racial or ethnic background of those who seek to immigrate, although it is important to recognize that the prominent role for family sponsorship in the United States, Australia, and Canada have to some extent the effect of muting changes in the status quo in terms of the racial and ethnic composition of each of the countries. The question, however, remains: can countries legitimately systematically exclude immigrants of certain nationalities, races, or ethnic or religious backgrounds with a view to preserving cultural and social homogeneity and community solidarity that more liberal immigration policies may threaten?

Political philosopher Michael Walzer is a prominent proponent of the position that in nearly all instances it is legitimate for nation-states, as sovereign entities freely dictating their relationships with other peoples and other nation-states, to choose to exclude outsiders.[36] Walzer suggests that nations are like clubs. As such, argues Walzer, nations should be able to define their own membership criteria. Walzer's fundamental claim is that:

> The distribution of membership is not pervasively subject to the constraints of justice. Across a considerable range of the decisions that are made, states are simply free to take in strangers (or not)—much as they are free, leaving aside the claims of the needy, to share their wealth with foreign friends, to honour the achievements of foreign artists, scholars, and scientists, to choose their trading partners, and to enter into collective security arrangements with foreign states. But the right to choose an admissions policy is more basic than any of these, for it is not merely a matter of acting in the world, exercising sovereignty, and pursuing national interests. At stake here is the shape of the community that acts in the world, exercises sovereignty, and so on. Admission and exclusion are at the core of communal independence. They suggest the deepest meaning of self-determination. Without them, there could not be communities of character, historically stable, ongoing associations of men and women with some special commitment to one another and some special sense of their common life.[37]

This position elevates nation-state sovereignty to a level where arguably almost any constraints a nation wishes to impose on immigrants in protection of its culture and its status as a cohesive community are legitimate—even those that are discriminatory on racial, ethnic, religious, or ideological grounds. There are at least two contestable aspects of Walzer's position. The first is that the continuing development and evolution of international human rights norms increasingly suggests that nation-state sovereignty is not as inviolate as Walzer seeks to suggest. The second surrounds Walzer's implicit assumption that "communities of character" cannot be defined by a common commitment to liberal democratic institutions and the corresponding values of tolerance, diversity, and inclusion. Liberals in developed countries are likely to argue strenuously that liberal values can and in many countries do serve as a basis for "communities of character."

In *The Disuniting of America*, Arthur Schlesinger Jr. argues a position that straddles the communitarian/liberal divide. Schlesinger believes that children of ethnic minorities should not be entitled to public education catering to their ethnic or national origin in terms of the language of instruction, the historical perspective emphasized, or the aspects of world geography concentrated upon. Instead, argues Schlesinger, the American public education system should be committed to furthering American culture and the importance of liberal democratic institutions. According to Schlesinger:

> The militants of ethnicity now contend that a main objective of public education should be the protection, strengthening, celebration, and perpetuation of ethnic origins and identities. Separatism, however, nourishes prejudices, magnifies differences and stirs antagonisms... Watching ethnic conflict tear one nation after another apart, one cannot look with complacency at proposals to divide the United States into distinct and immutable ethnic and racial communities, each taught to cherish its own apartness from the rest. One wonders: Will the center hold? or will the melting pot give way to the Tower of Babel?[38]

The liberal aspect of Schlesinger's prima facie communitarian position is that he apparently assumes that a relatively liberal immigration policy is demanded philosophically (giving rise to his factional concerns), but that within the bounds of a liberal immigration policy it is legitimate to seek to limit the degree to which the cultural values of immigrants are allowed to permeate the political culture of the United States through the accommodation of different ethnic beliefs, "histories," and languages in the education system, although it is important to acknowledge the major contributions that immigrants make to the culture of receiving countries in terms of cuisine, performing arts, other cultural pursuits, and academia.[39]

ii. Liberalism

Joseph Carens has outlined the consequences of favoring liberty over community from three different liberal perspectives: libertarianism, social contractarianism, and utilitarianism.[40] Libertarianism, as formulated by Nozick,[41] demands no more from government than the protection of property rights and the facilitation of exchange through the enforcement of contracts. From a libertarian perspective, then, immigration policies that go any further than preempting immigration that might impose any involuntary costs or burdens on residents are unacceptable because they will entail constraints on personal liberty.[42] From a social contractarianism viewpoint, arguably the appropriate immigration policy is the one that would be agreed to behind a Rawlsian "veil of ignorance" such that the drafters of immigration policy would not know the particularities of their own personal situation (morally arbitrary features such as country of residence, gender, education, ethnicity, etc.), beyond knowing that they represent some human personality in the world.[43] Although subject to subsequent reservations by Rawls as to its applicability across polities, the purpose of the veil is to ensure that the drafters of the ideal immigration policy would not be bargaining with known endowments and would therefore seek to ensure that the policy drafted would be fair to all concerned, especially the least advantaged. The social contractarian perspective, then, also arguably militates in favor of the relatively free international movement of people, with a similar caveat to libertarianism. Free immigration should occur only so far as the maintenance of public order and respect for rights, including social welfare entitlements, is not threatened by immigrant flows.[44] From a utilitarianism perspective, Carens argues that the utility of both citizens and immigrants ought to be considered,[45] with the result that immigration should be allowed to the point where the marginal net benefits accruing to immigrants (if there were no net benefits they would presumably not move) equal the marginal net costs to citizens of the immigration through, for instance, congestion effects and the economic (labor market and fiscal) effects reviewed above.

iii. Implications for Existing Immigration Policies

Current immigration policies in developed countries do not seem to be explained neatly by either the communitarian or liberal perspectives. For example, the widespread adoption (albeit debatable observance) of the 1951 UN Convention Relating to the Status of Refugees (the Geneva Convention) with respect to the admission of refugees undermines one of the core tenets of the communitarian position—community self-definition—by constraining a significant portion of national sovereignty through supranational commitments. Another delegation of state sovereignty with respect to immigration policy can be observed in the European Union, where the Treaty of Amsterdam commits member countries to the free internal movement of people, with no internal border checks. With these possible exceptions, however, the communitarian position has some salience in the current state of immigration policies among developed nations. Family-sponsored immigration policies reflect a concern that new immigrants should be like old immigrants. Independent admissions based on employer sponsorship, age, language ability, and possession of relevant training and work experience implicate both communitarian and liberal ideals. The screening process implicates communitarian ideals because such policies define criteria that attempt to maximize the benefit to insiders of immigration. Liberal ideals are implicated to the extent that the screening process does not take into account cultural or ethnic factors, but instead accepts all applicants who exhibit the qualities believed to be important indicators of the ability to succeed in the domestic economy. In many respects, liberal (especially utilitarian) and economic perspectives on immigration policy are closely aligned, and largely inform the reform options briefly canvassed below.

IV. Rethinking Immigration Policies

One of the key features of immigration policy in most developed countries is a quota system that restricts the number of immigrants that will be accepted each year in each admission class. These quotas are justified on the basis that completely open borders would be problematic because of negative externalities (e.g., congestion effects), labor market effects, and the political and fiscal stresses that would be placed on the redistributive programs of the welfare state due to fiscally induced migration.

Despite the problems perceived to be associated with illegal immigration (which are at least in part due to quotas),[46] quota systems are a practical (although arbitrary) way of limiting the number of immigrants arriving each year. One of the primary shortcomings of the quota method is that it unduly hampers the flow of immigrants who can demonstrate that they will not be a burden on the amenities of the welfare state. Many would-be immigrants, despite the fact that they are able to demonstrate that they will not be a burden through various means, such as the possession of adequate personal resources or through pre-arranged employment (independent immigrants), through the sponsorship of legally resident or citizen relatives (family immigrants), or through the sponsorship of a private party or organization (refugees selected overseas), are not able to immigrate due to quota restrictions.

Another problem associated with the quota system is that quotas must be set in advance, which places the very difficult (perhaps impossible) task of predicting the needs of the labor market (at least in the case of employment-based quotas) in the hands of a centralized bureaucracy. Central planning for the future needs of the domestic labor market is an assignment that to be undertaken accurately requires an almost unlimited and constantly changing flow of information on macroeconomic conditions and microeconomic information on labor markets in particular sectors. Moreover, given the administrative delays associated with processing immigration applications in virtually all developed countries, the lag between quota-setting and actual admissions is likely to prove highly problematic. In the case of the United States, wait times for employment-based permanent resident visas ("green cards") commonly run as long as 10 years.

Given these deficiencies of a quota system, there seems to be a a compelling case for devolving and decentralizing power over immigration decision-making to private parties to a much greater extent than currently prevails, although health, criminality, and national security checks by the state should be retained for the reasons noted earlier. This reorientation would allow the international movement of people to be much freer and would promote a more efficient mix of international movements in goods, services, capital, and labor. I now spell out in more detail how such a decentralized approach to immigration policy might operate.

A. INDEPENDENT APPLICANTS

As a starting premise, those who wish to immigrate who have already secured employment or who have financial resources sufficient to maintain independence from the amenities of the welfare state (except publicly subsidized education and basic healthcare) should be able to emigrate freely provided that they, either individually or through their employer, have taken out specified minimum coverage private social program insurance to cover any drawings that they may make against social programs of the state within a certain period of time after entry. This mandatory social program insurance requirement (akin to mandatory automobile accident insurance) is central to my thinking in seeking to screen out fiscally induced immigration by internalizing a significant portion of the social costs of immigration to would-be immigrants or their sponsors. To the extent that the prescribed minimum coverage proves to be inadequate to reimburse drawings on these social programs, immigrants and their sponsors would be jointly and severally liable for reimbursement of the deficiency.

The social programs that immigrants would be denied access to immediately after entry would include, inter alia, welfare payments, unemployment insurance, food stamps, public housing subsidies, and public pensions. Publicly subsidized education and basic healthcare would not be among the excluded benefits and would thus be available to all immigrants. Public education would not be included in the enumerated items because public education is one of the primary mechanisms through which liberal democratic states impart liberal values, such as tolerance, to succeeding generations—a function that is important in establishing and perpetuating the security of a nation's liberal democratic institutions. Publicly subsidized basic healthcare would not be among the excluded items because, given that the immigrant has presumably already passed a medical screen prior to landing, there is unlikely to be a significant adverse selection problem or abuse of the system in this regard. Given that education and basic healthcare are primary goods, it would take a considerable threat of fiscal abuse to preempt their use by newly landed immigrants. Furthermore, given the fact that all immigrants are taxed on their income at the same rates and in precisely the same way as are natives, there appears to be little justification for denying them the enjoyment of publicly provided education and publicly subsidized healthcare. Similarly, objections that increased immigration will result in increased negative congestion effects and thus generate demand for more infrastructure such as highways, schools, and hospitals are met by the fact that immigrants pay taxes just as do natives.

The responsibilities entitling one to sponsor an immigrant might include taking out specified minimum insurance coverage against any social benefits (excluding publicly subsidized education and basic healthcare) that the immigrant might draw on during the minimum residence period required for full social program eligibility. The selection of a minimum residence period is to some extent arbitrary. However, arguably it should not be longer than the period of residence required to qualify for citizenship: in Canada three years, in the United States five years. Longer periods would create normatively problematic categories of first- and second-class citizens. The social program insurance mechanism would entail a mandatory obligation on the part of the sponsor to pay the premiums required to insure the worker against any drawings he or she may make against the amenities of the welfare state. The sponsored worker would be free to draw on social programs (other than publicly subsidized education or basic healthcare, which would be provided as a matter of course), but the state would be entitled to be indemnified for these drawings by the insurance company underwriting the social program insurance policy held by the sponsor. One of the main advantages of this insurance scheme is that in a competitive private insurance market, insurance premiums would adjust to reflect the expected drawings of immigrants given their observable characteristics such as educational background, occupation, age, work experience, etc., as well as the projected state of the economy and hence the demand for their services, thus acting as an automatic stabilizer of immigrant flows. If it turns out that the fears of fiscally induced immigration are exaggerated and immigrants do not draw public benefits at a significant rate, insurance will be inexpensive and readily affordable for most sponsors. If fears of fiscally induced immigration are well-founded, then insurance premiums will be significantly higher, thereby increasing the costs of sponsorship and creating stronger incentives for sponsors to be more selective in screening potential immigrants.

Once a sponsored employee has arrived in the country, employers would be obligated to continue paying premiums on the insurance contract for the full minimum residence period, regardless of whether the employee remains employed by the employer (unless a new employer agrees to assume this responsibility). If the employer subsequently becomes insolvent, winds-up, or otherwise cannot be compelled legally to honor its obligation to pay premiums for the period, then the sponsored immigrant would become responsible for taking over the insurance premium payments or else could potentially be held to be in default of the conditions for permanent residence and be subject to deportation from the country.

A related concern in the context of employer-sponsored immigrants might be that fly-by-night or sham employers might sponsor dozens of immigrants, commit to paying their premiums for three years, then promptly declare bankruptcy and/ or wind-up their operations. To the extent that this is a concern, however, insurance companies have an incentive to sell insurance only to reputable, well-established businesses, or perhaps demand premium payments upfront from companies that present relatively poor or unknown default risks. Moreover, immigrants not covered by current social program insurance policies would incur the risk of deportation.

Independent immigrants who are admitted based on having financial assets sufficient to maintain independence from the amenities of the welfare state (for example, under investor immigrant programs) and are thus not sponsored by employers would remain responsible for obtaining social program insurance coverage of the required minimum amount for the requisite period, although one would generally expect the premiums to be minimal.

Those admitted to the country on student visas to study would benefit from this liberalized immigration policy regime, as would host countries.[47] Students from abroad admitted to study at the post-secondary level, especially postgraduate students, have in most cases established that they have the motivation, talent, and language skills required to succeed in an academic environment. This same motivation and talent is often translatable into considerable value in the labor market. If these students are able to secure employment and sponsorship upon graduation, there is little reason to preclude them from doing so. In fact, there appear to be several reasons to encourage them to stay. Most college and university graduates on student visas are fluent in at least one of the county's major languages, are well educated, talented, and motivated, and are therefore prima facie well-equipped to contribute productively to the domestic economy immediately. In addition, they are likely to be relatively young so that their presence can modestly improve the dependency ratio (which affects, inter alia, the sustainability of pay-as-you-go public pension schemes discussed in Chapter 3), and are likely to have already internalized to a considerable extent the values and social mores of the country, mitigating communitarian concerns.

To the extent that young students who stay after completing post-secondary education abroad contribute to a brain drain from the country of origin that is costly—a debatable proposition[48]—there may be scope for countries of origin to try to reduce the magnitude of these brain-drain costs. One option may be for countries of origin to demand that students leaving the country to study abroad (or their families) repay the publicly subsidized portion of their primary and secondary education if they ultimately elect to remain abroad after completing their studies (or to post a bond to this effect). Given that the scale and effects of a brain drain are empirically contestable, however, and may be largely offset by remittances from emigrants (currently estimated to be in excess of $400 billion per year—almost four times total foreign aid levels), and the further fact that it is unclear who actually pays for publicly subsidized primary and secondary education of emigrating students in the first place, such policies may not be warranted.

B. FAMILY PREFERENCE IMMIGRATION

An arrangement very similar to that envisaged for independent immigrants could be instituted for family preference immigrants. Under a decentralized family preference system, any individual who is sponsored by a relative (such as a spouse, or parent) would be eligible immediately for immigration, provided that the would-be immigrant has met health, criminality, and national security screens and his or her sponsor has secured social program insurance of a specified minimum amount on the immigrant's behalf. This would be a highly desirable development because of the extremely long waits currently imposed on family-sponsored immigrants in many developed countries. As with independent immigrants, family-sponsored immigrants admitted through the decentralized process would be eligible to receive publicly subsidized education and basic healthcare benefits, but any welfare payments, unemployment insurance, food stamps, public housing subsidies, or public pension payments received within a specified period of time after entry would be subject to reimbursement by the sponsor's insurer.

C. REFUGEES AND ASYLUM SEEKERS

The issue of refugee admissions is less amenable to a decentralized approach to immigration policy. There are two main types of refugees—those who arrive in the host country seeking admission (inland refugee claimants), and displaced persons who are selected overseas for admission to the host country (overseas refugee claimants). Those who arrive uninvited in the desired destination country claiming that they are refugees must be considered for admission in accordance with the host country's obligations under the Geneva Convention (unless, for instance, the country has enacted restrictions—as have Germany, the United States, and Canada—providing that the country will not consider the cases of asylum seekers arriving via a "safe third country" or from "safe countries of origin"). Because signatory countries have an obligation under international law by virtue of the Geneva Convention to consider the cases of inland refugee claimants on their merits, the decentralized approach is not readily applicable. For refugees selected overseas, however, the decentralized approach will generally be relevant. Developed countries often establish targets for the number of refugees selected overseas for admission to the host country. A complete abandonment of the quota approach in favor of decentralized overseas admissions may risk a deluge of overseas refugee claimants (although this seems unlikely). The current quotas are arbitrary, but are to some extent understandable because refugees selected overseas often lack valuable labor market skills such as fluency in the language of the country of landing and/or specialized human capital, and because they may take longer to integrate into the country's labor market (although the empirical evidence does not support fears of long-run non-integration).[49] Thus, an abandonment of the quota system for overseas refugees should not be ruled out altogether. Despite these concerns, however, many residents of developed countries and church and community organizations take great pride in extending aid to refugees and asylum seekers and are likely to gain utility from the knowledge that they are helping those in desperate need. In addition, to the extent that a decentralized system requires social program insurance similar to that advocated for the independent and family classes, there is little to fear fiscally from a higher influx of refugees selected overseas.

D. ILLEGAL IMMIGRANTS AND TEMPORARY WORKERS

For several reasons, illegal immigration should be discouraged despite its net positive welfare effects; this discouragement, however, should not be through increased border controls, but through accommodation. The psychic costs borne by illegal immigrants associated with the stigma attached to their status, as well as the continual fear of discovery, are considerable (but presumably outweighed by the expected benefits of staying). In addition, border patrols and infrastructure are often ineffective at keeping out those who desperately desire admission, and the costs associated with these controls are substantial. Finally, the existence of a permanent underclass of "others" who are unable to participate fully in the community and in social programs is undesirable for humanitarian reasons, while mass deportations would often entail enormous human costs as well as fiscal costs to the state, rendering them politically infeasible.[50]

One way to relieve the pressure exerted by illegal immigrants to immigrate is to liberalize immigration policy. By eliminating quotas for immigrant admissions, and by allowing those sponsored by employers or relatives (and supported with social program insurance) to gain entry so long as they pass health, criminality, and national security screens, some of the pressure exerted by illegal immigrants for admission will be relieved. Although obtaining employer sponsorship, securing social program insurance, and passing health, criminality, and national security screens impose transactions costs that would not accompany illegal immigration, being considered a "legitimate" or "legal" immigrant is likely to be of considerable economic and psychic value. In addition, once legally admitted to the country, under these proposals an immigrant would immediately begin fulfilling the period of residency required to participate fully in social programs and also to naturalize as a citizen.

If demanding employer sponsorship and social program insurance of unskilled immigrants proves to impose too great a burden in terms of transactions costs on employers or would-be immigrants to stem the tide of illegal immigration, another way to eliminate the pressure for illegal immigration would be to liberally distribute temporary worker visas to any employer-sponsored immigrant. Due to the problems associated with trying to expel or deport temporary workers, exemplified by the permanent guest worker phenomenon of Western Europe, this liberal temporary worker system should be accompanied by an automatic graduation to permanent legal immigrant status after a specified period of continuous employment in the host country. That is, if one held a temporary worker visa for, say, three to five years and worked continuously (or nearly continuously, even if not with the same employer) for the entire period, then one would be automatically extended legal permanent resident status, provided that medical, criminality, and national security screens are satisfied. During the period of residence as a temporary worker, the only social services available would be publicly subsidized education and basic healthcare. Upon the automatic grant of permanent resident status, the temporary worker would qualify for full participation in all social programs and would begin the period of residency necessary to naturalize as a citizen. Thus, there would be very little incentive for would-be workers to immigrate illegally because they would forgo the medium-to-long–term benefits associated with the relatively straightforward process to work legally. The host country would also benefit from the implementation of this system. Immigrants who would have possibly entered the country illegally otherwise would be registered as temporary workers and thus would be easily identifiable by the host country. The introduction of the temporary worker class of admission by creating a registry of temporary workers would help social program administrators curtail the consumption by such workers of social services to which they are not entitled, would (at least to some extent) reduce forgone tax revenues by reducing the incentives to pay workers "under the table," and would also allow many of the resources previously allocated to patrolling borders for illegal immigrants to be allocated to more productive uses.

V. Conclusion

The international movement of people lags far behind international movements of goods, services, and capital mostly because immigration policies in most developed countries are relatively restrictive. This state of affairs is undesirable because the potential benefits to global economic welfare are large in terms of increasing world economic output from freer international movement of people. In addition, liberalized immigration policies have the potential to decrease global income inequalities. One of the main barriers to opening up the borders of developed countries to unrestricted immigration flows, however, is fiscally induced migration. Impoverished immigrants may be drawn to developed countries by the amenities of the welfare state, which, at the limit, may threaten the viability of the social programs that constitute the welfare state.

In order to realize most of the economic benefits associated with liberalized immigration flows without impairing the viability of the welfare state, this case study has argued in the long term for abandoning numerical quotas on family-sponsored and independent immigrants and relying instead on the mechanisms of sponsorship and minimum mandatory social program insurance. The sponsorship/mandatory social program insurance system would protect the integrity of the welfare state by preventing its abuse by newcomers. At the same time, decentralization of immigration decision-making would generate improvements in the efficiency of labor markets in developed countries by decreasing the uncertainties associated with recruiting abroad, by decreasing the waiting period associated with the bureaucratic requirements of immigration agencies, and by allowing the needs of the labor market to indirectly determine the number of immigrants admitted each year. The delegation of immigration decision-making power to those benefiting most from the decisions, coupled with a policy requiring them to internalize the costs of social program utilization through insurance premiums, would generate a much better alignment of incentives than bureaucratic administration of admission requirements (beyond health, criminality, and national security screens).

The timing of immigration policy reforms may prove to be a key determinant of how much benefit individual countries will be able to realize from liberalization. Many industries already face increasingly fierce global competition for the recruitment of those possessing highly specialized human capital.[51] Given the empirical fact that once specialized clusters of complementary industries form in a particular locale they tend to be self-perpetuating (agglomeration economies),[52] an important first-mover advantage may be seized by those countries demonstrating a willingness to dispense with formal immigration quotas and allowing international labor markets to operate more freely. Such initiatives should be complemented by more effective public and private resettlement assistance programs, language training, credential equivalency determination mechanisms, and bridging programs to enable immigrants to upgrade their qualifications through appropriate classroom and on-the-job training.[53] These policies, along with inclusive public education policies, should be designed to promote full social and economic integration and minimize the prospect of impoverished and alienated immigrant enclaves (multiple solitudes) that Schlesinger, Putnam, Sen and Collier (among others) have rightly worried about.[54]

These clustering benefits are likely to be most concentrated in the recruitment of those with highly specialized human capital,[55] but may be realized to an indeterminate extent with the recruitment of relatively unskilled workers as well. As natives and highly skilled immigrants are drawn increasingly into employment demanding highly specialized human capital in the so-called "new" or "knowledge-based" economy, new complementary opportunities for unskilled workers arise. Dual-career households demand nannies, housekeepers, gardeners, and cooks. Aged parents require healthcare workers. To the extent that these positions cannot readily be filled by unskilled native workers, growth in highly skilled occupations may be hampered for lack of affordable ancillary services. Thus, the general liberalization of immigration policy in developed countries will facilitate the reaping of the greatest range of benefits possible. Not only will countries adopting such policies capture a potentially very important first-mover advantage, but they will be able to reinforce this advantage by admitting unskilled workers who are able to meet the requirements proposed above to provide the support services demanded by many highly skilled workers, their families, and their employers.

In short, I believe that in an increasingly globalized world economy, developed countries would find it prudent to integrate immigration policy fully and centrally into their external economic policies (along with international movement of goods, services, and capital) and to remove it from the largely protectionist, inefficient bureaucratic backwaters in which it has languished in most developed countries for much of their history. Although recent concerns over international terrorism may create pressures to render existing immigration policies more restrictive than they currently are, we should not allow these concerns to blind us to the substantial long-term domestic and global welfare gains likely to be realized from more liberal immigration policies—building stronger bridges, rather than higher or longer fences.

That an expansive immigration policy is politically feasible, if well-designed and its rationales well and consistently articulated by political leaders, is at least partly exemplified by the case of Canada, which admits about 250,000 migrants a year—almost 1 percent of its population (in relative terms about twice the level of entry of both legal and illegal immigrants into the United States). Despite the scale and increasing diversity of its immigration flows, and despite significant flaws in its policies,[56] international public opinion polls find that the net positive attitudes of respondents—the number of points by which positive attitudes to immigrants exceed negative attitudes—is far larger in Canada than any other country surveyed. Immigration policy is not an issue of "high politics" on the national political agenda.[57] Most Canadians perceive themselves as winners from immigration;

adverse labor market and fiscal effects have been largely mitigated by prevailing policies, and cultural diversity has mostly come to be seen as a virtue and not a vice in today's global economy—a view that stands in sharp contrast to the predicates of earlier, much more restrictive (indeed racist) Canadian immigration policies—which suggests the possibility of progressive policy evolution.

In a US context where political debates over liberalizing immigration policies are currently intense, and recognizing that significant segments of the public are sceptical of the virtues of more liberal immigration policies, feasible political compromises might accord high priority to the following reforms:

1) Substantial expansion over time (like progressive tariff reductions on imported goods described in Chapter 5) of the number of H-1B visas for temporary skilled workers (and entrepeneurs) and their families, including more liberal rules on workers changing employers and spouses seeking employment, with a clear and not unduly protracted path to permanent resident status (e.g., five years of more or less continuous employment), and ultimately the option of naturalization ideally accompanied by mandatory social insurance coverage prior to acquiring permanent resident status (or alternatively be disentitled to access to these programs).

2) For foreign graduate students with doctoral degrees from US universities, especially in, but not necessarily limited to, the STEM disciplines, and with employer sponsorship, an immediate right to permanent resident status and ultimately the option of naturalization.

3) More modest expansion over time of the number of H-2B visas for less skilled temporary workers, in sectors that typically attract an insufficient suply of domestic workers, but again with a clear path to permanent resident status (e.g., five years of more or less continuous employment), and ultimately the option of naturalization, again ideally accompanied by mandatory social program insurance coverage prior to acquiring permanent resident status (or alternatively be disentitled to access to these programs).

4) Expansion of the number of family preference immigrants, perhaps restricted to spouses and minority-age children, and perhaps with a longer period of mandatory social program insurance coverage (e.g., 10 years, mirroring Canadian family sponsorship obligations), given the absence of employment preconditions or qualifications, but with no quota limits on the number of immigrants who can meet the conditions for this category as defined.

5) For current illegal or unauthorized immigrants who are able to satisfy criminality, national security, and health screens (other than the criminal conduct implicit in their illegal status), a clear path to permanent resident status and ultimately the option of naturalization, perhaps by being issued temporary worker visas after satisfying these screens and being required to demonstrate thereafter more or less continuous employment for a period

(e.g., five years), during which they would not qualify for access to social entitlement programs, other than public education and basic healthcare, unless social program insurance coverage against claims on such programs had been obtainted. An excessively burdensome or protracted path to citizenship for the currently estimated 11 million illegal immigrants in the United States is likely to prove self-defeating and to leave many of them in legal limbo indefinitely, given the infeasibility and inhumanity of mass deportations.

Reforms along these lines seem likely to attract significant support from employers facing increasingly fierce global competition for highly skilled talent and from workers whose jobs depend on such talent. These reforms will assuage less skilled domestic workers, who may be among the country's least advantaged citizens, that they will not be facing unconstrained competition from waves of temporary unskilled foreign workers (who would be viewed more as complements than substitutes), and should appeal to existing permanent residents or citizens who wish to sponsor close family members without inordinate delays. To render these reforms politically feasible, broadly cast coalitions of these groups will need to publicly disemminate credible information about the benefits (especially economic) of immigration (underscoring the obvious fact that most Americans are, at one or more generation removed, immigrants and presumably feel that they, their forebears, and their country have been well-served by that fact). Framing the issues by an appeal to American pride in their origins and recalling the cherished values inscribed on the base of the Statue of Liberty and the constant need for regeneration of the country's settler spirit may open space for socially productive compromises on otherwise potentially highly divisive issues.

{ 8 }

Climate Change Policy: Managing More Heat in the World's Kitchens

I. Introduction

This case study relies on a number of propositions about climate change that I take to be convincingly established.[1] First and foremost among them is that anthropogenic (i.e., human-caused) climate change is real and it is increasing average global temperatures over the long term. Second, this warming has potentially disastrous consequences for large swathes of humanity, and is a problem requiring immediate, concerted, and sustained action. Third, it is possible to address this problem through a combination of behavioral modification, effective policymaking, and international cooperation and regulation.[2] Fourth, increasing the efficiency of energy generation, particularly in terms of carbon emissions, is an important aspect of any serious climate change mitigation strategy. Finally, the increased presence of carbon dioxide influences the global climate system in potentially dramatic and irreversible ways. Although carbon dioxide is not the only human influence on the climate system, it is an important one, and it is generally accepted that dealing with it ought to be a top policy priority.[3]

Even if we accept these premises, though, the global climate system is not fully understood. Thus, decisions regarding climate change policy will need to be made under conditions of uncertainty, contestation, and ignorance.[4] Energy conservation may lead to some emissions reduction, but, particularly in light of the rapid pace of economic development and population growth in much of the developing world, this is not a sufficient solution: increased efficiency in economic production will be necessary.[5] In practice, the perceived and political necessities of economic growth means that wide-scale reductions in energy use are unlikely.[6] Therefore, innovation in energy technology must be at the center of any successful decarbonization effort.[7]

The nature of the problem dictates that, at some level, solutions will need to have the near full participation of the international community.[8] Although the causes of climate change are located within political borders, their effects clearly transcend them. Nevertheless, the adoption of carbon abatement schemes by individual countries will lead to higher costs for domestic consumers and decreased competitiveness of domestically produced goods as producers will be facing higher production costs, leading to carbon leakage and capital relocation to countries that have more permissive policies.[9] Additionally, lowered demand for oil or coal in some countries as a result of abatement policies will likely result in increased use elsewhere as global prices decline.[10]

Why, then, has there been an absence of international agreement to address the issue? The most straightforward answer is that climate change is a classic collective action problem.[11] Because the benefits of carbon abatement cannot be restricted to those who contributed to creating them, all parties have an incentive to freeride. This, in turn, results in the suboptimal abatement of carbon.[12] However, although this understanding does offer a basic framework of analysis, an austere Public Choice approach to the matter rests, at least implicitly, on an insufficiently nuanced model of individual motivation and cognition and, concomitantly, is limited in its ability to offer advice for addressing the problem.

II. Policy Instruments

There are four principal types of policy instruments available to address carbon emissions: information and exhortation, mandates, subsidies, and pricing.[13] Informational and exhortative policies designed to draw public attention to the existence and potential consequences of global warming are likely to prove useful in raising awareness and, consequently, in inducing behavioral change. Over time, they may fundamentally alter how climate change is perceived, fostering an increased willingness on the part of the public to undergo sacrifices to address the problem.[14] On the other hand, the straightforward provision of scientific information is likely to be inneffective, at least directly and immediately, at changing public attitudes, except among a small audience. Nisbet, for example, finds that "as in other debates, such as stem cell research, abortion, or gun control, the rest of the public either ignores the coverage or reinterprets competing claims based on partisanship or self-interest, a tendency confirmed across several decades by public opinion research."[15] Although this assertion may be too deterministic, it certainly contains a kernel of truth. Nonetheless, informational measures tend to be relatively low-cost and, in one way or another, are likely vital to addressing the issue of climate change in the long run as public attitudes and beliefs will need to be altered. This is all the more true if one seeks to promote democratic decision-making by an informed citizenry.

Mandates may take a number of forms: one of the most common is the establishment of an emission standard for production of a megawatt hour (MWh) of power that applies to all sources.[16] This type of policy may prove useful in overcoming hurdles to innovation as it necessitates compliance. However, it does not provide business with incentives to develop cleaner or more efficient techniques beyond the regulatory requirement, and may actually discourage such behavior if firms fear a tightening of standards should they become more efficient than required.[17] One possible means of addressing this concern would be to assign credits to firms that emit greenhouse gasses (GHG) at a rate per MWh below the required level, while forcing those that emit above it to purchase those credits.[18] This approach shades into a cap-and-trade system, a policy instrument discussed further below.

Another means of addressing carbon emissions is the subsidization of green technology. At the production stage this might take the form of guaranteeing an above-market price for green power sold to the grid. From an economic efficiency perspective, subsidies of this type are generally considered a poor idea except in limited circumstances (i.e., where the support is for basic research) as they are seen as distortionary.[19] At the consumption stage, subsidization might take the form of a tax credit for those purchasing energy-efficient products such as hybrid vehicles. In addition to the high cost to government, subsidization of this type may also impair the fundamental shift in public attitudes toward the environment that many believe necessary to effectively address climate change.[20] More generally, the subsidization of climate-friendly technologies will artificially lower the cost of energy (via subsidies to green generation technology) or of energy use (via subsidies to appliance efficiency), leading to socially excessive levels of energy supply and consumption.[21] In pursuing this course, the government is also engaging itself in the business of picking technological winners, creating the possibility of locking-in inefficient, early-generation technologies and providing little incentive for novel or revolutionary technological development.[22]

The standard economic policy prescription for efficient carbon abatement is a market-based instrument such as a tax on emissions or a tradable permit system. Serious concerns arise that any unilateral (i.e., non-global) pricing will cause the leakage of jobs and emissions to other jurisdictions.[23] Indeed, Helm notes that leakage of this type may actually increase emissions. For example, while the United Kingdom reduced its carbon production by 15 percent between 1990 and 2005, its carbon consumption went up by 19 percent over the same period. A large portion of carbon-intensive products came from China, meaning that additional carbon was generated per unit as a result of the shipping-driven fuel consumption and less carbon-efficient (i.e., coal-powered) industry in China.[24] At the same time, however, a substantial amount of emissions in developed countries occur in non-tradable sectors such as transportation and residential buildings.[25] An additional concern is the regressive nature of carbon pricing. As the price will ultimately be borne by consumers, it will negatively impact those with lower incomes who spend proportionately more on non-discretionary goods and services such as heating and electricity.[26]

In principle, taxation is the simpler form of carbon pricing.[27] Most proponents suggest that the tax rate should be priced equal to the marginal benefits of emission reductions, represented by estimates of the social cost of carbon, and that it should be applied economy-wide. Advocates also tend to prefer "upstream" (taxing energy producers and importers) rather than "downstream" (taxing retail sales) approaches. An upstream approach would be administratively simpler due to the relatively small number of primary energy producers in an economy compared to the number of retailers.[28] Although somewhat more complex to administer, cap-and-trade systems have advantages, not the least of which is their relatively greater political acceptability as a result of a public aversion to taxes in general.[29] One drawback of the cap-and-trade approach relative to carbon taxes is the uncertainty of the cost of emitting carbon, arising from the government setting the quantity of allowances and supply and demand setting the price. This has the potential to undermine political support and investment in the research and development of abatement technologies as the uncertainty of prices will increase the risks associated with investment in abatement research. This has led to suggestions for price floors and ceilings, as well as offset provisions for allowances.[30]

One of the basic truths about climate change policy is that it necessarily involves uncertainty. Current technologies are not able to reduce emissions without seriously impacting the economy, making them politically costly, if they are feasible at all.[31] Although various carbon minimizing or sequestering technologies hold the promise of future low-cost improvements in efficiency or abatement, the cost, time, and extent of these gains remain indeterminate. Uncertainty is also inherent with respect to price signalling. A tax-based approach creates a predictable cost of carbon but the actual level of abatement is nearly impossible to predict in advance as it is dependent on elasticities of supply and demand in various markets. On the other hand, cap-and-trade systems create a predictable level of abatement, but leave the actual price of emissions uncertain, which will be determined via the market demand for emissions permits.

III. Ethical Considerations

From an ethical perspective, three of the primary problems relating to compensation or mitigation as a result of regulatory or policy change are determining what the status quo is, how certain it is to continue, and whether an actor suffering a loss as the result of a change ought to bear that loss alone. In other words, did the loss occur as a result of a risk that the loser was (or ought to have been) aware of? In order to address this issue, I have divided the following section into three parts, each dealing with an important aspect of the matter at hand. Although I do not purport to provide a definitive answer to the problem, I seek to unpack some of the key issues involved in making decisions in the area and the ethical concerns they raise.

A. LIABILITY FOR PAST EMISSIONS

Historical saturation is a significant matter with respect to fairness and the allocation of burden. Carbon released into the atmosphere has an impact on atmospheric absorption capacity and, in turn, climate for something like 200 years.[32] As such, there is an argument to be made that those responsible for such emissions ought to be held accountable. Conversely, it could be ethically problematic to punish current generations for the behavior of their forebears, or to suggest that those forebears are liable for those emissions given their ignorance of the harmful effects on the global environment.

Based on tort principles, Posner and Weisbach have argued that it would be unethical to hold the current generation liable for past behavior of members of their country, particularly if there is no evidence of negligence.[33] A lack of moral culpability could also be advanced if those emissions occurred prior to scientific understanding of their harmful effects on the environment. Conversely, one might argue that the current generation has benefitted—in terms of power and prosperity—as a result of those emissions, and ought to pay the cost, albeit retroactively. Moreover, just because individuals are not morally culpable does not mean they are not liable for the consequences of their actions. Culpability and liability are both analytically and ethically distinct.[34] Indeed, this distinction is foundational to the separation of tort and criminal liability.

From the perspective of developing countries, it can be argued that: (1) they have not contributed nearly as much as developed countries to the existing stock of atmospheric carbon, and therefore should not be forced to bear the costs of abatement equally; and, (2) they are entitled to per capita emissions on a par with developed countries. However, the large scale transfers of wealth from developed to developing countries that would be necessary to give effect to an equal per-capita approach is highly unlikely as it would impose significant costs on producers—who tend to exercise substantial political influence—as well as voters more generally in developed countries.[35] As McKibbin and Wilcoxen note, despite the validity of arguments on both sides, "neither is a realistic basis for designing a policy that sovereign nations will have to ratify and to implement."[36] Here, as elsewhere in politics, the moral high ground is neither clearly defined nor sufficiently strong to cause substantive change.

Another concern is the allocation of abatement costs. As a basic proposition, the impacts of a "business as usual" approach to carbon emissions will vary considerably across countries, imposing greater or lesser costs of not addressing climate change on particular actors. One line of reasoning suggests that the costs of carbon abatement ought to be allocated according to the benefits achieved from carbon emission reduction. On this view, countries such as the United States and Canada that are less vulnerable to climate change—and may even end up as net benficiaries due to longer growing seasons and increases in arable land and ease of access to primary resources—ought to bear less of a burden than those countries such as Maldives or Bangladesh that are likely to suffer catastrophic consequences even if the widely proposed 2° C cap on global average temperature increase is achieved.[37] Conversely, if it is accepted that any nonnatural (i.e., man-made) deviation from global norms or equilibrium points is an externality and (at least morally) warrants compensation, then the opposite conclusion would be reached.[38] Thus, for example,

Maldives should receive the greatest level of compensation, rather than contributing the most.

Related to the ethical responsibility attributed to causation, there is also a question as to whether there is a moral duty to assist developing countries in addressing climate change. As discussed above, one possible answer is that the developed world's overwhelming contribution to the problem means that there is a direct obligation to assist the developing world in mitigating the effects. On the other hand, in seeming contrast to the ethos of *A Theory of Justice* and *Political Liberalism*, Rawls argued that distributive justice concerns do not extend to those outside the boundaries of one's political community.[39] At a basic level, this can be seen as aligning with a deliberative concept of democracy as it implies that only individuals who are subject to the coercive authority of a state are also entitled to its benefits. As members of other countries are not subject to its coercive authority, they are also not entitled to its benefits (i.e., redistribution). However, even if there is no moral imperative to treat extra-nationals as equals in terms of distribution, this does not mean that there are no limits to what a particular jurisdiction can lay claim to. As the result of international human rights obligations, it is not unreasonable to assert that providing assistance to developing countries is required by both morality and international law.

B. JUSTIFYING DIFFERENT EMISSIONS LEVELS

The idea of equal per-capita emissions is intuitively appealing as a global standard for a number of reasons: it resonates with basic liberal notions of fairness and justice, it is administratively straightforward, and its simplicity is aesthetically appealing. However, Kaplow, among others, suggests that the equal per-capita argument is not grounded in any comprehensive moral principle.[40] Moreover, there are a number of principled rationales that support an unequal per-capita allocation of emission quotas.

For a variety of structural reasons, including factor endowments, climate, and proximity to trading partners, some countries will be induced toward higher carbon emissions and/or greater costs associated with meeting a given reduction target. For example, in parts of Canada the climate (i.e., the North) is relatively more harsh than many other regions of the world, requiring a greater per-person expenditure of energy on shelter.[41] Similarly, Canada's economy is resource-based—leading to a generally greater amount of carbon emissions per dollar of GDP—although this may not be as compelling an argument: the price of carbon could reasonably be built in via exports.[42] Borders are not perfectly fluid and there are broader issues of community membership and identity tied into geographic residence. As such, it could be ethically justifiable for jurisdictions that are structurally induced to emit more carbon per capita to do so without penalty.

Positive externalities are also a potential justification for unequal allocation. For example, there is a question as to whether countries with carbon sinks such as forests should be compensated for them, or, more specifically, for not slashing and burning them to make way for agriculture. From one perspective, cutting them down is effectively a carbon emission, and not cutting them down is simply maintaining the status quo—why should a political entity be compensated for not doing environmental damage? On the other hand, if carbon emissions and sequestration are to be taken seriously, with a particular focus on controlling externalities, then why should jurisdictions that refrain from putting forests to other productive uses not receive compensation for doing so? They are, after all, creating a generalized benefit by forgoing private gain.

Reliance may also serve as a justification for the differential allocation of emissions. It can be argued that investments made at a time when they were morally unproblematic (i.e., prior to a general consensus about the potential dangers of carbon emissions in terms of climate change) ought to be taken into account when implementing policy changes. A real world example of this can be found in the EU's allocation of fishing quotas in the face of declining stocks. In that situation the allocation of quotas was based on the relative importance of the fisheries to national economies.[43] In general, this argument could be used to justify transitional rules, but probably not a crystallization of differential access for all time.[44]

More generally, to allow per capita emissions in rapidly growing developing economies such as China and India to increase to levels prevailing in developed countries such as the United States would be ruinous in terms of environmental outcomes, while compelling developed countries such as the United States to reduce their emissions to per capita levels prevailing in less developed countries would be economically ruinous (in addition to being politically untenable).

IV. Political Factors

A. STRUCTURAL

The nature of a given jurisdiction's geography and its factor endowments are likely to play a strong role in shaping attitudes toward carbon abatement measures both directly and via their impact on the organization of the economy. Differences in these respects will impose differential costs in terms of both material subsistence (i.e., shelter, heating, transportation) as well as strongly condition the comparative advantage of a given jurisdiction, thus affecting the structure of a given economy. This, in addition to raising ethical issues (discussed in the previous section), is likely to shape public opinion regarding the legitimacy of climate change science and the willingness to accept the economic costs imposed by measures designed to address those issues.[45] One probable source of this differentiation is self-interest. Although not conclusive, it is suggestive that on average residents of the more carbon-intensive subnational economies in Canada, for instance, are substantially less likely to believe in climate change.[46]

A related factor is the presence of focusing events, something determined largely by environmental conditions beyond the scope of political manipulation. The general argument here is that public opinion is highly responsive to anecdotal but personally observed effects of policy problems (the availability heuristic, noted in Chapter 2). Thus, in jurisdictions where severe weather events occur—for example, droughts and bush fires in Australia, floods in Bangladesh—the issue of climate change is more readily accepted and more highly prioritized as its effects are tangible and hence salient.[47] It is, however, notable that these severe events need not be tied directly to carbon emissions or GHGs more generally.[48]

Another macro-level consideration is the robustness of the economy. Indeed, public opinion has shown itself to be relatively elastic, responding to changes in the economic fortunes of the jurisdiction. In the United States, for example, willingness to pay a tax on carbon emissions was notably higher prior to 2008 than it was during the 2008 economic crisis; and, there is evidence that as the United States emerges from that crisis, the acceptability of carbon pricing and the acceptance of global warming as a real and current problem may be increasing.[49]

B. INSTITUTIONAL

The impact of formal institutions on the feasibility of a given climate change policy are likely to be manifest in the presence or absence of federalism (as well as the allocation of powers therein), the nature of the electoral system, and the organization of the legislative process, as well as the landscape of existing taxes and subsidies that affect carbon emissions (e.g., gasoline taxes, price floors for power from renewable sources). One intuitive consequence of federalism is that the diffusion of power makes concerted action less likely than in unitary states.[50] That said, a majority of individuals in both Canada and the United States—relatively decentralized federal systems—support action on climate change by their subnational governments independent of the actions of the central government.[51] Of course, support for an approach does not translate directly into its adoption. Nonetheless, two Canadian provinces—British Columbia and Quebec—have implemented carbon taxes, despite a clear absence of action on climate change at the national level.[52]

Another important aspect of federalism for climate change is the constitutional allocation of powers within the federation. For example, in most, if not all federal systems, only the central government is empowered to negotiate international obligations. However, the allocation of power within a given system will impact both the strength of a jurisdiction's bargaining positions and adherence to any agreements made at the national level, as the negotiating government may not be able to enact all of the necessary measures to comply with an agreement because they are matters of subnational jurisdiction.[53] Many federal countries are subject to potential normalizing and/or disciplining forces at the international level and must also contend with domestic pressures. For example, the Australian federal government's sweeping treaty power allows it to pass legislation that is binding on subnational units in support of international obligations. This is simply not possible in Canada or the United States due to their respective Constitutions' allocation of powers. An additional advantage of the Australian system is that intergovernmental relations are conducted in a more coordinated fashion through the institutionalization of federal-state relations via the Council of Australian Governments (COAG).[54]

Although the greater overall success in addressing climate change in the European Union relative to North America can be at least partly attributed to fundamental economic and social differences such as a tradition of more active state involvement in the economy,[55] electoral systems also play a role. The proportional representation system of electoral representation employed by most member states and the European Parliament have led to an institutionalization of green parties that has not occurred in the United States or Canada, in no small part because of their majoritarian systems.[56] The branch or division of the government tasked with producing the first draft of legislation or policy that impacts climate change will also likely play a large role in shaping its parameters, and vice versa.[57] In the United States, for example, the finance committee of Congress would likely produce the initial draft of a carbon tax, whereas a cap-and-trade bill would start in environment and public works; the core of the former bill would likely focus on revenue creation whereas that of the latter would focus on environmental goals;[58] the original draft would impact the framing of the issue and, in turn, the legislation's political feasibility.

Conceived of as norms and standard operating procedures, institutions also play a role in shaping the political viability of climate change policies. The prior trajectory (i.e., the inertia) of an institution will shape the nature of its policies and actions, manifest in the internalized norms of its managers and staff, absent a force of sufficient strength to overcome the status quo bias. For example, in a parliamentary system such as Canada, in the absence of strong and active leadership from the prime minister or an experienced and trusted cabinet minister, the nature of recommendations and action by a given department is unlikely to change tack.[59] Similarly, the Canadian experience with climate change has led to a department tasked with the issue (Environment) that has little power, few allies, and a bureaucracy that is reticent to advance substantive climate policies.[60] Moreover, the Ministry of Finance, as an organization, has been described as displaying "an almost religious hostility to cluttering the tax system with specific measures aimed at producing behavioural change in consumers or taxpayers,"[61] the primary function of a carbon tax.

It has also been suggested that the journalistic norm of presenting a "balanced" perspective in lieu of direct attempts at objectivity (particularly where the technical complexity of an issue generally precludes journalistic expertise in the area) has led to a general misrepresentation about the degree of consensus regarding the existence of anthropogenic global warming, at least in the United States.[62] In other words, by giving both positions on the existence of man-made global warming equal, or at least some, consideration, in media representations of the issue, it accords those refuting its existence a legitimacy that they simply do not possess in the scientific community.

C. IDEATIONAL

As a general principle, "public opinion can fundamentally compel or constrain political, economic and social action to address particular risks."[63] There may be slack between the wishes of the public and the actions of their elected representatives, but on some level public opinion shapes (and is shaped by) the political agenda, as well as altering the political costs and benefits associated with adopting particular measures or positions. It also influences politicians' notions of what the appropriate action or policy is in a given situation. Of course, vested interests are unlikely to sit idly by. They, too, play a role in shaping political agendas and public discourse, and do so in a manner that is likely to give disproportionate weight to their preferences via lobbying, strategic messaging, campaign financing, and other means.[64]

As noted in Chapter 2, substantial evidence indicates that individuals are willing to make personal sacrifices in order to punish what they believe to be unfair or unjust behavior on the part of others. In other words, "self-interest maximization can be somewhat tempered by the affirmative desire to treat others fairly."[65] This leads us to a basic premise that international agreements that are not perceived as fair are less likely to be signed, and more likely to be shirked if they are signed.[66] This suggests that the framing of climate change policies as fair and equitable will play an important role in their public acceptability and, in turn, their political feasibility. In this vein, it is worth noting that public opinion data indicates that large majorities of people in developing countries agree with the statement "poorer countries should be required to take significant action immediately along with richer countries." Additionally, a relatively small number in any country believe that developing countries should not be required to take any action.[67]

However, although there is widespread support for addressing climate change, it is frequently of a low intensity, particularly relative to economic concerns. This is clearly evident during times of economic recession.[68] This low prioritization lends substantial credence to Pielke's concept of the "iron law of climate change." Pielke's basic premise is that economic gains come at environmental costs, and environmental gains come at an economic cost; although individuals are willing to accept a personal price to address climate change, that willingness only goes so far. Where the economy and the environment are in direct conflict, economic concerns will nearly universally win out. Any successful attempt to address climate change must recognize the (at least) medium-term reality of this and operate—and be framed—accordingly.[69] Another possible reason for the consistently low prioritization of climate change is a lack of public understanding of its causes and consequences. For example, a 1999 GlobeScan survey found that the single most (and incorrectly) identified "cause" of global warming was the depletion of the Earth's ozone layer, while relatively few respondents correctly identify the use of fossil fuels as a principal cause.[70] The absence of focusing events in many jurisdictions likely plays a role in the level of intensity and immediacy attached to climate change. There is a perception in many developed countries that they are not directly vulnerable, and that global warming is a threat that is geographically distant.[71]

Another relevant issue is the "quality" of the public opinion held, insofar as it forms a coherent set of policy prescriptions that could conceivably be implemented and that are not internally inconsistent. On the one hand, Americans have expressed moderate levels of concern regarding the impact of global warming and strongly believe that the United States should reduce GHG emissions. They also support international treaties seeking to address the relevant issues. On the other hand, there is public opposition to tax policies that would directly affect them, such as gas taxes. This suggests that the US public has yet to develop an internally coherent understanding of the interrelation between economics and climate change and remains in the "wishful thinking" stage of opinion formation.[72]

A further contributor to misperception and limited (or erroneous) understanding of climate change are the active challenges to the legitimacy of the Intergovernmental Panel on Climate Change and climate science more generally. Mobilized interests—for example, the fossil fuel industry—have mounted campaigns to protect their interests. These campaigns tend to rely on (1) challenging validity of the science and/or the advisability of the precautionary principle, and (2) framing the issue as a direct conflict between the economy and the environment, in which case the "iron law of climate change" dictates that the economy will win.[73] In contrast, a positive example of issue framing in this area is that of E.O. Wilson and others, who by focusing on the moral aspects of stewardship and responsibility for humanity more generally convinced many religious leaders of the importance of addressing climate change.[74]

D. PSYCHOLOGICAL

Behavioral economics suggests that individuals' mental processes are related to the political feasibility of climate change policies in at least two ways: via the availability heuristic and as a result of confirmation bias associated with an individual's core beliefs. The availability heuristic describes the tendency of individuals to base their estimates of probability and importance on particularly salient events they can readily call to mind. The problem with this is that memorable events are often unrepresentative.[75] For example, the most prominent reason cited for a belief in climate change in both the United States and Canada is individual perception of local weather changes.[76] As Nisbet notes, "the tendency to dismiss the urgency of climate change is exacerbated given the problem's complexity and its lack of immediate, visible impacts."[77] In the past, mobilizing or focusing events have proved to be important drivers of environmental policy change,[78] but climate change seems different—we cannot observe it in the same way. It is less real.[79] Australia (at least until recently) has been more successful than North America at instituting climate change policies. Public opinion on the importance of climate change has persisted much longer in Australia than elsewhere, a fact that is logically attributable to a series of major weather events, including a near decade of drought. The less substantial financial downturn experienced by Australia likely also played a role by not displacing the salience of climate change to the degree experienced in countries more deeply affected by the recent recession.[80]

There are four basic types of individual worldview: hierarchical, fatalistic, individualist, and egalitarian. Each of these views includes a set of assumptions about appropriate social organization and will lead adherents to perceive different risks and to support different policy responses. A hierarchical worldview is fearful of threats to the status quo and supportive of the active management of policy problems by experts. A fatalistic worldview is sceptical that anything we might feasibly do will make much of a difference to such an overwhelming problem. An individualistic one is most fearful of restrictions of individual autonomy, inherently skeptical of regulation and supportive of market-based solutions. Egalitarians, on the other hand, are most concerned with (re)distributive justice in terms of risks and benefits.[81]

In general, ideas about the role of the state can be linked to these fundamental values. For example, individuals with libertarian or individualist values are significantly less likely to support climate change initiatives than those with egalitarian values.[82] Kahan et al. suggest that individuals with values that favor hierarchy and/or individualism are more likely to be skeptical of environmental risks as widespread acceptance would justify restricting commerce and industry, activities that they prize. The reverse would be true for individuals with relatively egalitarian and communitarian values. These values, they contend, are likely to shape individuals' opinions of the quality of a given expert's opinion and the degree of consensus within the scientific community through at least three mechanisms, each of which is supported by both prior work in the field and compelling large-n survey data.

First, as discussed above, the availability heuristic suggests that individuals tend to base decisions on the information they can readily call to mind, such as events they have personally experienced. Because instances of expert support for one's existing values are more likely to be recalled, individuals will tend to perceive scientific opinion in a manner more consistent with their values than it might actually be. Second, individuals tend to work harder to uncover information that confirms their predispositions. Third, individuals are also likely to exhibit bias in their assimilation of information, basing their evaluation of the credibility of the information source on the information's conformity with their own predispositions.[83] These predispositions appear to manifest in both Canada and the United States, where the best predictor of individual attitudes toward climate change science is partisan identification. In the United States, 41 percent of those identifying as Republicans believe in climate change, while 69 percent of Democrats do. In Canada, Conservative Party supporters are nearly three times as likely as supporters of other parties to disbelieve the reality of climate change.[84]

V. Transition Strategies

A. TAXES AND PERMITS

The two principal forms of carbon pricing are taxes and cap-and-trade schemes. Both have merits and demerits. However, as Simpson et al. aptly note "[e]conomists leery about command-and-control approaches feel more comfortable with taxes. They don't have to get elected of course."[85] In Canada, for example, political opportunism, business denunciations, and media scepticism mean that carbon taxation appears, at least in the near future, to be a political dead letter at the national level.[86] In addition to this, even where carbon taxes have been successfully implemented, the loopholes and exceptions they contain may undermine the fundamental logic of a tax and create perverse incentives.[87] That said, in the long term, imposing a tax may be useful in and of itself by serving as a touchstone for future advocacy and a benchmark for the costs of various abatement strategies, and by acclimatizing the public to the idea of carbon emissions as being harmful.[88]

In addition to overcoming a general public aversion to increased taxation in many, if not all, developed economies,[89] it may be necessary to gain support from concentrated interests. Arguably, the best-suited policy for this kind of politicking is the cap-and-trade system, as modifications can be made to the initial allocation system independent of the equilibrium allocation (because the allocations can be tradable).[90] However, as will be discussed below, this approach can severely impair the effectiveness of pricing carbon in terms of emissions reduction. Additionally, the monitoring of offset purchases has proven problematic, particularly with respect to the substantial possibility of fraud.[91]

That being said, the revenue-raising possibilities of an allocation auction may also be politically attractive. This may be particularly true during times of fiscal austerity: where new revenue sources are sought, ongoing budget deficits may increase the political feasibility of new sources of revenue.[92] Cap-and-trade systems also avoid the need to overcome inbuilt institutional inertia, particular within finance and revenue ministries,[93] who are often opposed to using taxes as a means to induce behavioral change.[94] Thus, although a "tax" on carbon may not be feasible due to the negative connotations of the term or institutional bias against it, a policy with similar effects might be feasible to implement under the rubric of cap-and-trade.

B. CARBON TARIFFS AND EQUITY

A principal concern with respect to the unilateral (domestic) implementation of a carbon pricing scheme is that it imposes additional costs on domestic firms vis-à-vis foreign producers with no or less stringent regulations on carbon emissions. One way to address this issue is the imposition of a "carbon tariff" or border tax adjustment aimed at imposing similar costs on imported goods.[95] Doing so would serve three interrelated purposes. First, it would prevent the "leakage" of carbon emissions to foreign countries as a result of increased foreign market share or the "offshoring" of production by domestic producers. Second, it would prevent foreign producers from experiencing a de facto comparative advantage. Third, it may serve as a means to alleviate domestic political concerns surrounding job loss and hardship placed on the already struggling manufacturing sectors in much of the developed world. There are, however, questions as to the legality of carbon tariffs under current World Trade Organization (WTO) rules (although these seem surmountable), as well as a moral-ethical issue of how to address equity concerns regarding the undue imposition of costs on developing countries via such a system of unilateral import-based adjustments.[96]

An additional way to address domestic producers' concerns would be to apply the border tax adjustment on exports as well—that is, to rebate the cost of carbon on domestically produced goods destined for export. This would address additional concerns about domestic competitiveness in the global market. However, absent the widespread adoption of carbon pricing schemes, there would likely be little overall impact on global emissions levels. This highlights the potential conflict of ethical and political demands. On the one hand, moral and ethical concerns regarding the imposition of costs on the developing world may necessitate differential treatment of imports depending on their place of origin (i.e., lower or no carbon tariffs on goods imported from the least developed countries), while politics may require the uniform treatment of imports in order to prevent the politically nightmarish perception of the leakage of jobs and production to developing countries.[97]

C. REVENUE NEUTRAL CARBON PRICING

The more visible a price on carbon, the less politically palatable it is likely to be.[98] In ecnomic terms, pricing carbon is problematic because it will increase firms' production costs and product prices, thereby reducing real household incomes.[99] The effects on industry, however, will vary across sectors as a function of their carbon intensity. Indeed, the logic of the instrument relies on this: by internalizing the environmental costs of production, the substitution of a lower carbon-intensity product for a higher-intensity one will be induced, resulting in lower carbon emissions and incentivizing research and development.

One way to render carbon pricing more economically and politically palatable would be to make it revenue neutral. Indeed, this has been done successfully in the Canadian province of British Columbia.[100] The simplest way of doing so would be to directly translate revenue gained from the pricing scheme into broad-based tax cuts (e.g., personal or corporate income taxes or consumption taxes). Public opinion, however, does not necessarily support such an approach. When asked their preferences for how revenues from carbon pricing should be spent, 51 percent of Canadians and 43 percent of Americans indicated alternative energy research and development. Only 32 percent in each country indicated tax rebates, payroll tax cuts, or deficit reduction as their preferred use of such revenues[101] The revenue neutrality argument may also be hard to make in light of apprehensions of political opportunism and an ever-present temptation to divert carbon taxes into general revenues, especially at a time when many countries are contending with major budget deficits.[102] That said, with respect to regional concerns (either inter or intra-nationally) a tax may be made more palatable by distributing the revenues back to their source jurisdiction.[103] For example, Albertan opposition to any form of national carbon taxation could be alleviated by directing some or all of the revenues back to the Alberta government.[104] A harmonized global carbon tax could function in the same way.[105] In order to maintain the effectiveness of the tax at reducing carbon emissions, it would likely be necessary to establish ground rules as to the use of the remitted monies in order to prevent direct, and minimize the indirect, subsidization of the taxed industries.[106]

D. GRANDFATHERING AND EXEMPTIONS

Revenues from taxation or auctioned permits can be used to offset the impact on consumer prices by lowering other taxes, fund basic research, or engage in any number of other socially beneficial government initiatives. Grandfathered (non-auctioned) permits do not allow for this.[107] Grandfathered permits actually work in favor of vested interests, as subsequent entrants into a given sector or industry will face an additional entry barrier—emissions permits. In this respect, then, the grandfathering of permits may actually have the opposite effect of that desired.[108] Making entry into a given sector more difficult reduces competition as well as incentives to innovate, as entrenched players will be steered toward the extraction of rents rather than research and development.

A second concern is that grandfathered or otherwise freely distributed permits are regressive.[109] The establishment of a regulatory scheme limiting carbon emissions imbues permits with value. If these permits are distributed on a past use or other non-priced fashion, shareholders reap windfall gains. On the other hand, with carbon taxation or auctioned permits, revenues can be used to fund tax reductions in other areas (i.e., revenue-neutral taxation).[110] Basing initial allocations on historical levels also has the effect of rewarding laggards and penalizing early-adopters as firms or sectors that had taken the initiative to develop and employ lower carbon technology will effectively be penalized (via a lower allocation of emissions) than those that did not.[111]

E. PRICE CEILINGS, FLOORS, AND COLLARS

A key drawback of cap-and-trade schemes is the uncertainty they introduce into firms' bottom lines. As noted above, the price of an emissions permit cannot be reliably predicted ex ante as elasticities of supply and demand in affected sectors are often not known in advance with any degree of certainty. One way to avoid imposing excessive costs on business would be to establish a price ceiling on permits.[112] This so-called "safety-valve" would allow firms facing excessive costs in the market to purchase emissions permits from the government at a fixed rate. Doing so would have the effect of preventing too high a price on carbon at any particular time stagnating economic growth. At the other end of the spectrum, there is a concern that the uncertainty of carbon prices may preclude the types of long-term, capital-intensive investments likely to be necessary to achieve substantial advances in emissions efficiency. If firms are uncertain of the payoffs of investing in more energy-efficient methods of production, then the risks associated with the development of that technology become untenable and advances in energy efficiency—the primary goal—become suboptimal. In order to counteract this concern, price floors on emissions permits have been suggested as a means of facilitating investment in innovation.[113] A floor could be implemented in a similar fashion to a ceiling except instead of the government selling permits for a fixed price, it would agree to buy them for one.[114]

F. INFORMATION AND EXHORTATION

The relatively low prioritization of climate change relative to issues such as the economy, job creation, and national security has proven a substantial barrier to effective climate change. In many respects, this appears to be linked to the lack of focusing events that, as a result of the availability heuristic, might cause individuals to accord a greater priority to climate change.[115] In some respects, this is a structural-environmental problem that is beyond the control of political leaders. However, the provision of information regarding the human costs of climate change, as well as its potential close-to-home effects, would likely be invaluable in increasing the public's relative prioritization of the matter.

A second informational strategy would be to provide clarity in terms of the causes of climate change, the way in which policy instruments aimed at addressing it would function, and the impacts of that policy on both the economy and individuals. Although the evidence is clear that scientific "truth" is not in and of itself determinative,[116] there is evidence that greater information about climate change, particularly regarding its effects and the manner in which proposed policies would operate to address it, may increase support for those policies. At very least, it ought to reduce the credibility of opposition voices.[117]

G. FRAMING

Leisorwitz argues that "messages about climate change need to be tailored to the needs and predispositions of particular audiences; in some cases to directly challenge fundamental misconceptions, in others to resonate with strongly held values."[118] Complementing this assertion, Nisbet identifies a typology of frames applicable to climate change. These include addressing climate change as a means of fostering social progress, as an economic investment in global competitiveness, as a moral issue, as a matter of scientific uncertainty, and others.[119]

In addition to the direct provision of information discussed above, there are at least three methods of overcoming the inbuilt psychological biases that may negatively impact the political acceptability of climate change policy proposals.[120] The first is *Identity Affirmation*. This strategy is premised on a belief that effective communication shows its audience information in a way that supports a conclusion that supports their cultural values rather than threatening them. For example, this might involve framing carbon pricing as an investment in future economic stability or as a service to one's children. Related to this concept is the idea of *Pluralistic Advocacy*. The recommendation here is that policy proposals ought to be presented and advocated by as diverse a set of experts and opinion leaders as possible, on the grounds that information is more likely to be accepted from experts whom individuals perceive to have values in line with their own, and the more diverse the advocates, the broader the appeal. The third strategy is *Narrative Framing*. This approach involves the crafting of messages to evoke narrative templates that are congenial to target audiences. In the context of climate change, this might include portraying carbon pricing as a way in which individuals can foster social progress and contribute to the betterment of humanity.

VI. Conclusion

A global solution—in some form or another—will eventually be necessary to address the problem of climate change. A key element of any such solution will be creating an incentive structure that encourages participation and discourages free-eriding and shirking at the national level. An important point to remember here is that this can involve carrots *and* sticks. That is to say, although it will be important to ensure that all countries feel that they will gain from a given agreement,[121] the mobilization of shame—as manifest in appeals to fairness, appropriateness, or justice—may be an equally effective tool. In fact, in some cases it may be the only viable means to induce participation; direct material costs to a given economy can be outweighed by losses in international prestige and domestic public opinion, making participation the least costly of the options available. Pielke asserts that although pricing schemes, cap-and-trade in particular, sound appealing, "[they] cannot work because [they run] smack into the iron law of climate policy... putting a high price on carbon causes economic pain and discomfort to energy consumers, who also happen to be citizens and, often, voters. Politicians who want to continue in their jobs spend every waking hour trying to protect their constituents from economic pain. They will not rush to cause it intentionally."[122] This, I think, is an overstatement. Although economic consequences are likely a primary motivator, this view falls prey to the reductionist analysis of Public Choice theory. Politicians do, in fact, have other goals for their time in office. As discussed in Chapter 2, explanations for political behavior are varied—from individuals seeking individual gains as the result of political leadership, to acting out of a sense of moral compulsion or merely responding to mobilized environmental groups. Nevertheless, it is clear that politicians will sometimes impose short-run costs on their constituents for greater long-run social gains, albeit subject to more concerns than what is morally correct or the most technically efficient policy.[123]

In the long run, addressing climate change will require changing public attitudes. However, we are unlikely to get there in a single bound. Rather, this problem will need to be adressed in stages. One potential course of action would be the gradual imposition of carbon pricing, preferably via taxation but acceptably via cap and trade, at the domestic level coupled with commensurate border adjustments on both imports and exports. This will facilitate a gradual reallocation of resources in the economy and should both develop an institutional capacity to administer a carbon-pricing regime and foster a general sense of acceptance among the attentive public. Once an effective domestic regime is established, movement toward international cooperation becomes viable through the negotiation of border adjustment reciprocity agreements. These agreements are more likely to be reached bilaterally at first, but once a sufficient density of agreements is established, a cascade effect may follow.

This approach reflects very much proposals developed by Dieter Helm in a recent, widely acclaimed book.[124] Helm despairs of top-down negotiation of international treaties on climate change policy, which he views as having largely been an exercise in futility over the past two decades, reflecting a classic Prisoners' Dilemma collective action problem with massive free-riding incentives. Instead, he proposes that major jurisdictions adopt a carbon tax, initially at a relatively low level, but with commitments to raise it at periodic intervals until some target level of CO_2 emissions (e.g., 450 CO_2 PPM) is reached. In order to avoid carbon leakage and migration, and in recognition of the fact that it is carbon consumption, wherever it originates, that needs to be discouraged, he favors a carbon tariff at the border on imports reflecting the CO_2 intensity of their production. Countries with similar measures in place would receive a credit against the carbon tariff, creating incentives for countries to adopt such measures in order to retain the revenue so generated. Although designing a carbon tariff that conforms to international trade rules presents significant challenges,[125] such a regime seems legally feasible, as long as it avoids arbitrary or unjustifiable forms of discrimination between domestic and foreign producers, and among foreign producers from different countries. Over time, Helm is optimistic that countries may converge on a harmonized carbon tax.

However, there are some signficant drawbacks to a purely unilateral approach. First, it may create few incentives for countries to adopt a carbon tax in non-traded goods sectors. For example, according to Helm, China and India, over the next decade, are planning to build the equivalent of three new coal-fired generation plants a week. Presumably, much of this new generation will service domestic electricity needs, particularly in the residential sector, or otherwise for domestically demanded goods and services. Second, exporters will be concerned that they will be disadvantaged when competing in foreign markets against firms that do not face such a tax in their home markets. Although rebating the tax on exporters would address the problem of decreased export competitiveness, it would also significantly undermine the environmental rationales for the tax.

In order for Helm's scenario to reach the level of plausibility, however, there must first be a reasonably large number of domestic climate policy regimes—something that has proven remarkably problematic, though as we have seen, not entirely impossible. In order to facilitate the development of domestic regimes a number of the strategies discussed above will likely be necessary. In terms of information, the public's attention ought to be drawn toward such focusing events as occur in order to drive home the neceessity of addressing climate change.

Persuading citizens that a carbon tax that is revenue-neutral or—in the case of countries struggling to finance large deficits—a more attractive source of additional revenue than income or consumption taxes, and akin to "sin taxes" such as taxes on cigarettes and alcohol, may be partly responsive to this challenge. Phasing in such taxes over a significant transitional period, perhaps accompanied by tax credits for low-income households to offset disproportionate consumer costs, may enhance public acceptability.[126]

Ultimately, the "best" approach to induce carbon efficiency is one that effectively reduces the carbon output of a given jurisdiction through the inducement of investment in research and development in more efficient means of energy production and/or manufacturing in a way that is economically efficient, politically feasible, and administratively viable. The nature of these criteria are shaped by a plethora of variables that will make the calculus for each jurisdiction more or less unique. What I have sought to accomplish herein is to provide both conceptual insight—insofar as there is no universally applicable solution—and to highlight some of the more significant factors that contribute to the advisability of one approach or another in the pricing of carbon.

{ 9 }

Institutional Reform and Development: The Perils of Utopianism

I. Introduction

There is no area of public policy, domestic or foreign, where transition costs are of such central importance as institutional reform in developing countries. The field of development theory and practice, at least in the postwar years, has been peculiarly susceptible to all manner of fads and fashions with respect to both the ends and the means of development. Various schools of thought have come in and out of favor: capital fundamentalism, dirigiste central planning, dependency theory, the Washington consensus (market fundamentalism), and eclectic combinations of all of the foregoing.[1] As well, various economic conceptions of development, principally economic growth, have been juxtaposed with more holistic conceptions of development, such as human well-being or freedom.[2]

Many of the theories of development that dominated over this period—economic, cultural, and geographic—were largely institution-free. However, over the past two decades, an institutional perspective on development has become increasingly prominent in development thinking, captured in the mantra "institutions matter" or "governance matters." Beginning in the 1990s, based on the assumption that the quality of a country's institutions are an important determinant of its development prospects—supported by an increasing body of empirical evidence—there has been a massive surge in development assistance for institutional reform projects in developing and transition economies, involving investments of many billions of dollars. However, the reform experience thus far—whether directed at promoting democracy, promoting the rule of law, or reforming discrete areas of law such as property rights—suggests that if institutions do indeed matter for development, we still do not have a firm understanding of how to transform dysfunctional institutions. Or as Douglass North puts it, "we may know a lot about polities, but not how to fix them."[3]

This mixed-to-weak record of institutional reform in developing countries has prompted a growing recognition that institutional reformers are never writing on a blank slate and that existing institutions are typically the product of a long process of evolution, often reflecting conditions that prevailed early in these countries' histories. Hence, path dependency heavily constrains the options open to institutional reformers going forward—that is to say, history casts a long shadow on the present and indeed the future.[4] Thus, utopian visions of rapidly transforming lawless or repressive regimes into robust rule of law societies, or transforming deeply entrenched forms of autocratic government into flourishing democracies, have begun to fade.

II. Path Dependence Theory

As discussed in Chapter 2, with respect to positive theories of the political process, growing bodies of literature in economics, political science, and elsewhere describe how the reinforcement of a given set arrangements over time raises the cost of changing them.[5] Applied to institutions, the theory helps to explain how institutions (or networks of institutions) take shape through self-reinforcing mechanisms and why—as a consequence—they are difficult to change. The key insight associated with path dependence theory is that, under certain conditions, economic and other activities may be subject to increasing returns, whereby the benefits of engaging in them increase, rather than decrease over time as more and more people invest in a given way of doing things. As these investments—of time, money, skills, and expectations—add up, the relative cost of exploring alternatives steadily rises. A simple model of path dependence would therefore emphasize three features of an arrangement: (1) an initial set of choices or random events that determine the starting position, (2) the subsequent reinforcement of those choices or events through "feedback effects," and 3) the degree to which switching costs may preclude good alternatives from being explored in the long run.

Self-reinforcement mechanisms increase switching costs, locking in certain legal, political, and institutional arrangements. In addition, mutually reinforcing mechanisms suggest that institutional interdependencies that are the historical legacy of myriad past events may undermine the success of nodal institutional reforms, implying that we cannot easily modify any of these institutions in isolation. However, path dependence theory is not entirely deterministic, in that it recognizes the notion of "critical junctures"—interaction effects between distinct causal sequences that conjoin at particular points in time—that place institutional arrangements on particular paths or trajectories. The literature recognizes that critical junctures may be cathartic events in a country's history or minor perturbations that precipitate feedback or cumulative effects that place a country on a new or modified trajectory. Unfortunately, "critical junctures" are difficult to define prospectively, or even to identify with high levels of confidence while they are happening, without the benefit of hindsight in terms of the feedback effects that they trigger.

III. Rule of Law Reform and Development

Although the rule of law ostensibly commands wide support across the world, in fact understandings of the meaning of the rule of law diverge widely, ranging from "thick" conceptions that equate the rule of law with a substantively just legal system to "thin" conceptions that are procedurally oriented and emphasize notions of due process and neutral adjudication of disputes. Some conceptions of the rule of law emphasize its intrinsic value, others its instrumental value in fostering investment and growth through the protection of property rights and the enforcement of contracts.[6]

I and colleagues have extensively reviewed elsewhere recent experience with rule of law reform in developing countries.[7] We focus principally on legal institutions, in particular the judiciary, prosecutorial institutions, the police, correctional institutions, specialized administrative or regulatory agencies, the organized bar, and legal education institutions. Despite the massive investment of resources by external donors in rule of law reform initiatives in many developing countries over the past 20 years, rule of law ratings for many developing countries remain weak, and in some cases have deteriorated over time.

We conclude that approaches to rule of law reforms that do not take into account adaptive behavior with respect to the particular institutional context in question, as well as mutually reinforcing effects among interdependent institutions, are unlikely to be successful. If one takes path dependence seriously, future reform strategies will be significantly constrained and shaped by the legacies of history. The lessons of path dependence lead to a conundrum. Path dependence shows that isolated institutional reforms are likely to ignore both self-reinforcing mechanisms and institutional interdependencies, and are therefore often doomed to failure. However, system-wide ambitious reforms during "normal times" are disruptive and likely to fail because of the extensive switching costs that they are likely to entail for a myriad of actors within and outside the institutions in question (and the resistance that these will engender on that account). Thus, despite institutional interdependencies, all-encompassing reforms are simply not feasible. This is true during normal times, and there seems to be evidence that, even in post-conflict societies (which may present more opportunities or at least greater urgency for change), all-encompassing reforms often achieve only very limited success.[8]

Are reformers then left only with windows of opportunity (critical junctures) in which major reforms can be implemented successfully? Is there any way that reformers can account for the lessons of path dependence theory without being in a potentially eternal waiting period for the right moment? As Rodrik puts it, "the challenge for the empirical literature on institutions is to explore these [path dependent] patterns without falling into the trap of reductionism or of historical and geographical determinism."[9]

There are two potential (and complementary) strategies for dealing with this conundrum. First, adopting an institutional bypass strategy, reformers may be able to identify some institutions that can be more easily detached from a broader mutually reinforcing institutional matrix or be created de novo, such as semiautonomous revenue agencies; new constitutional or human rights courts or commissions; semi-independent regulatory agencies; one-stop government agencies (such as the Brazilian Poupatempo)[10] for issuing, for example, passports, driving licenses, ID cards, and health cards; and alternative forms of dispute resolution.[11] This strategy may enable more ambitious stand-alone reforms that nevertheless have important showcase effects that demonstrate lower switching costs or greater benefits than sceptics had assumed, although even here the experience with semiautonomous revenue agencies and independent regulatory agencies suggests that these institutions are likely to be fragile without complementary reforms, over time, to the surrounding institutional matrix.

The second strategy is to reform existing institutions that are interconnected and mutually reinforcing in a time-sensitive manner by prioritizing a sequence of reforms, beginning with certain core reforms but recognizing that further complementary reforms will be necessary in the future to reinforce the initial reforms. This implies that reforms should be incremental, which is quite different from many current reform practices that are either stand-alone without being incremental or are so encompassing as to be infeasible.

One of the lessons of path dependence is that we are not writing on a blank slate. It is true that in abnormal times—"critical junctures" (for example, the aftermath of economic collapse, civil war, or military invasion)—the credibility and legitimacy of incumbent elites may be weakened by such crises, creating new political openings for marginalized constituencies.[12] At the same time, it is unlikely that all preexisting economic, social, and cultural factors that create costs for switching to new institutional regimes can be ignored entirely[13] (as contemporary challenges to institutional reform in, for example, Iraq, Afghanistan, Egypt and Libya exemplify). Reformers should recognize not only the importance of switching costs, but also be sensitive to the different kinds of switching costs associated with reform.[14]

First, in terms of political economy considerations, switching costs may be high for those who benefit from the institutional status quo (however socially dysfunctional).[15] These costs may be mitigated by reforms that create or strengthen a countervailing political constituency that benefits from the reforms.[16] Alternatively, vested interests may need to be bought off or grandfathered in some way to mute opposition to the reforms. Second, switching costs may also reflect individual learning costs in adapting to a new regime (the "installed base" problem). These can be mitigated by state-sponsored public education programs and gradual processes of transition that avoid the need for abrupt adaptation to a new regime. Third, switching costs may reflect the scarcity of financial and human resources required to implement new institutional regimes, which can be mitigated by external financial and technical assistance. Finally, switching costs may reflect deeply embedded cultural beliefs or practices that are resistant to change.[17] Here, reforms that adapt traditional institutions (such as traditional forms of alternative dispute settlement or communal property rights) may mitigate problems of cultural dissonance. Moreover, institutional reforms implemented over time may in turn lead to modifications in cultural belief systems. Obviously, the salience of these switching costs will vary from one context to another, hence implying a tailored, country-specific set of transition cost mitigation strategies.

IV. Democratic Reform and Development

Although democracy can be a means to better development outcomes, it also has intrinsic value.[18] In *The Idea of Justice*, Sen argues that the relationship between public reason and justice demands some form of participatory governance, or "government by discussion," as government decisions must be publicly justified. He rejects the idea that democracy has a uniquely Western heritage and points to many historical examples of "government by discussion" in widely different societies (albeit taking many different forms).[19]

Most of the rich countries in the world are democracies, and most of the poorest countries are not, or have not been for most of their histories.[20] Recently, however, this reality seems to be changing. The last quarter century has seen a wave of democratization.[21] In 2010, some 116 countries claimed to be democracies, compared to only 39 in 1974.[22] Many of these countries have also adopted new constitutions, entrenched bills of rights, and made provision for constitutional judicial review (the so-called "new constitutionalism").[23]

Despite the euphoria in many development circles over the recent wave of democratization, Carothers offers a sobering assessment.[24] According to Carothers, of the nearly 100 countries considered as being in transition to democracy, only a relatively small number—probably fewer than 20—are clearly on their way to becoming successful, well-functioning democracies. According to Diamond, the 1999 Pakistani coup initiated the reversal of the wave of democratization from its peak, and there has been democratic recession ever since.[25] Diamond argues that this reversal was symptomatic of deep-seated problems of governance with which many other new and fragile democracies were also struggling.[26] The troubled attempts to install democratic political regimes in Iraq, Afghanistan, Libya, and Egypt are some of the more prominent contemporary examples of the challenging task of democratic reform.[27] In a 2010 report, Freedom House found that liberty, human rights, and the number of free democracies in the world had been declining for four consecutive years.[28]

Carothers argues that five questionable assumptions define the conventional transition paradigm. First, any country moving away from dictatorial rule can be considered to be a country in transition toward democracy. Second, democratization tends to unfold in a set pattern of stages: the opening, the breakthrough, and the consolidation. Third, elections are of determinative importance. Fourth, the underlying conditions in transitional countries—their economic level, political history, institutional legacies, ethnic makeup, sociocultural traditions, or other "structural" features—will not be major factors in either the onset or the outcome of the transitional process. Fifth, democratic transitions making up the recent wave of democratization are being built on coherent, functioning states.

Carothers considers all of these assumptions to be problematic. In contrast, he argues that many countries in transition from authoritarianism to democracy reflect two persistent syndromes: "feckless pluralism" and "dominant power politics." "Feckless pluralism" refers to situations in which small, deeply entrenched political elites periodically alternate power and enrich themselves at the expense of the general population. "Dominant power politics" refers to situations where one party, despite periodic elections, dominates government over long periods of time and often governs with little heed for the general interests of the population.

Some scholars caution that the deliberation, cooperation, and compromise ideally associated with democracy cannot readily be imposed through top-down measures. Instead, reform must occur from the bottom up, through thick prior networks of associational activity—civil society or "social capital"—that have already cultivated these norms, which can then be scaled up to regional or national democratic governments.[29] However, other scholars point out that many forms of social capital are parochial, exclusionary, discriminatory, or repressive, such as the social capital that resides within the Klu Klux Klan and the Mafia. These scholars argue that desirable forms of social capital cultivate a wider radius of trust, and that these forms of social capital evolve organically and are not readily constructible by deliberate public policies.[30]

In designing reforms of political institutions, it is important to be sensitive to the specific characteristics of each country. Generalizations about the relationship between democracy and development or binary distinctions between democracy and autocracy[31] offer very little useful guidance or policy-relevant information on the design of particular political regimes.

Even democratic political regimes in the developed world vary vastly in their formal institutional features: some are presidential, others parliamentary; some are unicameral, some bicameral; some are unitary states, others federal states; some have tight political party structures, while others have much looser structures; some employ majority or first-past-the-post voting, while others have adopted some form of proportional representation; some tightly regulate election campaign expenditures, others subsidize these expenditures from public resources, while still others do little of either; some have adopted an entrenched bill of rights and constitutional judicial review as constraints on legislative and executive action while others have not, and so on.[32] The political arrangements that are feasible in a country will, to an important extent, be a function of each country's history, culture, and institutional legacies.[33] As with the rule of law and other institutional reforms, path dependence may significantly constrain the reform options that are feasible for a country's political regime, at least in terms of the organizational form if not the underlying rationale.

V. Property Rights and Development[34]

Perhaps most reflective of the importance of property rights in contemporary thinking on economic development has been the success and influence of Hernando de Soto's *The Mystery of Capital: Why Capitalism Triumphs in the West and Fails Everywhere Else*,[35] in which he argues that strong protection for private property rights is the key factor in explaining the economic success of the developed world and the economic stagnation of many developing countries. Indeed, on de Soto's account, the potential benefits of formalization of property rights are significant. De Soto claims that "the total value of the real estate held but not legally owned by the poor of the Third World and former communist nations is at least $9.3 trillion," which he characterizes as "dead capital."[36]

This broad assertion is unsatisfactory, however, as it leaves a great deal of indeterminacy in terms of the actual policies implied in achieving the objective of strengthening the protection of property rights. The theoretical and empirical literature that has emerged in support of this claim has been used by some to advocate titling and registration programs as a general solution to the problem of property rights insecurity. However, this blanket approach toward the establishment of stronger property rights may well be unwarranted and counterproductive, and instead a more nuanced approach is required to craft successful development policies regarding property rights.[37]

It is important at the outset to highlight briefly some of the reasons that property rights have occupied such a prominent place in the development literature in recent years. Although many sweeping claims have been made about the benefits of private property, especially by economists who often conceive of the rule of law as centrally concerned with the protection of property rights and the enforcement of contracts, the literature has also disaggregated the benefits by analyzing a number of distinct economic benefits that private property can bring:

1) Exclusive use leads to resources being used more efficiently.
2) Security of tenure and easy transferability of property increase access to credit.
3) Security of tenure increases incentives for investment.
4) Security of tenure decreases inefficient and wasteful competition for resources.

Many development scholars and policymakers contend that these benefits of private property are best achieved by a formal state-run property system, because when fully functional and accessible such a system provides clearer and more secure allocation of property rights than could any informal measures to protect private property. Where there is a credible third-party enforcer of property rights—in particular the state—uncertainty is reduced or completely eliminated. Moreover, a formal property system can also reduce transaction costs in market interactions by providing increased information to third parties about the rights that an individual has over land. Similar arguments are also often made for formalizing title to personal property, in particular for facilitating the granting and taking of security interests in personal property to enhance access to credit. Notwithstanding these claims, other scholars have pointed out that in many developing countries, informal or customary mechanisms for securing reasonably high levels of certainty in property rights are often good substitutes for a formal property rights regime.

Although there may be some benefits in the formalizing of property rights regimes, such regimes also entail various costs:

1. Significant costs are entailed in setting up a land registration or recordation system, including initial surveys and the cost of updating the registry or recordation system through time to reflect changes in the composition of land-owing groups or intervening transactions.
2. Formalization and individualization of land tenure may seriously undermine the possibility of communal tenure providing an insurance role for members of the land-owning group, and through time may result in the emergence of a landless class with few, if any, other economic opportunities, sources of insurance, or social safety nets.
3. Formal rules may undermine effective informal institutions by creating dysfunctional conflicts between the two classes of regime in ignoring the significance of cultural switching costs.[38] This problem is likely to be particularly acute if formal mechanisms are predicated on spatial notions of ownership, while informal regimes recognize a much more functional conception of property rights, including a wide variety of usufructuary rights, such as the right to gather firewood, collect water, gather fruit, or hunt, fish, or traverse land owned by other groups or individuals.
4. Formalization programs, depending on how they are designed and implemented, can expose latent divisions between or among claimant groups that had previously lain dormant, but are likely to be provoked or exacerbated by the relative finality of formalizing property rights, and hence lead to increased social conflict.
5. Flaws in the titling process are likely to be exploited by politically or economically powerful groups at the expense of women and other marginalized groups who face various barriers to accessing a formal property rights system.
6. Even assuming that a formal property rights system is well designed, deeply entrenched informal norms may impede the successful implementation of

a formal property rights regime where they are sharply antithetical to the latter and may result in the latter being largely ignored or becoming quickly outdated.
7. As in the case of rule of law reforms, there are important institutional interconnections: a land titling system is predicated on effective complementary institutions, including the judiciary, the legal profession, and the police. Formalizing property rights without complementary reforms to these other institutions may therefore achieve very little.

This is not to say that informal regimes are always efficient. For example, they may only be efficient for members of close-knit groups and may entail negative externalities for non-members. Informal regimes themselves may also reflect path dependence and time lags in responding to changes in the economic or technological environment, so that there may well be efficiency gains to be realized, at least potentially, from a more formal property rights regime.[39]

Because of the complex interactions between a property rights regime and the social, economic, political, and legal framework within which such a regime operates, it is not fruitful simply to argue for or against the formalization of a property rights regime or for "strong and clear" property rights. Rather, the relationship between property rights and development is much more complex, and a more nuanced approach to these issues is required. As David Kennedy writes:

> "Clear and strong" property rights is a misleading recipe. Property rights have no ideal form which will be rendered clear and strong. Their allocation everywhere is a matter of economic, social and political choice for which no formula can substitute.[40]

The context dependence of successful property regimes leads to three important considerations. First, property formalization programs cannot be considered as isolated economic development projects as one might consider certain physical infrastructure projects. Rather, such programs must be considered as a part of a general framework for economic development, typically including a wider set of reforms aimed at the promotion of the rule of law.[41] Contrary to the optimistic rhetoric of de Soto's work, property formalization programs are not, standing alone, the key to unlocking the potential of the developing world.[42]

Second, in determining what role outsiders can play in helping to promote a state's formal property regime, it is essential to ask a broader question about the similarities among optimal property regimes. If the optimality of a property rights regime is context-independent, then a titling program developed by theorists in Washington or from elsewhere in the developed world may indeed be applicable and beneficial to extremely diverse countries. However, although the functions performed by property rights may be similar in many countries, the characteristics of a property regime are in fact highly dependent on local context and thus it is unrealistic to expect that one model of a successful regime would be applicable across various societies. In fact, one would expect that the characteristics of such regimes, as well as strategies for their implementation, will differ substantially across societies. This suggests that, in practice, local or regional models of property regimes may be more successful than Western models.[43]

Finally, significant changes to property regimes should be approached with caution and drastic, uniform top-down property changes should be avoided.[44] Contrary to conventional economic thinking, the formalization of property rights is not necessarily desirable at all states of development or for all property owners.

Because of these considerations, unless there is clear and compelling evidence pointing to the need for a systematic state-led formalization program, the optimal response may be an optional or sporadic system of title registration. Although a sporadic program of title representation is not without its own costs,[45] such a program brings substantial benefits relative to a systematic formalization program. As I have argued elsewhere, in the face of limited resources and state capacity, a sporadic system of land registration has the benefit of providing the additional security and clarity of formal property rights to those desiring it most.[46] By simply providing an additional vehicle or option for owning property, a sporadic registration program does not require disturbing the arrangements of those groups that are content with the status quo. Where customary arrangements limit individuals' economic opportunities, the option of formalization is present. Moreover, a voluntary system overcomes the collective action problem of providing the machinery for the enforcement of property rights by having the state provide it and allowing people to opt into it.

Perhaps the strongest benefit, however, of a sporadic and voluntary formalization system is that it avoids the myriad unforeseeable and potentially negative consequences that can result from the top-down imposition of a uniform system of property arrangements. As I have stressed, a property rights regime is not an isolated institution, but rather an institution that has strong interrelationships within a variety of other institutions. In such circumstances, and where policymakers have imperfect or limited information, it may be impossible to predict all the potential consequences flowing from drastic institutional changes, and unpredictable negative consequences may emerge from imposed changes.[47] A gradual and reversible process of voluntary change at the individual level can mitigate such potentially harmful consequences.

Even in situations where a systematic program is clearly superior to a voluntary program, drastic and irreversible changes should be avoided.[48] Rather, changes should be incremental in nature. For example, where communal property is prevalent, rather than registering individual, fully alienable freehold titles to specified plots of land to the exclusion of all others, a rudimentary titling program could be undertaken utilizing simple compass-and-chain surveys rather than full-scale cadastral surveys where only the base group title would be registered without prejudice to the various functional or usufructuary rights that others might possess under customary law. Landowning groups might also be given a more formal legal structure and clearer decision or governance rules (akin to private corporations with restrictions on share transferability), while maintaining some limits on outright alienability of group land.⁴⁹ Such programs lessen the potential for serious social conflict or disruption from abrupt legal change and facilitate an evolutionary process for the emergence of strong private property rights.⁵⁰

VI. Conclusion

Although in many poor developing countries it is often possible to identify a better "there" than "here," the institutional entailments in getting from here to there pose major challenges for institutional reform. Contemporary institutional reformers have come to recognize that reforms cannot be imposed from the outside by pretending that "Djibouti is Denmark" (or can easily become Denmark), or by "skipping straight to Weber."⁵¹ Formulating effective strategies for mitigating transition (switching) costs—political, cognitive, economic, and cultural—whose salience will vary greatly from one context to another is now increasingly recognized as central to the reform enterprise.⁵² Viewing externally promoted institutional reforms as a largely technocratic exercise that can ignore the political economy of the domestic reform process has been revealed as a chimera.⁵³

{ 10 }

Conclusion: Taking Transition Costs Seriously

I. Introduction

Otto von Bismarck, the first Chancellor of Germany from 1871 to 1890, once famously remarked that "politics is the art of the possible...[it] is not a science, as the professors are apt to suppose." Accepting the wisdom of these remarks (as I do), it is important to emphasize that what is possible in politics is not predetermined, and cannot be reduced to a formal model. It can, however, be fashioned—within limits—by astute political leadership. Although Public Choice theory emphasizes the disproportionate political influence of concentrated interest groups over diffuse interest groups and voters at large, more nuanced positive understandings of the dynamics of political decision-making (such as those explored in Chapter 2) suggest a greater scope for political leadership than more static, "iron triangle" theories of the policymaking process that emphasize the close and often incestuous relationships between legislators, the bureaucracy, and organized interest groups.

On this more nuanced view of the political process, political leaders with a sensitivity to deep-seated cultural beliefs and historical development as well as an understanding of the currents and cadences of political discourse and debates are often able to craft policies that move a generally socially beneficial reform agenda forward. Constructing coalitions of often unlikely interest groups and appealing to broader unorganized cross sections of voters by framing issues in a way that resonates with their basic normative values, and hence constructing a reasonably broad social consensus in favour of reform, may pave the way for policy change. This perspective also recognizes that citizens can often be encouraged to support policies that do not reflect their direct material self-interest, and may on occasion be antithetical to it, by appealing to their notions of fairness or related moral reference points. On this view, effective political leadership entails more than a passive reading of the political "tea leaves"; it requires proactively crafting political compromises that move generally socially beneficial reform agendas forward in stages. In private markets, suppliers of goods and services do not assume that consumer preferences are fixed and immutable. Rather, it is accepted that advertising and marketing efforts can induce consumers to try new products or services in substitution for old. The same is true of political markets. Policy entrepreneurs have the ability to shape what is politically possible through advocacy, framing of issues, the provision of new information, and the creation of new fora for public consultation and debate that empower previously marginalized groups of citizens or introduce new perspectives on policy reform options. Addressing squarely and self-consciously the transition costs typically engendered by significant policy changes is central to this enterprise—particularly in increasingly pluralistic societies where a homogeneous set of core values may be absent.

While I have referred to effective political leaders seeking to pursue generally socially beneficial policy objectives by seeking to mitigate transition costs that may yield losers who will obstruct the adoption of these policies, I have largely bracketed what constitutes "generally socially beneficial," recognizing that these virtues will often lie in the eye of the beholder and may differ, even among reasonable people.[1] However, I am, for the most part, content to adopt, for present purposes, a conventional, utilitarian-based social welfare function (as advanced, for example, by Kaplow and Shavell).[2] My essential point is that however the objective function is defined, those facing the political imperative of election or re-election in order to effectuate their policies (assuming, for my purposes, a full-franchise, reasonably competitive, representative democracy), will need to address transition costs as an essential feature of their political strategies.

This is not to gainsay the possibility that unenlightened (even ill-intentioned) leaders pursuing policies that may ultimately be socially destructive, according to most people's lights (at least with the benefit of hindsight), may attempt to co-opt, buy off, or even dupe political losers from these policies in order to effectuate them, or alternatively offer token compensation to the losers to assuage the majority of their citizenry that the losers are not being treated unfairly. Thus, if the Nazis had bought one-way tickets out of Germany for its Jewish citizens, instead of consigning them to the gas chambers, or Idi Amin had adopted a similar policy for Asians expelled from Uganda, or had Robert Mugabe adopted similar policies for white farmers whose farms he expropriated without compensation in Zimbabwe, it is possible that these token policies may have assuaged a majority of citizens that this was adequate compensation or mitigation for the losers. Although, as Kaplow and Shavell argue, the intensity of the disutilities experienced by the losers may well exceed any gains in utility by the rest of the population, and should in principle be accounted for in a utilitarian calculus, political systems that, at least in theory, are designed to equalize political influence (one person, one vote) are not well adapted to constraining a tyranny of the majority. Hence the case for constitutionally enshrined bills of rights or recognition of international human rights as protections against minority oppression (as adverted to in Chapter 2, although potential majoritarian abuses of minorities are by no means confined to encroachments on private property rights). Authoritarian regimes may, of course, pose the opposite problem of a tyranny of the minority.

Without gainsaying the importance of such protections against abuse of power, the focus of this book has been on the role of compensation or other transition cost mitigation strategies in representative democracies in forging an effective political coalition (or a reasonably broad social consensus) in favor of generally socially beneficial reforms, where the absence of attention to transition costs is likely to render the policy status quo ante the default option, irrespective of its perversity.

II. The Virtues of Incrementalism and Compromise

On occasion, countries will be beset by cataclysmic shocks—economic collapse, military conflict, civil war, or natural disasters—that call for drastic and immediate policy responses without the opportunity to canvas all the possible second- and third-order effects of these responses, where the law of unintended consequences is likely to reveal, over time, a variety of impacts that were not, and perhaps could not, be anticipated at the time of the initial, immediate response. However, most policy reforms lack this cataclysmic character, and are typically more incremental in nature, where unintended consequences can be mitigated by a more cautious and exploratory strategy of policy change. David Lloyd George, prime minister of the United Kingdom from 1916 to 1922, once advised: "Don't be afraid to take a big step if one is indicated. You can't cross a chasm in two small jumps. The most dangerous thing in the world is to try to leap a chasm in two jumps." In many, perhaps most, policy contexts this is not helpful advice. Attempting to cross a chasm in two small steps is likely to be suicidal but the same is often true of attempts to cross a large chasm in one leap. Feasible public policy options may often entail building a bridge across the chasm in stages, or working one's way around its edges.

I began this book with a reference to William Wilberforce's role in the enactment of the Slavery Abolition Act in the United Kingdom and its colonies in 1833. After enduring chronic and debilitating illnesses in his later years, Wilberforce died just three days after hearing that the passage of the Act through Parliament was assured. However, the passage of this Act was not a single cataclysmic event where slavery was pervasive before its enactment, and disappeared immediately upon its enactment. In fact, Wilberforce, a Member of Parliament for much of his career, headed a parliamentary campaign against the British slave trade for 26 years until the passage of the Slave Trade Act of 1807 (and similar legislation in the United States in 1808), which abolished the international slave trade, but not slavery itself—something that took a further 26 years in the United Kingdom and its colonies and much longer elsewhere. But even the enactment of the Slavery Abolition Act in 1833, with its provisions for compensation of plantation owners and a short phaseout period of slavery in British colonies where it then existed, did not, obviously, address slavery in other countries throughout the world, including, perhaps most notably, a former British colony, the United States. Only an enormously convulsive civil war from 1861 to 1865 would achieve this—with President Lincoln's Emancipation Proclamation in 1863, and the passage of the Thirteenth Amendment to the US Constitution in 1865. However, despite these reforms many of the entailments of slavery persisted. In a landmark US Supreme Court decision in 1896, *Plessy v. Ferguson*,[3] the constitutionality of state laws requiring racial segregation in public facilities was upheld under the doctrine of "separate but equal." This doctrine promoted racial segregation in public school systems and other public services, and a wide variety of so-called "Jim Crow" laws, especially in the southern States. Many of these persisted until the repudiation of the "separate but equal" doctrine by the US Supreme Court in its famous 1954 decision in *Brown v. Board of Education*.[4] This decision was followed a decade later by congressional action with the enactment of the Civil Rights Act of 1964 and the Voting Rights Act of 1965. Thus, the formal abolition of slavery, and all its direct and indirect entailments, in today's developed world spanned a period of more than a century-and-a-half; and, of course, its legacy persists in various ways today.

This brief reprise of the history of the abolition of slavery and its entailments is not in any way an attempt to defend the protracted nature of the political enterprise in ridding humanity of one of the worst moral blights ever to have afflicted it, nor is it to indulge the naturalistic fallacy of arguing that what is (or was) must be optimal because if it was not, things would have happened differently. Rather, it is intended to emphasize that even with an issue as morally indefensible as slavery and all its entailments, its abolition was not a one-time cataclysmic event, but a protracted process of policy evolution, which more generally characterizes most major policy reform processes. As Charles Lindblom argued in his famous essays on the virtues of "muddling through," analytical and policy incrementalism is the norm, not the exception, in policy change.[5] In many policy contexts, incrementalism has many virtues in forging and sustaining minimum winning political coalitions (and a reasonably broad social consensus favoring change), while addressing the law of unintended consequences—often manifested in the unexpected nature and scale of adverse impacts on losing interests—as the reform process evolves. I believe that the merits of incrementalism equally hold whether the policy reform in question involves "more state" or "more market." Although Friedrich Hayek classically emphasized the virtues of markets in economizing on the need for information relative to centralized, collective decision-making,[6] radical moves to privatize and marketize goods or services previously provided by, or regulated by, the state may equally have unintended consequences. These are exemplified in recent experiences with the sweeping privatization of state-owned enterprises in the former Soviet Union ("shock therapy"), World Bank/IMF structural adjustment programs in developing countries, in Western countries with the deregulation of aspects of financial services markets, radical austerity programs, the deregulation of some electricity markets, privately provided correctional services, and the deployment of private security forces in foreign wars,[7] just as with radical moves to "more state" as with Mao Zedong's catastrophic

"Great Leap Forward" or Stalin's collectivization of agriculture. As James C. Scott has eloquently argued,[8] centralized collective decision-makers (whether in my view proposing "more state" or "more market") often lack the detailed local knowledge of complex human, social, and economic interactions that is necessary to anticipate all the consequences of their decisions. Most of us are averse to the risk of major disruptions in our lives, whatever the source.

A closely related political virtue to that of incrementalism is compromise. As political philosophers Amy Gutmann and Dennis Thompson persuasively argue in a recent book, in pluralistic representative democracies (especially those with many checks and balances and potential veto points), compromises of principles and interests among different constituencies within and across political parties will often be necessary to advance generally socially beneficial policy changes: a wide range of constituencies may agree that various aspects of the status quo are unsatisfactory, and that a compromise is an improvement overall on the status quo, even if from a single normative perspective the compromise is contradictory or even incoherent (recalling Bismarck's famous analogy between law-making and sausage-making).[9] In other words, shades of gray are often to be celebrated as partial progress, not denigrated as unprincipled compromises measured against an unattainable state of perfectionism (an example of the Nirvana fallacy). As they state in the conclusion to their book:

> If politics is the art of the possible, compromise is the artistry of democracy. Democracy calls on politicians to resist compromise and to accept it. They may resist it more when they campaign, but they need to accept it more when they govern... The compromising mindset focuses on the critical question for governing: is the proposed law better than the status quo? In a democracy, the spirit of the laws depends on the spirit of compromise.[10]

Or as political philosopher Michael Walzer puts the same point:[11]

> I don't think I could govern innocently; nor do most of us believe that those who govern us are innocent... But this does not mean that it isn't possible to do the right thing while governing. It means that a particular act of government (in a political party or in the state) may be exactly the right thing to do in utilitarian terms and yet leave the man who does it guilty of a moral wrong. The innocent man, afterwards, is no longer innocent. If on the other hand he remains innocent, he not only fails to do the right thing (in utilitarian terms): he may also fail to measure up to the duties of his office (which imposes on him a considerable responsibility for consequences and outcomes).

III. Lessons From Experience

I believe that the seven brief case studies and other examples that I have discussed in this book reveal the importance of incrementalism, compromise, and transition cost mitigation strategies in widely disparate contemporary public policy contexts in forging and sustaining minimum winning political coalitions (and a reasonably broad social consensus) supporting generally socially beneficial policy reforms. But is it possible to draw out some general lessons about the politically optimal configuration of transition cost mitigation strategies across various policy contexts?

As I have emphasized throughout this book, transition cost mitigation strategies include not only explicit compensation of losers from policy change (which account for a tiny proportion of all such strategies), but also the much more common strategies of grandfathering, postponed implementation, and phased or graduated implementation. It is to choices among this broader portfolio of transition cost mitigation strategies that I address some brief concluding thoughts.

As I noted in Chapter 2, "ganging-up on," or singling out isolated individuals to bear all or most of the costs of generally socially beneficial reforms (the classic eminent domain case, where, e.g., a citizen's home is expropriated for a public school), when this will typically entail complete loss of the enjoyment of the asset in question, will strike many citizens as grossly unfair and engage widespread sympathies (on the reasoning that "there, but for the grace of God, go I"). In the typical expropriation case, there is no adaptive strategy reasonably available to the property owner short of full compensation for the loss of the asset in question, so that he or she is put in a position of being able to acquire a reasonably close substitute elsewhere. Hence, the prevalence of constitutional and statutory expropriation protections in most developed legal systems.

Other cases bear a close resemblance to the classic eminent domain case. For example, revised setback laws requiring buildings to be setback a greater distance from property lines or street allowances may require many existing structures to be demolished. Here policymakers are likely to face a choice between explicit compensation, or grandfathering of existing non-conforming uses if the social benefits of requiring adaptation of existing structures are unlikely to exceed the costs of adaptation.[12]

Canada's dairy supply management regime may be another case in point where the existing regime has deliberately induced individual dairy farmers to invest in acquiring dairy quotas worth on average $2 million per farmer in current market value. To simply cancel this scheme overnight is likely to strike many citizens (beyond dairy farmers) as akin to an expropriation of a major part of dairy farmers' wealth. Hence, a gradual phaseout reflected in commitments in trade treaties to substantially reduce tariffs over time complemented by partial compensation (e.g., for diminution in the book or acquisition value—not market value—of quotas).

The abolition of slavery also entailed large one-time capital losses for slave owners that in the United Kingdom and its colonies attracted substantial compensation, whereas the issue was resolved in the United States by civil war (followed by de jure or de facto segregation in many parts of the country to the present day). Although it would clearly be tendentious to claim that compensation was a viable alternative in the US context (where it was periodically proposed in national and state legislatures and formally endorsed by President Lincoln in 1862), it never attracted broad-based support from either pro-slavery or antislavery constituencies,[13] underscoring the fact that the political economy of policy transitions is not easily generalizable across polities with very different institutional structures and histories.

Termination of mortgage interest tax deductability in the United States (like termination of dairy quotas in Canada) also entails undermining investments (partially impounded in house prices) deliberately induced by public policies. Although likely to have a much less draconian impact on average homeowners' wealth (and more impact on wealthy homeowners in higher marginal tax brackets, for whom this provision entails a largely regressive wealth transfer), a gradual phaseout perhaps accompanied with more finely targeted time-limited assistance to first-time homebuyers with below-average household incomes (to signify continuing public support for the "American Dream") may be a politically feasible reform strategy.

Phased implementation of policy reforms also seems appropriate in the case of negotiated trade liberalization commitments and implementation of more liberal immigration policies in order to avoid sudden and highly disruptive impacts on job markets to which many workers may have limited capacity to adapt (e.g., by relocation, job training, etc.), at least in the short term. Public pension reform, designed to ensure long-term fiscal sustainability, given increased life expectancies and lower fertility rates, exhibits many of the same characteristics. Reducing benefits to curent or imminent retirees who have very limited ability to adapt to diminished benefits will seem to many citizens (not only retirees) as reneging on the social contract, while burdening younger workers with the entire burden of sustainability through higher contributions will seem to many citizens (not only younger workers) to be grossly inequitable. Hence, the principal feasible policy reform option is to raise the minimum retirement age in gentle stages to avoid sudden and disruptive impacts on workers nearing retirement age with limited adaptation options.

In other policy contexts, postponed implementation may be the optimal strategy for mititgating transition costs. For example, proposals to increase energy efficiency or emission standards for automobiles or industrial or electricity plants might be implemented on a future committed date if the technological adaptations required of producers (and their cost) are reasonably well-known in advance, while at the same time providing consumers with a limited lead time to adapt their consumption patterns. In contrast, in the case of climate change policy, major—even radical—technological breakthroughs (presently, at best, only sketchily understood) are required in order to render major CO_2 emission reductions both technologically feasible and economically bearable. Thus, a lengthy graduated phase-in period for increasingly stringent carbon taxes or cap-and-trade regimes to incentivize long-term technological innovation may be the most politically feasible option, given the unknown scale of the costs entailed, provided that equivalent burdens are placed on imports (i.e., taxing carbon consumption, whatever its source), with duty remissions for countries adopting similar policies (with a view to motivating the evolution of a harmonized global carbon tax).

In the case of major institutional reforms—in effect, changing the rules of the political game—in developing countries (or elsewhere), path dependency, reflecting the contingencies of history (exemplified in recent reform experiences in countries such as Iraq, Afghanistant, Egypt, Libya, and elsewhere), cautions against abrupt or radical departures from the institutional status quo (however socially dysfunctional), and argues instead (in most cases) for a strategy of incrementalism in the institutional reform agenda, which is likely to be shaped by highly context-specific circumstances that external reformers are often ill-equipped to appreciate.

The disparate nature of the transition cost challenges that arise in a vast range of widely divergent policy reform contexts, of course, precludes strong generalizations, but the case studies and other examples discussed in this book hopefully offer useful analogies (or disanalogies) in many such contexts, even where not discussed explicitly herein.

IV. Conclusion

Returning to my review of prominent normative perspectives on transition issues in Chapter 2, Kaplow's strong presumption against compensation or other transition-cost mitigation strategies for adverse impacts of policy changes, on the grounds that these are just another probabilistic risk like any other that will influence risk reduction behavior ex ante, is largely unhelpful in the real world of policymaking, and may often be a prescription for either political suicide or political paralysis by failing to take the opposition of losers and their sympathizers seriously as a matter of political economy. Although it is useful to be reminded that all transition-cost mitigation strategies entail some social costs, and that some strategies entail more costs than others (most prominently in the form of moral hazard and consequential over-investment in the pre-reform activity in question), and of the need to be sensitive to concerns raised by the theory of second-best,[14] where removing one economic distortion while leaving other related distortions unaddressed may actually reduce social welfare, these concerns can hardly justify foreswearing such policies altogether if politically strategic adoption of them is a sine qua non for advancing generally socially beneficial policy changes.

Conversely, Epstein's opposing view that all policy changes that significantly impair the value of private property rights presumptively warrant compensation, however foreseeable, risks taking certain classes of losers too seriously by vesting in them (and the courts) something close to a veto power over policy changes, unjustifiably privileging the status quo and paralyzing the political process. A major irony of these two sharply antithetical views of the case for mitigating transition costs from policy changes is that they yield a common policy implication: policy reforms will be difficult to effectuate on both views, either because losers are not taken seriously enough, or because certain classes of losers are taken too seriously. On both views, policy stasis becomes the default option.[15]

One hopes that in his dying days William Wilberforce was able to take great pride and solace in the accomplishments wrought by himself and his fellow abolitionists, not because they achieved nirvana overnight, but because they marked important progress, despite the political compromises involved, in achieving full human equality (racial, religious, and sexual)—a quest that may never end.

{ NOTES }

Chapter 1

1. This phrase is borrowed from the title of the superb travelogue by Rory Stewart, who walked across Afghanistan in 2002, shortly following the fall of the Taliban: RORY STEWART, THE PLACES IN BETWEEN (2004).
2. This was later abridged in the face of protests and desertions.
3. *See, e.g.*, WILLIAM HAGUE, WILLIAM WILBERFORCE: THE LIFE OF THE GREAT ANTI-SLAVE TRADE CAMPAIGNER (2007); WILLIAM LAW MATHIESON, BRITISH SLAVERY AND ITS ABOLITION 1823–1839 (1926); HOWARD TEMPERLEY, BRITISH ANTISLAVERY, 1833–1870 (1972); NICHOLAS DRAPER, THE PRICE OF EMANCIPATION: SLAVE OWNERSHIP, COMPENSATION AND BRITISH SOCIETY AT THE END OF SLAVERY (2010).
4. I am grateful to my colleague, Stephen Waddams, for drawing this example to my attention.
5. Guido Calabresi, *The Pointlessness of Pareto: Carrying Coase Further*, 100(5) YALE L.J. 1211 (1991).
6. *See* Michael Trebilcock & Mariana Prado, WHAT MAKES POOR COUNTRIES POOR?: INSTITUTIONAL DETERMINANTS OF DEVELOPMENT ch. 4 (2012).

Chapter 2

1. *See* LOUIS KAPLOW & STEVEN SHAVELL, FAIRNESS VERSUS WELFARE (2006).
2. DANIEL N. SHAVIRO, WHEN RULES CHANGE: AN ECONOMIC AND POLITICAL ANALYSIS OF TRANSITION RELIEF AND RETROACTIVITY (2000).
3. Louis Kaplow, *An Economic Analysis of Legal Transitions*, 99(3) HARV. L. REV. 509 (1986); *see also* Lawrence Blume & Daniel L. Rubinfeld, *Compensation for Takings: An Economic Analysis*, 72(4) CAL. L. REV. 569 (1984); Lawrence Blume, Daniel L. Rubinfeld & Perry Shapiro, *The Taking of Land: When Should Compensation Be Paid?*, 99(1) Q.J. ECON. 71–92 (1984); THOMAS J. MICELI, THE ECONOMIC THEORY OF EMINENT DOMAIN: PRIVATE PROPERTY, PUBLIC USE (2011); SHAVIRO, *supra* note 2.
4. Louis Kaplow, *Transition Policy: A Conceptual Framework*, 13 J. CONTEMP. LEGAL ISSUES 161 (2003).
5. *Id.* at 190.
6. *Id.* at 208–09.
7. *See, e.g.*, JAMES M. BUCHANAN & GORDON TULLOCK, THE CALCULUS OF CONSENT: LOGICAL FOUNDATIONS OF CONSTITUTIONAL DEMOCRACY 80–90 (1965); Gordon Tullock, *Achieving Deregulation: A Public Choice Perspective*, 2(6) REGULATION 50–54 (1978); Blume & Rubinfeld, *supra* note 3, at 620–22; Blume et al., *supra* note 3, at 88–90; Frank I. Michelman, *Property, Utility, and Fairness*, 80(6) HARV. L. REV. 1165 (1967).
8. ROBERT D. COOTER & HANS-BERND SCHAFER, SOLOMON'S KNOT: HOW LAW CAN END THE POVERTY OF NATIONS ch. 14 (2013) ("The Many versus the Few").

9. John Quinn & Michael J. Trebilcock, *Compensation, Transition Costs, and Regulatory Change*, 32(2) U. TORONTO L.J. 117 (1982).
10. Kaplow, *supra* note 4.
11. *See* Saul Levmore, *Just Compensation and Just Politics*, 22 CONN. L. REV. 285 (1989).
12. Blume & Rubinfeld, *supra* note 3.
13. *See also* Thomas Merrill, *Rent Seeking and the Compensation Principle*, 80 Nw. U. L. REV. 1561, 1581 (1986).
14. *See* EDWARD IACOBUCCI, MICHAEL TREBILCOCK & HUMA HADER, ECONOMIC SHOCKS: DEFINING A ROLE FOR GOVERNMENT ch. 5 (2001).
15. *See* Steven Shavell (Working Paper, Harvard Law School, 2013).
16. *See* Jonathan S. Masur & Jonathan R. Nash, *The Institutional Dynamics of Transition Relief*, 85 N.Y.U. L. REV. 391, 421–26 (2010).
17. Steven Shavell, *On Optimal Legal Change, Past Behavior, and Grandfathering*, 37(1) J. LEGAL STUDIES 37 (2008).
18. W.A. FISCHEL, REGULATORY TAKINGS: LAW, ECONOMICS, AND POLITICS 216–17 (1995).
19. Michelman, *supra* note 7
20. Fischel, *supra* note 18, at 147–48.
21. JOHN RAWLS, A THEORY OF JUSTICE (1971).
22. For various strands of communitarianism, see, e.g., Alasdair MacIntyre, *Ideology, Social Science, and Revolution*, 5:3 COMP. POLIT. 321 (1973); MICHAEL SANDEL, LIBERALISM AND THE LIMITS OF JUSTICE (2d ed. 1998); CHARLES TAYLOR, SOURCES OF THE SELF: THE MAKING OF THE MODERN IDENTITY (1989); MICHAEL WALZER, SPHERES OF JUSTICE: A DEFENSE OF PLURALISM AND EQUALITY (1983); AMITIAI ETZIONI, THE MORAL DIMENSION: TOWARD A NEW ECONOMICS (1990); ROBERT D. PUTNAM, BOWLING ALONE: THE COLLAPSE AND REVIVAL OF AMERICAN COMMUNITY (2000).
23. ERNEST J. WEINRIB, THE IDEA OF PRIVATE LAW (1995); ERNEST J. WEINRIB, CORRECTIVE JUSTICE (2012).
24. Levmore, *supra* note 11.
25. *See, e.g.*, ROBERT NOZICK, ANARCHY, STATE, AND UTOPIA (1974).
26. MICELI, *supra* note 3, ch. 2.
27. RICHARD ALLEN EPSTEIN, TAKINGS: PRIVATE PROPERTY AND THE POWER OF EMINENT DOMAIN (1985).
28. *Id.* at 93; for a more austere version of libertarian theory in the takings context, see ELLEN FRANKEL PAUL, PROPERTY RIGHTS AND EMINENT DOMAIN (2008).
29. EPSTEIN, *supra* note 27, at 281.
30. BUCHANAN & TULLOCK, *supra* note 7; Tullock, *supra* note 7.
31. *See* Ellen Frankel Paul, *Moral Constraints and Eminent Domain*, 55 GEO. WASH. L. REV. 152 (1987).
32. *See* Mark Kelman, *Taking Takings Seriously: An Essay for Centrists*, 74 CAL. L. REV. 1829 (1986).
33. *See* Note, *Richard Epstein on the Foundations of Takings Jurisprudence*, 99 HAR. L. REV. 791 (1986).
34. *See, e.g.*, Merrill, *supra* note 13; Paul, *supra* note 31.
35. *See, e.g.*, Joseph Fox, *Takings*, 53 U. CHI. L. REV. 279 (1986); Rogers M. Smith, *Don't Look Back, Something Might Be Gaining on You: The Dilemmas of Constitutional Neoconservatives*, AM. BAR FOUND. RES. J. 280 (1987).

36. *See* Merrill, *supra* note 13.

37. Smith, *supra* note 35. Conversely, a number of scholars have argued that an increased judicial role in the economy and state policy is a necessary step in the evolution of the economy, a means by which to facilitate dispute resolution in an increasingly complex and interdependent global economy. *See, e.g.*, Martin M. Shapiro & Alec Stone-Sweet, On Law, Politics, and Judicialization (2002).

38. Miceli, *supra* note 3, at 113.

39. Shaviro, *supra* note 2, at 3.

40. Anthony Downs, An Economic Theory of Democracy (1957).

41. Mancur Olson, The Logic of Collective Action: Public Goods and the Theory of Groups (1971).

42. Buchanan & Tullock, *supra* note 7.

43. George Stigler, "The Theory of Economic Regulation," *in* The Citizen and the State: Essays on Regulation (1975).

44. *See generally* The Encyclopedia of Public Choice (Charles Rowley & Friedrich Schneider eds., 2004); Dennis Mueller, Public Choice III (2003).

45. Andrew McFarland, *Neopluralism*, 10 Ann. Rev. Political Sci 45 (2007).

46. For critiques of public choice theory, see Ian Shapiro & Donald Green, Pathologies of Rational Choice Theory: A Critique of Applications in Political Science (1994); Albert Breton, Competitive Governments: An Economic Theory of Politics and Public Finance (1996); Donald Wittman, The Myth of Democratic Failure: Why Political Institutions Are Efficient (1995); Steven Croley, Regulation and Public Interests: The Possibility of Good Regulatory Government (2008); Daniel Farber & Philip Frickey, Law and Public Choice (1991); Jerry Mashaw, *The Economics of Politics and the Understanding of Public Law*, 65 Kent L. Rev. 123 (1990); Daniel Farber, *Democracy and Disgust: Reflections on Public Choice*, 65 Kent L. Rev. 161 (1989); Michael Trebilcock, *The Choice of Governing Instrument: A Retrospective, in Designing Government: From Instruments to Governance* (Pearl Eliadis, Margaret Hill & Michael Howlett eds., 2005).

47. Craig Parsons, How to Map Arguments in Political Science (2007).

48. Other approaches include: ideas, interests, and institutions (e.g., Geoffrey Garrett & Barry Weingast, *Ideas, Interests, and Institutions: Constructing the EC's Internal Market, in* Ideas and Foreign Policy (J. Goldstein & R. Keohane eds., 1993); rationality, culture, and structure (e.g., Comparative Politics: Rationality, Culture, and Structure (Mark Irving Lichbach & Alan S. Zuckerman eds., 1997); and, the "Funnel of Causality" (e.g., Richard Simeon, *Studying Public Policy*, 9(4) Can. J. Political Sci. 548 (1976).

49. As with nearly all aspects of the study of human behavior, the categories are not truly discrete and there is significant overlap and interaction between and among them; many theories plausibly fall within multiple categories.

50. This aspect of the argument can lead to a slightly ambiguous, and potentially problematic interpretation of the concept of structure (see, e.g. John Gerring, *Craig Parsons's How to Map Arguments in Political Science*, 7(2) Perspectives on Politics 432 (2009) (book review). Herein, it is not suggested that structural elements have specific, constant, and universal effects (i.e., a strictly positivist understanding). Rather, the matter is somewhat sidestepped by conceptually bounding the scope of analysis such that certain deeply entrenched institutions and values (e.g., representative democracy, liberalism) are taken as constants

for the purposes of analysis. At the same time, other structural elements (e.g., factor endowments) do remain relatively constant (or are depleted in predictable ways).

51. Daron Acemoglu, Simon Johnson & James A. Robinson, *The Colonial Origins of Comparative Development: An Empirical Investigation*, 91(5) AM. ECON. REV. 1369 (2001).

52. Rafael La Porta, Florencio Lopez-de-Silanes & Andrei Shleifer, *The Economic Consequences of Legal Origins*, 46(2) J. ECON. LIT. 285 (2008).

53. *See, e.g.*, Douglass C. North & Barry R. Weingast, *Constitutions and Commitment: The Evolution of Institutions Governing Public Choice in Seventeenth Century England*, 29(4) J. ECON. HIST. 803 (1989); Barry Weingast, *Rational-Choice Institutionalism*, in POLITICAL SCIENCE: STATE OF THE DISCIPLINE (Ira Katznelson & Helen V. Milner eds., 2002); more generally, see Ellen M. Immergut, *The Theoretical Core of the New Institutionalism*, 26(1) POLITICS AND SOCIETY 5 (1998).

54. George Tsebelis, *Decision Making in Political Systems: Veto Players in Presidentialism, Parliamentarianism, Multicameralism and Multipartism*, 25(3) BRIT. J. POLITICAL SCI. 289, 293 (1995).

55. *See, e.g.*, Giovanni Sartori, *Parties and Party Systems: A Framework for Analysis*, in HOW PARTIES ORGANIZE: CHANGE AND ADAPTATION IN WESTERN DEMOCRACIES 71 (Richard Katz and Peter Mair eds., 1976).

56. Similarly, Béland and Cox suggest that politics is not only a struggle for power and control among those seeking to maximize their own interests, material or otherwise, but also a contest among individuals whose communications with one another shape not only what they want, but "what they deem to be appropriate, legitimate and proper." For them, ideas are causal beliefs that are products of cognition, connected to the "real" world via perception, and are more or less formal conceptualizations of causal relationships that serve as guides for action. Daniel Béland & Robert Henry Cox, *Introduction: Ideas and Politics*, in IDEAS AND POLITICS IN SOCIAL SCIENCE RESEARCH 301–02 (Daniel Béland & Robert Henry Cox eds., 2010).

57. *Id.* at 4.

58. Peter A. Hall & Rosemary C.R. Taylor, *Political Science and the Three New Institutionalisms*, 44(5) POLITICAL STUD. 936, 956 (1996).

59. *See, e.g.*, VICTOR PETER, MANAGING WITHOUT GROWTH: SLOWER BY DESIGN NOT DISASTER (2008).

60. FRANK FISCHER, REFRAMING PUBLIC POLICY: DISCURSIVE POLITICS AND DELIBERATIVE PRACTICES 83 (2003).

61. Jan-Erik Lane, *Public Policy and Implementation*, in INSTITUTIONAL REFORM: A PUBLIC POLICY PERSPECTIVE 36 (1990).

62. William H. Sewell, Jr., *Three Temporalities: Toward an Eventful Sociology*, in THE HISTORIC TURN IN THE HUMAN SCIENCES 245, 263 (Terrence J. McDonald ed., 1996).

63. There are at least four positive feedback mechanisms. First, large setup or investment costs such as specialized infrastructure create a strong incentive to stay the course once the investment is made. Second, as complex systems operate they tend to become more efficient as a result of "learning-by-doing," resulting in higher returns on investments and rendering the opportunity costs (or "switching costs") of adopting an alternative policy higher. Third, there is the idea of coordination or network effects—where the benefits an individual receives from a particular activity increase as others adopt the same option (i.e.,

use of similar technology or the development of mutually beneficial supply chain management systems). Fourth, individuals may begin to tailor their investments and choices to expectations based on the continuation of a given policy or path. Thus, a change in that course may negatively affect the outcome of those choices, provoking individuals or organizations that have a vested interest in the status quo to actively resist change (a central focus of this book). Paul Pierson, *Increasing Returns, Path Dependence, and the Study of Politics*, 94(2) AM. POLITICAL SCI. REV. 251 (2000); *see also* Mariana Prado & Michael J. Trebilcock, *Path Dependence, Development, and the Dynamics of Institutional Reform*, 59(3) U. TORONTO L.J. 341 (2009).

64. With respect to the impact of "policy legacies" (i.e., prior policies in a similar area) on the uptake and development of future policy, see Margaret Weir & Theda Skocpol, *State Structures and the Possibilities for "Keynesian" Responses to the Great Depression in Sweden, Britain, and the United States*, in BRINGING THE STATE BACK IN) 107–64 (Peter B. Evans, Dietrich Reuschemeyer & Theda Skocpol eds., 1985.

65. *See, e.g.*, ROBERT D. PUTNAM, MAKING DEMOCRACY WORK: CIVIC TRADITIONS IN MODERN ITALY (1993).

66. A more fulsome elaboration of the concept of layering and other processes on endogenous institutional change can be found in James Mahoney & Kathleen Thelen, *A Theory of Gradual Institutional Change*, in EXPLAINING INSTITUTIONAL CHANGE: AMBIGUITY, AGENCY, AND POWER (Mahoney & Thelen eds., 2010).

67. *See, e.g.*, Amos Tversky & Daniel Kahneman, *The Framing of Decisions and the Psychology of Choice*, 211(448) SCI. 453 (1981).

68. Russell B. Korobkin & Thomas S. Ulen, *Law and Behavioral Science: Removing the Rationality Assumption from Law and Economics*, 88 CAL. L. REV. 1051, 1108–10 (2000); *see also* Tversky & Kahneman, *supra* note 67.

69. Daniel Kahneman, *Maps of Bounded Rationality: Psychology for Behavioral Economics*, 93(5) AM. ECON. REV. 1449, 1457 (2003).

70. Some recent scholarship disputes the existence of an endowment effect. For example, Plott and Zeiler suggest that the effect is the product of experimental conditions and not a distinct psychological trait. (*See* Charles R. Plott & Kathryn Zeiler, *The Willingness to Pay—Willingness to Accept Gap, the "Endowment Effect," Subject Misconceptions, and Experimental Procedures for Eliciting Valuations*, 95 AM. ECON. REV. 530–45 (2005); Charles R. Plott & Kathryn Zeiler, *Exchange Asymmetries Incorrectly Interpreted as Evidence of Endowment Effect Theory and Prospect Theory?*, 97 AM. ECON. REV.1449–66 (2007). However, Plott and Zeiler's conclusions have also been challenged; *see* Andrea Isoni et al., Comment: *The Willingness to Pay—Willingness to Accept Gap, the "Endowment Effect," Subject Misconceptions, and Experimental Procedure for Eliciting Valuations*, 101 AM. ECON. REV. 991–1011 (2011); *see also* Jack L. Knetsch & Wei-Kang Wong, *The Endowment Effect and the Reference State: Evidence and Manipulations*, 71 J. ECON. BEHAVIOR & ORG. 407–14 (2009). For a rejoinder, *see* Gregory Klass & Kathryn Zieler, "*Against Endowment Theory*," 61 U.C.L.A. L. REV. 2 (2013).

71. Korobkin & Ulen, *supra* note 68, at 1100. For example, one study indicates that the minimum acceptable selling price of a home is heavily influenced by an arbitrarily proposed asking price. Half of the study respondents—real estate agents all—saw a booklet of information on the house, which included a substantially higher-than-the-actual asking price; the other half saw the same information but the asking price was substantially below

the actual asking price. The agents were then asked to state their minimum selling price. Although both groups regressed toward the mean the movement toward the actual price accounted for only 60 percent of the difference between the proposed and market prices. That is, the difference between the average acceptable price for those shown the low and high proposed prices was 41 percent of the distance between the low and high proposed prices. DANIEL KAHNEMAN, THINKING, FAST AND SLOW (2011), citing G.B. Northcraft & M.A. Neale, *Experts, Amateurs, and Real Estate: An Anchoring-and-Adjustment Perspective on Property Pricing Decisions*, 39(1) ORGANIZATIONAL BEHAVIOR & HUM. DECISION PROCESSES 84 (1987). However, it has been suggested that the reverse might be true in other circumstances (e.g., in the valuation of stock prices). SHAVIRO, *supra* note 2, at 23.

72. *See* CASS SUNSTEIN, GOING TO EXTREMES: HOW LIKE MINDS UNITE AND DIVIDE (2009); JONATHAN HAIDT, THE RIGHTEOUS MIND: WHY GOOD PEOPLE ARE DIVIDED BY POLICIES AND RELIGION (2012).

73. ALAN M. JACOBS, GOVERNING FOR THE LONG TERM: DEMOCRACY AND THE POLITICS OF INVESTMENT (2011).

74. Korobkin & Ulen, *supra* note 68, at 1135–36.

75. *Id.* at 1136.

76. PARSONS, *supra* note 47, at 131. For a more comprehensive review of the role and nature of ideas, see Yves Surel, *The Role of Cognitive and Normative Frames in Policy-Making*, 7(4) J. EUR. PUB. POLICY 495 (2000); John Campbell, *Institutional Analysis and the Role of Ideas in Political Economy*, 27 THEORY & SOCIETY 377 (1998); Grace D. Skogstad & Vivien A. Schmidt, *Introduction: Policy Paradigm Development, Transnationalism, and Domestic Politics, in* INTERNATIONALIZATION AND POLICY PARADIGMS (Skogstad & Schmidt eds., 2011); Béland & Cox, *supra* note 56; Martin Carstensen, *Paradigm Man vs. the Bricoleur: Bricolage as an Alternative Vision of Agency in Ideational Change*, 3(1) EUR. POLITICAL SCI. REV. 147 (2011).

77. PARSONS, *supra* note 47, at 97–98; *see also* Skogstad & Schmidt, *supra* note 76; Peter A. Hall, *Conclusion: The Politics of Keynesian Ideas, in* THE POLITICAL POWER OF ECONOMIC IDEAS: KEYNESIANISM ACROSS NATIONS 361 (Peter A. Hall ed., 1989).

78. It is also likely that there will be systematic differences between the way that individual members of the public and decision-makers such as politicians or interest group leaders come to decisions about the desirability of given policies and the type of information available to them in doing so (JACOBS, *supra* note 73). Decision-makers or "policy elites" are likely to have substantially more background knowledge (albeit still imperfect) in a given area than the average citizen. They are also likely to have substantially greater resources available to them to consider, and come to reasonably reliable conclusions about, the long-run costs and benefits of a particular policy proposal for their constituency. In short, although the understanding of policy elites will be far from perfect, it is reasonable to believe that their understanding of the situation will be more sophisticated and, likely, more accurate than that of the average member of the public.

79. *See, e.g.*, Dan M. Kahan, Hank Jenkins-Smith & Donald Braman, *Cultural Cognition of Scientific Consensus*, 14(2) J. RISK RES. 147 (2011).

80. In some respects, ideas of this type can be seen as culturally institutionalized—indeed the distinction between ideational and institutional explanations is often somewhat blurry—but normative beliefs of this type can be seen as somewhat more pervasive than institutionalized logics of appropriateness.

81. A prime example of this can be seen in the construction of narratives surrounding dairy supply-management in Canada, where the idea of a free market can be invoked to support a deregulation of production, and the notion of protecting hard-working farmers can be invoked in favor of the maintenance of existing quota systems. See Chapter 6 for a further discussion of this matter.

82. These groups might also be thought of as "epistemic communities," that is, as "network[s] of professionals with recognized expertise and competence in a particular domain and an authoritative claim to policy-relevant knowledge within the domain or issue are." Peter M. Haas, *Introduction: Epistemic Communities and International Policy Coordination*, 46(1) INT'L ORG. 1, 3 (1992).

83. Margaret E. Keck & Katheyn Sikkink, *Transnational Advocacy Networks in International and Regional Politics*, 159 INT'L SOC. SCI. J. 89–101 (1999).

84. Peter A. Hall, *Policy Paradigms, Social Learning, and the State: The Case of Economic Policymaking in Britain*, 25(3) COMP. POLITICS 275–96 (1993).

85. Paul A. Sabatier & Christopher M. Weible, *The Advocacy Coalition Framework: Innovations and Clarifications, in* THEORIES OF THE POLICY PROCESS 65 (Sabatier ed., 2d ed. 2007).

86. MARGARET E. KECK & KATHRYN SIKKINK, ACTIVISTS BEYOND BORDERS: ADVOCACY NETWORKS IN INTERNATIONAL POLITICS (1998).

87. In many respects, these groups can be seen as operating in a fashion similar to more traditional interest groups (e.g., business associations), albeit with somewhat different goals and arguably, more legitimate appeals to notions of fairness and moral force.

88. KECK & SIKKINK *supra* note 86, at 2–3.

89. *Id.* at 16–25; *see also* Sanjeev Khagram, James V. Riker & Kathryn Sikkink, *From Santiago to Seattle: Transnational Advocacy Groups Restructuring World Politics, in Restructuring World Politics: Transnational Social Movements, Networks, and Norms* 3 (Khagram ed., 2002)

90. Frank Dobbin, Beth A. Simmons & Geoffrey Garrett, *The Global Diffusion of Public Policies: Social Construction, Coercion, Competition, or Learning?*, 33 ANN. REV. SOCIOLOGY 449, 460 (2007).

91. Fabrizio Gilardi, *Who Learns from What in Policy Diffusion Processes?*, 54(3) AM. J. POLITICAL SCI. 650, 652–53 (2010).

92. For a more thorough discussion of the concept of framing, see, e.g., Dennis Chong & James N. Druckman, *Framing Theory*, 10(1) ANN. REV. POLITICAL SCI. 103–226 (2007).

93. FRANK BAUMGARTNER & BRYAN D. JONES, AGENDAS AND INSTABILITY IN AMERICAN POLITICS 26 (1993).

94. *Id.* at 27.

95. Skogstad & Schmidt, *supra* note 76. This may be particularly successful in light of what Sabatier et al. and others dub the "devil shift" whereby the preferred policy options of alternative advocacy coalitions are perceived to be far more detrimental to the interests and values of members of the first coalition than they actually are. *See, e.g.*, Paul Sabatier, Susan Hunter & Susan McLaughlin, *The Devil Shift: Perceptions and Misperceptions of Opponents*, 40(3) W. POLITICAL Q. 449 (1987); Sabatier & Weible, *supra* note 85.

96. *See* Charles Reich, *The New Property*, 73 YALE L.J. 733 (1964).

97. Kaplow, *supra* note 4.

Chapter 3

1. Kim Willsher, *French Strike over Pension Reform Set to Disrupt Travel and Schools*, GUARDIAN (June 23, 2010), GUARDIAN, *available at* http://www.guardian.co.uk/world/2010/jun/23/france-general-strike-pension-reforms?INTCMP=SRCH (last visited June 26, 2012).

2. *French Strikes and Protests: As It Happened*, GUARDIAN, http://www.guardian.co.uk/world/blog/2010/oct/20/french-strikes?intcmp=239, (last visited Sept. 9, 2012).

3. Angelique Chrisafis, *Nicolas Sarkozy Orders Break-Up of Blockades as French Protests Continue*, GUARDIAN (Oct. 20, 2010), *available at* http://www.guardian.co.uk/world/2010/oct/20/nicolas-sarkozy-france-protests-blockades (last visited June 26, 2012).

4. *Id.*

5. Kim Willsher, *French Pension Reform Vote Passed by Parliament*, GUARDIAN (Oct. 22, 2010), *available at* http://www.guardian.co.uk/world/2010/oct/22/french-pension-reform-vote (last visited June 26, 2012).

6. Kim Willsher, *Hollande Pushes Ahead with Pledge to Undo Sarkozy Pension Change*, GUARDIAN.CO.UK (May 23, 2012), *available at* http://www.guardian.co.uk/world/2012/may/23/hollande-reverses-sarkozy-election-reform (last visited June 26, 2012). The Hollande administration subsequently came under pressure from the European Commission to return to Sarkozy's policy, but in May 2013 was still holding its ground (Bruno Waterfield, *Francois Hollande Tells European Commission It Can't Dictate to France*, TELEGRAPH.CO.UK (May 29, 2013), *available at* http://www.telegraph.co.uk/finance/financialcrisis/10088005/Francois-Hollande-tells-European-Commission-it-cant-dictate-to-France.html (last visited October 21, 2013).

7. Alan M. Jacobs, *Governing for the Long Term: Democracy and the Politics of Investment* (2011).

8. OECD STAFF, PENSIONS AT A GLANCE 2011: RETIREMENT-INCOME SYSTEMS IN OECD AND G20 COUNTRIES 13 (2011).

9. *Id.*

10. *Id.*

11. Axel Borsch-Supan, *Rational Pension Reform*, 32 GENEVA PAPERS 430, 432 (2007).

12. OECD Staff, *Putting Pensions on Auto-Pilot*, *in* OECD PENSIONS OUTLOOK 2012, at 45 (2012); OECD STAFF, *supra* note 8, at 66–67.

13. For example, the Canada Pension Plan experienced a sustainability problem in the mid-1990s, which prompted the reforms described below (page 83, *supra*.) For examples of current sustainability problems in European public pension schemes, see OECD Staff, *Putting Pensions on Auto-Pilot*, *supra* note 12 at 49–50. *See also* Alan J. Auerbach & Ronald Lee, *Welfare and Generational Equity in Sustainable Unfunded Pension Systems* (NBER Working Paper 14682), National Bureau of Economic Research, Cambridge, MA (2009), *available at* http://www.nber.org/papers/w14682, (last visited June 26, 2012); Martin Hering & Thomas R. Klassen, *Strengthening Fairness and Funding in the Canada Pension Plan: Is Raising the Retirement Age an Option?* (SEDAP Research Paper No. 263), Social and Economic Dimensions of an Aging Population, McMaster University, Hamilton, ON, (2010), *available at* http://socserv.mcmaster.ca/sedap/p/sedap263.pdf, at 4–5 (last visited June 26, 2012); John B. Williamson & Diane M. Watts-Roy, *Aging Boomers, Generational*

Equity, and Framing the Debate over Social Security, in BOOMER BUST?: ECONOMIC AND POLITICAL ISSUES OF THE GRAYING SOCIETY (Robert B. Hudson ed., 2009); Borsch-Supan, *supra* note 11 at 431.

14. Hering & Klassen, *supra* note 13, at 8. Some plans have also had sustainability problems exacerbated by lower-than-expected investment returns and labor force participation among older workers. *See, e.g.*, OECD STAFF, *Pensions at a Glance 2011, supra* note 8, and Jacobs, *supra* note 7, at 155–56.

15. OECD STAFF, *supra* note 8, at 166. Also known as "dependency ratio" (e.g., Borsch-Supan, *supra* note 11, at 435.)

16. OECD STAFF, *supra* note 8, at 40.

17. *Id.* at 25.

18. *Id.* at 13.

19. Hering & Klassen, *supra* note 13, at 3.

20. OECD STAFF, *supra* note 8, at 163. Immigration has in some countries mitigated this trend.

21. For example, the United States' Social Security trust funds are expected to be exhausted by 2035. (Brian Faler, *U.S. Social Security Program to Run out of Money by 2035*, BLOOMBERG NEWS, Apr. 23, 2012), *available at* http://business.financialpost.com/20 12/04/23/u-s-social-security-program-to-run-out-of-money-by-2035/, (last visited Sept. 9, 2012)).

22. Hering & Klassen, *supra* note 13, at 29.

23. The benefits of declining fertility include greater autonomy (especially for women) and more rapid accumulation of capital, which in turn produces growth. (*Go Forth and Multiply a Lot Less*, ECONOMIST.COM (Oct. 29, 2009), *available at* http://www.economist.com/node/14743589.

24. Jacobs, *supra* note 7.

25. OECD STAFF, *supra* note 8, at 63.

26. *Id.*; Borsch-Supan, *supra* note 11.

27. Hering & Klassen, *supra* note 13; Canada Revenue Agency, *Canada Revenue Agency Announces Maximum Pensionable Earnings for 2012*," *available at* http://www.cra-arc.gc.ca/nwsrm/rlss/2011/m11/nr111101-eng.html (last visited Sept. 9, 2012).

28. Although contributions can be collected from employers, the evidence suggests that employer payroll taxes are passed through to employees in the form of lower wages. (Peter Dungan, *The CPP Payroll Tax Hike: Macroeconomic Transition Costs and Alternatives*, 24 CAN. PUBLIC POLICY 395, Queen's Economics Department, *available at* http://qed.econ.queensu.ca/pub/cpp/Sept1998/2Round3Paper.pdf (last visited June 26, 2012).)

29. Cato Institute, *Social Security, in* CATO HANDBOOK FOR POLICYMAKERS, Cato Institute, CATO.ORG (2009), *available at* http://www.cato.org/pubs/handbook/hb111/hb111-17.pdf (last visited June 26, 2012).

30. Robert J. Shiller, *Social Security and Individual Accounts as Elements of Overall Risk-Sharing* (Cowles Foundation Paper No. 1061, Yale Department of Economics) (2003), *available at* http://aida.wss.yale.edu/~shiller/pubs/p1061.pdf (last visited June 26, 2012).

31. OECD STAFF, *supra* note 8, at 13.

32. Hering & Klassen, *supra* note 13, at 26 and 37. However, the effect on labor force participation is not as dramatic as it would once have been. This is because many OECD plans have been reformed to allow a benefit recipient to continue working, and/or to cease working before starting to receive the benefits.

33. U.S. GENERAL ACCOUNTING OFFICE, IMPLICATIONS OF RAISING THE RETIREMENT AGE 7 (1999), *available at* www.gao.gov/archive/1999/he99112.pdf (last visited June 26, 2012).

34. LONG TERM STATE PENSION SUSTAINABILITY: INCREASING THE STATE PENSION AGE TO 67, at 2 (IMPACT ASSESSMENT) (2011), *available at* http://www.dwp.gov.uk/docs/ia-increasing-state-pension-age-to-67.pdf (last visited June 26, 2012).

35. Dungan, *supra* note 28.

36. OECD STAFF, *supra* note 8, at 54; FRANK T. DENTON & BYRON G. SPENCER, AGE OF PENSION ELIGIBILITY, GAINS IN LIFE EXPECTANCY AND SOCIAL POLICY 14–15 (SEDAP Research Paper No 276, 2010), *available at* http://socserv.mcmaster.ca/sedap/p/sedap276.pdf (last visited June 26, 2012); Hering & Klassen, *supra* note 13, at 30.

37. Hering & Klassen, *supra* note 13, at 10.

38. PETER HICKS, LATER RETIREMENT: THE WIN-WIN SOLUTION 19 (Commentary No. 345) (C.D. Howe Institute, 2012), *available at* http://cdhowe.org/pdf/Commentary_345.pdf (last visited June 26, 2012).

39. Jacobs, *supra* note 7, at 174, 198, and 225.

40. *Id.* at 17.

41. *Id.* at 17.

42. *Id.* at 21.

43. *Id.* at 18.

44. DENTON & SPENCER, *supra* note 36, at 13–14.

45. Borsch-Supan, *supra* note 11, at 435.

46. OECD STAFF, *supra* note 8, at 86.

47. Frank I. Michelman, *Property, Utility, and Fairness: Comments on the Ethical Foundations of Just Compensation Law*, 80 HAR. L. REV. 1165, 1214 (1967).

48. Hering & Klassen, *supra* note 13, at 38–39.

49. *Id.* at 36.

50. U.S. CONGRESSIONAL BUDGET OFFICE, GROWING DISPARITIES IN LIFE EXPECTANCY (2008), *available at* http://www.cbo.gov/sites/default/files/cbofiles/ftpdocs/91xx/doc9104/04-17-lifeexpectancy_brief.pdf (last visited June 26, 2012).

51. Hering & Klassen, *supra* note 13, at 36.

52. Polls showed that, although less than 40 percent of Canadians supported the eligibility age increase, enacting it had no significant impact on support for the Conservative government. (Éric Grenier, *Pension Tinkering Fails to Dent Tory Support among Older Canadians*, GLOBE & MAIL (Mar. 12, 2012), *available at* http://m.theglobeandmail.com/news/politics/pension-tinkering-fails-to-dent-tory-support-among-older-canadians/article2366369/?service=mobile (last visited June 26, 2012).

53. Teresa Smith, *Federal Changes to Oas Mirrored Poll Research; Firm Held Focus Groups across Country*, CALGARY HERALD (July 2, 2012), *available at* <http://www2.canada.com/calgaryherald/news/story.html?id=7ce04591-767c-4d48-bfc0-599cf4115b1f (last visited June 26, 2012); Joe Friesen & Bill Curry, *Prime Minister Harper Unveils Grand Plan to Reshape Canada*, GLOBE & MAIL (Jan. 26, 2012), *available at* http://www.theglobeandmail.com/news/politics/prime-minister-harper-unveils-grand-plan-to-reshape-canada/article542480/ (last visited June 26, 2012).

54. OECD STAFF, *supra* note 8; Hering & Klassen, *supra* note 13, at 45.

55. OECD STAFF, *supra* note 8, at 10.

56. Sébastien LaRochelle-Côté, John Myles & Garnett Picot, *Income Security and Stability during Retirement in Canada* 14–15 (2008), *available at* http://www.statcan.gc.ca/pub/11f0019m/11f0019m2008306-eng.pdf (last visited June 26, 2012); Jinyan Li, *Separation, Linkage and Blurring in the Public and Private Pillars of Canada's Retirement Income System, in* NEW FRONTIERS OF RESEARCH ON RETIREMENT 95, 97 (Leroy O. Stone ed., 2006), *available at* http://www.statcan.gc.ca/pub/75-511-x/75-511-x2006001-eng.pdf (last visited June 26, 2012).

57. OECD STAFF, *supra* note 8, at 118.

58. CBC News, *6 Big Canada Pension Plan Changes Arrive in 2012: New Rules Could Affect Retirement Planning* (Jan. 31, 2012), *available at* http://www.cbc.ca/news/business/taxseason/story/2012/01/30/f-cpp-changes.html (last visited Sept. 9, 2012).

59. At present in Canada, there is no further increase to benefit levels for those who delay receipt after age 70: DENTON & SPENCER, *supra* note 37, at 9.

60. William B.P. Robson, *What to Do about Seniors' Benefits in Canada: The Case for Letting Recipients Take Richer Payments Later* 5 (2012), *available at* http://www.cdhowe.org/pdf/e-brief_131.pdf (last visited June 26, 2012).

61. Arguably, to be truly actuarially neutral the benefit adjustment for date of receipt should reflect both (1) the change in the projected period of benefit receipt, and (2) the change in tax revenues caused by exit from the workforce.

62. RICHARD THALER & CASS SUNSTEIN, NUDGE (2009).

63. Service Canada, *Age of Eligibility for Old Age Security Benefits from 2023 to 2029*, *available at* http://www.servicecanada.gc.ca/eng/isp/oas/changes/oasgis_age_chart.shtml#agechart (last visited Sept. 9, 2012).

64. DENTON & SPENCER, *supra* note 36, at 5–6.

65. International Social Security Administration, *The 2010 Reform of the French Old-Age Pension Program*, *available at* http://www.issa.int/Observatory/Country-Profiles/Regions/Europe/France/Reforms/The-2010-Reform-of-the-French-Old-Age-Pension-Program (last visited Sept. 9, 2012).

66. Hering & Klassen, *supra* note 13, at 44.

67. Casey B. Mulligan & Xavier Sala-i-Martin, *Gerontocracy, Retirement, and Social Security* (NBER Working Paper No. 7117, 1999), *available at* http://www.nber.org/papers/w7117 (last visited June 26, 2012); OECD STAFF, SOCIETY AT A GLANCE: OECD SOCIAL INDICATORS 102 (2007).

68. Vincenzo Galasso & Paola Profeta, *Lessons for an Ageing Society: The Political Sustainability of Social Security Systems*, 19 ECON. POLICY 63 (2004). Canada sought to reduce public pension benefits once in 1985, and again in 1996. On both occasions, public resistance forced the government to back down. (Daniel Béland & John Myles, *Stasis Amidst Change: Canadian Pension Reform in an Age of Retrenchment* 11–18 (SEDAP Research Paper No. 111, 2003), *available at* http://socserv.mcmaster.ca/sedap/p/sedap111.pdf (last visited June 26, 2012).

69. Jacobs, *supra* note 7, at 246.

70. *Id.* at 23.

71. Russell B. Korobkin & Thomas S. Ulen, *Law and Behavioral Science: Removing the Rationality Assumption from Law and Economics*, 88 CAL. L. REV. 1051, 1135–38 (2000).

72. Hering & Klassen, *supra* note 13.

Chapter 4

1. *See* DANIEL SHAVIRO, WHEN RULES CHANGE: AN ECONOMIC AND POLITICAL ANALYSIS OF TRANSITION RELIEF AND RETROACTIVITY 7–15, 25–27 (2000) ("when the transition consequences of a rule change depend on people's past decisions that might have been different had they correctly predicted it—thus implying a government decision after they acted—one can describe the government decision as applying 'retroactively.' The rule change has, in effect, reached back into the past to alter the consequences of private decisions that preceded it"). Michael Graetz has shown that "nominally prospective" changes (i.e., those with an effective date in the future) have very similar wealth effects to those that are nominally retroactive. *See* Michael Graetz, *Legal Transitions: The Case of Retroactivity in Income Tax Revision*, 126 U. PA. L. REV. 47, 49–50, 59–60 (1977).

2. *See* Internal Revenue Code of 1986, as amended, section 163(h)(3) [hereinafter the "Code"] (allowing a so-called "itemized deduction" for "qualified residence interest," which means "any interest which is paid or accrued during the taxable year on—(i) acquisition indebtedness with respect to any qualified residence of the taxpayer, or (ii) home equity indebtedness with respect to any qualified residence of the taxpayer"). Note that the determination of whether any property is a qualified residence of the taxpayer is made as of the time the interest is accrued. *See* Code § 163(h)(3)(A). A "qualified residence" is the principal residence of the taxpayer, as well as "1 other residence of the taxpayer which is selected by the taxpayer for purposes of this subsection for the taxable year and which is used by the taxpayer as a residence (within the meaning of section 280A(d)(1))." *See* Code § 163(h)(4).

3. According to the most recent estimates published by the Staff of the Joint Committee on Taxation, the top three tax expenditures in the US Internal Revenue Code are: the exclusion from income of employer contributions for healthcare, health insurance premiums, and long-term care insurance premiums (estimated cost of $117 billion in 2012); reduced rates of tax on dividends and long-term capital gains (estimated cost of $108.4 billion in 2012), and the MID (estimated cost of $68.5 billion in 2012). STAFF OF THE JOINT COMMITTEE ON TAXATION, ESTIMATES OF FEDERAL TAX EXPENDITURES FOR FISCAL YEARS 2012–2017, JCS-1-13 (Feb. 1, 2013) [hereinafter JCS-1-13], at Table 1.

4. *Id.* at 35 (Table 1).

5. *See* SHAVIRO, *supra* note 1, at 144 (noting that "[a]mongst tax scholars, few provisions in the Internal Revenue Code are as roundly (and I would say correctly) condemned as the home mortgage interest deduction"). The mass of scholarly critiques of the MID is too long for a footnote, but important (recent) contributions include Edward L. Glaeser & Jesse M. Shapiro, "The Benefits of the Home Mortgage Interest Deduction," *in* TAX POLICY AND THE ECONOMY, Vol. 17 (James M. Poterba ed., 2003), *available at* http://www.nber.org/books/pote03-1.; John E. Anderson et al., *Capping the Mortgage Interest Deduction*, 60 NAT'L TAX J. 769 (2007); James Poterba & Todd Sinai, *Revenue Costs and Incentive Effects of the Mortgage Interest Deduction for Owner-Occupied Housing*, 64 NAT'L TAX J. 531–64 (2011).

6. *See What Do Tax Policy Experts Think about U.S. Tax Policy?*. UNIVERSITY OF MICHIGAN NEWS SERVICE (Apr. 11, 2013), *available at* http://ns.umich.edu/new/releases/21386-what-do-tax-policy-experts-think-about-u-s-tax-policy; *see also* Janet Novack, *Tax Geeks: Make Tax Filing Easy, Kill the Mortgage Deduction, Tax CPAs*, FORBES (Apr. 15, 2013), *available at* http://www.forbes.com/sites/janetnovack/2013/04/15/tax-geeks-make-tax-filing-easy-kill-the-mortgage-deduction-tax-cpas/.

7. For instance, *see* Mark Koba, *End the Mortgage Interest Deduction? Expect a Fight*, CNBC (Feb. 28, 2013), *available at* http://www.cnbc.com/id/100506426 (quoting a representative of the National Association of Home Builders as promising to "fight...tooth and nail" any proposals to eliminate or modify the MID).

8. *See* discussion in Dennis J. Ventry, Jr., *The Accidental Deduction: A History and Critique of the Tax Subsidy for Mortgage Interest*, 73 LAW & CONTEMPORARY PROBLEMS 233, at 233, 281, 283 (2010); Bruce Bartlett, *Tax Reform's 'Third Rail': Mortgage Interest*, 139 NCPR POLICY BACKGROUNDER 1 (1996), *available at* http://www.ncpa.org/pub/bg139.

9. *See* Roberta Mann, *Housing and the Mortgage Interest Deduction*, in BEYOND ECONOMIC EFFICIENCY 18 (David A. Brennan, Karen B. Brown & Darryl Jones eds., forthcoming) (citing CENTER FOR RESPONSIVE POLITICS, TOP INDUSTRIES GIVING TO MEMBERS OF CONGRESS, 2008 CYCLE, (last visited October 24, 2013) *available at* http://www.opensecrets.org/industries/mems.php?party=A&cycle=2008).

10. The standard deduction depends on filing status (single, head-of-household, or married filing jointly). *See* Code § 63(e).

11. *Id.*

12. *But see* Mark Pitt & Joel Slemrod, *The Compliance Cost of Itemizing Deductions: Evidence from Individual Tax Returns*, 79 AM. ECON. REV. 5 (1989) (noting that some taxpayers choose not to itemize where they would save taxes by doing so, speculating that this is because the compliance cost of itemizing exceeds their tax benefit from itemizing).

13. The litany of allowable itemized deductions has churned significantly in the postwar period. *See* Allan J. Samansky, *Nonstandard Thoughts about the Standard Deduction*, 1991 UTAH L. REV. 531, 533 n.12 (1991) ("the items currently qualifying as itemized deductions have changed significantly since 1944 [the year in which Samansky begins his history]").

14. *See* Code § 164.

15. *See* Code § 165(a). Such losses are described in Code § 165(c)(2) (losses incurred in any transaction entered into for profit, not connected with a trade or business) or Code § 165(c)(3) (losses of property not connected with a trade or business or a transaction entered into for profit, if the losses arise from casualty or theft).

16. *See* Code § 165(d). These are gambling losses of nonprofessional gamblers deductible as itemized deductions only to the extent of gambling winnings.

17. *See* Code §§ 170 and 642(c) (describing amounts paid or permanently set aside for a charitable purpose).

18. *See* Code § 213.

19. *See* Code § 67(d).

20. Miscellaneous itemized deductions include: unreimbursed vehicle expenses of rural mail carriers, investment expenses and expenses for the production or collection of income, tax determination expenses, and expenses allowed under the "hobby loss" rules of Code § 183. *See* Code § 67(a).

21. In 2011, the most recent data year for which summaries are available from the Internal Revenue Service's Statistics of Income, approximately 66 percent of individual returns filed claimed the standard deduction instead of itemizing. Calculated using data from INTERNAL REVENUE SERVICE, STATISTICS ON INCOME, INDIVIDUAL INCOME TAX RETURNS PUBLICATION 1304 (Complete Report); Table A (Selected Income and Tax Items for Tax Years, 1990–20011), *available at* http://www.irs.gov/uac/SOI-Tax-Stats-Individual-Inco

me-Tax-Returns-Publication-1304-(Complete-Report)#_tbla (last accessed October 24, 2013; click on "Table A" to access spreadsheet).

22. Code § 163(h)(3)(A).

23. *Id.*

24. *See* Code § 163(h)(4). The designation of the other property as a "residence" must accord with the meaning of "residence" under Section 280A(d)(1); the determination of whether any property is a qualified residence of the taxpayer is made as of the time the interest is accrued.

25. *See* Rev. Rul. 2010-25, 2010-44 IRB 571, Oct. 14, 2010 (finding that $1,000,000 can be treated as acquisition debt under Code § 163(h)(3)(B) and $100,000 can be treated as home equity debt under Code § 163(h)(3)(C); any excess is considered nondeductible personal interest).

26. Notice 88-74, 1988-2 CB 385.

27. *See* JCS-1-13, *supra* note 3, at 35. *See also* discussion in Mann, *supra* note 9.

28. *See* Ventry, *supra* note 8, at 257 ("Without the imputation of rental income from owner-occupied housing, the mortgage interest deduction was indefensible"). It would, of course, be an even bigger subsidy if homeowners were permitted depreciation deductions on their homes.

29. United States Revenue Act of 1913 (ch. 16, 38 Stat. 114, Oct. 3, 1913), at section II.B, first paragraph [hereinafter 1913 Code]. This is true even though the standard deduction was not added until 1944. See Individual Income Tax Act of 1944, Pub. L. No. 78-315, 58 Stat. 231, 236–37 (1944).

30. 1913 Code, *supra* note 29, at section II.B, second paragraph ("[t]hat in computing net income for the purpose of the normal tax there shall be allowed as deductions: First, the necessary expenses actually paid in carrying on any business, not including personal, living, or family expenses; second, all interest paid within the year by a taxable person on indebtedness; third, all national, State, county, school, and municipal taxes paid within the year, not including those assessed against local benefits; fourth, losses actually sustained during the year, incurred in trade or arising from fires, storms, or shipwreck, and not compensated for by insurance or otherwise; fifth, debts due to the taxpayer actually ascertained to be worthless and charged off within the year; sixth, a reasonable allowance for the exhaustion, wear and tear of property arising out of its use or employment in the business..."). The ability to deduct "all interest...on indebtedness" was not circumscribed until 1986, when it was limited to interest on home mortgages.

31. *See* discussion in Ventry, *supra* note 8, at 241–42 (2010) ("Congress provided full deductibility of interest on debt for business expenses in addition to debt for pseudo-business and personal expenses [such as a debt to purchase owner-occupied housing]"). Ventry identifies the rationale for allowing deductibility of interest payments as the difficulty of distinguishing between debt taken on for business reasons and personal debt.

32. *Id.* at 250.

33. *Id.* at 242, providing statistics on prevalence of mortgage-financed homeownership ("[b]y 1920, 40 percent of homeowners carried a mortgage on their primary residences").

34. *Id.* at 250–52 and note 68 (until the mid-1960s, the top marginal rate fell below 91 percent only briefly). *See* also Lawrence H. Seltzer, The Personal Exemptions in the Income Tax 62, tbl. 9 (1968) (showing that the percentage of households paying income tax grew from 5 percent before World War II to 74 percent after). Moreover, between 1939

and 1944, the highest marginal tax rate rose from 79 percent to 94 percent, and the lowest marginal rate rose from 4 percent to 23 percent. *See* John Brozovsky & A.J. Cataldo, *A Historical Analysis of the "Marriage Tax Penalty,"* ACCOUNTING HISTORIAN'S J. 168–70 (June 1993) (discussing these trends in the context of marriage bonuses and penalties).

35. *See* Carolyn Jones, *Class Tax to Mass Tax: The Role of Propaganda in the Expansion of the Income Tax during World War II*, 37 BUFF. L. REV. 685, 686 (1988) ("[f]or government officials, the income tax came to be seen as both a war financing device and as a means of decreasing excess purchasing power. The result was that the income tax rolls increased from about 7 million taxpayers in 1940 to more than 42 million in 1945").

36. *See* John R. Brooks II, *Doing Too Much: The Standard Deduction and the Conflict between Progressivity and Simplification*, 2 COLUM. J. TAX L. 203, 210 (2009) (arguing that the standard deduction attempts to promote progressivity at the same time that it tries to simplify compliance, but that these two objectives operate at cross-purposes) and Samansky, *supra* note 13, at 533 ("[t]he legislative history of the 1944 tax act describes the mechanics of the newly enacted standard deduction, but does not discuss either Congress' motivation in enacting it or its effect on distribution of the tax burden. Probably its only purpose was simplification").

37. *See* Ventry, *supra* note 8, at 251 and 265 (noting that "[f]ewer taxpayers were taking the standard allowance due to Congress's failure to index its value and due to rising real incomes and other inflationary pressures").

38. *Id.* at 250 (detailing the trends that caused mortgage debt to soar in the postwar period).

39. *Id.* at 237–38.

40. *Id.* at 238.

41. *See* IRS, SOI BULLETIN, TABLE 7, STANDARD, ITEMIZED AND TOTAL DEDUCTIONS REPORTED ON INDIVIDUAL INCOME TAX RETURNS, 1950–2006 (2008), *available at* www.irs.gov/pub/irs-soi/histab7.xls.

42. President Ronald Reagan, Third State of the Union Address (Jan. 25, 1984).

43. *See* Ventry, *supra* note 8, at 271.

44. *See id.*, citing Lou Cannon, *Reagan to Keep Home Mortgage Tax Deduction*, Wash. Post, May 11, 1984, at F1.

45. *See* Code § 163(h)(3) (1986).

46. *See* Ventry, *supra* note 8, at 274–75.

47. *Id.*, citing James R. Follain & David C. Ling, *The Federal Tax Subsidy to Housing and the Reduced Value of the Mortgage Interest Deduction*, 44 NAT'L TAX J. 147, 154 (1991) (stating the $42,500 figure).

48. Glaeser & Shapiro, *supra* note 5, at 50–52.

49. *Id.*

50. *Id.* at 51–53 (noting that "the American Housing Survey tells us that home problems, such as leaks and rats, are very rare among any but the poorest Americans. Indeed, in the entire AHS, more than 40 percent of the housing problems occur in the poorest 25 percent of the population and less than 15 percent of this population itemizes, even if they own").

51. *Id.* at 52.

52. *Id.* at 54–56.

53. *Id.* at 57–58.

54. *Id.* at 60.

55. *Id.* at 65–70.
56. *Id.* at 63.
57. *Id.*
58. *Id.*
59. *See* Richard Voith, *Does the Federal Tax Treatment of Housing Affect the Pattern of Metropolitan Development?*, Fed. Reserve Bank Phila. Bus. Rev. 3–16 (1999).
60. *See* discussion in Glaeser & Shapiro, *supra* note 5, at 57–59.
61. *See further* discussion of racial dimensions of housing assistance in Mann, *supra* note 9, at 9–11 (noting that "[t]he disparity between tax benefits for housing and direct assistance [rental subsidies] has both a racial and an income component, although the two components are interrelated").
62. *See* Glaeser & Shapiro, *supra* note 5, at 59.
63. *See* summary of economic literature in Rebecca Morrow, *Billions of Dollars Spent Inflating the Housing Bubble: How and Why the Mortgage Interest Deduction Failed*, 17 Fordham J. Corp. & Fin. L. 751, 761–70 (2012).
64. Glaeser & Shapiro, *supra* note 5, at 79.
65. *Id.* at 79–80.
66. *See, e.g.*, Cong. Budget Office, Pub. No. 3191, Budget Options Volume 2188 (2009). *See also* Roberta Mann, *The (Not So) Little House on the Prairie: The Hidden Costs of the Home Mortgage Interest Deduction*, 32 Ariz. St. L.J. 1347 (2000).
67. *See* Jacob Goldin & Yair Listokin, *Tax Expenditure Salience* (Working Paper, 2012), (on file with author) Goldin and Listokin].
68. *Id.* at 14–15 (explaining that "the mistakes caused by hyper-salience have real welfare costs to the taxpayers who act on those misperceptions. For example, low-income households may suspect that the 'tax advantages' associated with home ownership justify what would otherwise be an imprudent housing purchase. If this household ultimately takes the standard deduction, the tax advantages will never materialize, possibly leading to default and foreclosure. All in all, the fact that so many taxpayers appear to misunderstand the HMID's incentives (in both directions) is worrisome because it suggests the presence of widespread budgeting mistakes").
69. *See id.* for a summary of literature, at 771–74.
70. *See* Dennis Capozza et al., *Taxes, Mortgage Borrowing, and Residential Land Prices*, *in* Economic Effects of Fundamental Tax Reform (Henry Aaron & William Gale eds., 1996); *see also* Anderson et al., *supra* note 5, at 769. This suggests that, in response to increased demand for housing, supply may not be elastic enough to dampen the price increase. *See also* Richard K. Green et al., *Metropolitan-Specific Estimates of the Price Elasticity of Supply of Housing and Their Sources*, 95 Am. Econ. Rev. 334, 335 (2005).
71. *See* Shaviro, *supra* note 1, at 144.
72. *See* Steven C. Bourassa & Ming Yin, *Tax Deductions, Tax Credits and the Homeownership Rate of Young Urban Adults in the United States*, 45 Urban Studies 5–6, 1141–61 (2008) (finding that price capitalization of the MID disproportionately deters younger potential homeowners due to life-cycle constraints and their effect on gathering funds for a down payment).
73. *See* Shaviro, *supra* note 1, at 144. *See* also Martin Gervais, *Housing Taxation and Capital Accumulation*, 49 J. Monetary Econ. 7, 1462 (Oct. 2002) ("housing tax provisions distort the lifetime profile and composition of individuals' savings. In both cases,

distortions are due to the fact that the tax code makes the return on housing capital larger than that on business capital. The wedge between the two rates of return arises from the failure to tax implicit rental income from owner-occupied housing. The presence of mortgage interest deductibility, although neither sufficient nor necessary for the existence of a wedge between the two rates of return, increases the size of the wedge").

74. See Morrow, *supra* note 63, at 789–91.

75. See Andrew Hanson, *The Incidence of the Mortgage Interest Deduction: Evidence from the Market for Home Purchase Loans*, 40(3) PUB. FIN. REV. pages 340–42 (2012).

76. *Id.*

77. *Id.* at 340.

78. *Id.* at 341.

79. *Id.*

80. Lower-income taxpayers who will not find it advantageous to itemize their deductible expenses, even when they take out a mortgage, will face the same higher interest rates and inflated house prices, but will not be able to take advantage of the subsidy on their annual tax returns.

81. Ventry, *supra* note 8, at 264.

82. *See generally* Poterba & Sinai, *supra* note 5.

83. As calculated using second tax expenditure column of table. STAFF OF THE JOINT COMMITTEE ON TAXATION, PRESENT LAW, DATA AND ANALYSIS RELATING TO HOMEOWNERSHIP, prepared for a Public Hearing Before the Senate Committee on Finance, Oct. 6, 2011, *available at* https://www.jct.gov/publications.html?func=startdown&id=4366.

84. *See* Morrow, *supra* note 63, at 795.

85. *See* Gordon Tullock, *The Transitional Gains Trap*, 6 BELL J. ECON. 671 (1975).

86. *See* Martain Gervais & Manish Pandey, *Who Cares about Mortgage Deductibility?*, 34 CAN. PUB. POLICY 1, 14 (2008). Admittedly, this shift in households' balance sheets may itself have unintended consequences—for instance, encumbering other assets to retire mortgage debt that is no longer deductible may dampen demand to the extent that those assets would have been encumbered for other purposes.

87. *See* Goldin & Listokin, *supra* note 67.

88. *See infra*, Chapter 9: Conclusion.

89. Note, however, that there is a case to be made that the MID functions as partial insurance for homeowners against the risk of increased tax rates. If marginal rates increase, the value of the MID would increase proportionally and would become capitalized in house prices. The capitalization effect (partially) protects the homeowner against wealth shocks from government policy. (Thanks to Benjamin Alarie for this interesting suggestion.)

90. SHAVIRO, *supra* note 1, at 145.

91. *See* Gervais & Pandy, *supra* note 86, at 14–15.

92. *See* Morrow, *supra* note 63, at 802–09.

93. *See, e.g.*, Brady Dennis, *Mortgage Tax Break May Lose "Untouchable" Status*, WASH. POST, Dec. 1, 2012, *available at* http://bostonglobe.com/business/2012/12/01/mortgage-tax-break-may-lose-untouchable-status/E9aVAY7yTmq18NZ6Roz0TK/story.html.

94. *See* Mann, *supra* note 9, at 17–18, citing REPORT OF THE NATIONAL COMMISSION ON FISCAL RESPONSBILITY AND REFORM, THE MOMENT OF TRUTH 30–31 (2010), *available at* http://www.fiscalcommission.gov/ (last visited June 12, 2012). Ventry also recommends a shift to a credit. *See* Ventry, *supra* note 8, at 282–83 ("Assuming that national policymakers

and the American public still consider homeownership a worthy goal, repealing the MID would remove an obstacle to achieving that objective. Using the money saved from repeal ($108 billion in 2010) to fund a tax credit rather than a deduction would positively promote homeownership").

95. *See* discussion in Morrow, *supra* note 63, at 802–08.

96. U.S. GOV'T ACCOUNTABILITY OFFICE, GAO 10-1025R, TAX ADMINISTRATION USAGE AND SELECTED ANALYSES OF THE FIRST-TIME HOMEBUYER CREDIT 1 n.1 (Sept. 2010).

97. *See* SHAVIRO, *supra* note 1, at 146.

98. Daniel Shaviro, *The Bucket and Buffett Approaches to Raising Taxes on High-Income U.S. Individuals* (New York University School of Law, Law & Economics Research Paper Series Working Paper No. 12-44, Jan. 2013) (noting that "such approaches create odd MRR patterns, characterized by the sudden emergence of a zero MRR [marginal rate reduction] at an artificially determined point that seems unlikely to reflect sound design").

99. For discussion, *see* Peter Eavis, *Mortgage Interest Deduction, Once a Sacred Cow, Is under Scrutiny*, N.Y. TIMES DEALBOOK, Nov. 26, 2012, *available at* http://dealbook.nytimes.com/2012/11/26/mortgage-interest-deduction-once-a-sacred-cow-is-Seen-as-vulnerable/.

100. *See* Brett Ferguson et al. *Some Itemized Deduction Limits Considered Likely as Obama, Boehner Negotiate Deal*, DAILY TAX REPORT, 228 DTR GG-1, Nov. 28, 2012.

101. *Id.*

102. *See* Len Burman, *No, Ari, the Cliff Deal Will Raise the Economic Incentive to Give to Charity*, TAX POLICY CENTER BLOG (Jan. 8, 2013), *available at* http://taxvox.taxpolicycenter.org/2013/01/08/no-ari-the-cliff-deal-will-raise-the-economic-incentive-to-give-to-charity/?utm_source=feedburner&utm_medium=email&utm_campaign=Feed%3A+taxpolicycenter%2Fblogfeed+%28TaxVox%3A+the+Tax+Policy+Center+blog%29.

103. *Id.*

104. *Id.*

105. *See* Goldin & Listokin, *supra* note 67.

106. *See, e.g.*, Richard H. Thaler, *Some Empirical Evidence on Dynamic Inconsistency*, in QUASI RATIONAL ECONOMICS (Richard H. Thaler, ed., 1991) and Ted O'Donoghue & Matthew Rabin, *Doing It Now or Later*, 89 AM. ECON. REV. 1 (1999) (discussing the prevalence of "present-biased preferences").

Chapter 5

1. Paul Krugman, *The Narrow and Broad Arguments for Free Trade*, 83(2) AM. ECON. REV. 362 (1993).

2. *See generally* MICHAEL TREBILCOCK, MARSHA CHANDLER & ROBERT HOWSE, TRADE AND TRANSITIONS: A COMPARATIVE ANALYSIS OF ADJUSTMENT POLICIES (1990); EDWARD IACOBUCCI, MICHAEL TREBILCOCK & HUMA HAIDER, ECONOMIC SHOCKS: DEFINING A ROLE FOR GOVERNMENT ch. 9 (2001), upon which much of this case study is based.

3. ADAM SMITH, THE WEALTH OF NATIONS (Modern Library 1937) (1776).

4. For a sophisticated but accessible account of the evolution of trade theory, see ELHANAN HELPMAN, UNDERSTANDING GLOBAL TRADE (2011).

5. TREBILCOCK ET AL., *supra* note 2, at 42–76.

6. Robert Crandall, *Import Quotas in the Automobile Industry: The Costs of Protectionism*, 2 BROOKINGS REV. 4 (1983).

7. Economic Council of Canada, *Managing Adjustment: Policies for Trade-Sensitive Industries*, 2 ECON. COUNCIL CAN. 61 (1988).

8. J. DAVID RICHARDSON, UNDERSTANDING INTERNATIONAL ECONOMICS (1980) [Richardson].

9. Joseph Francois, Marion Jansen & Ralf Peters, *Trade Adjustment Costs and Assistance: The Labour Market Dynamics*, in TRADE AND EMPLOYMENT: FROM MYTHS TO FACTS (2011).

10. *Id.*

11. *Id.* at 23.

12. Louis Jacobson, Robert LaLonde & Daniel Sullivan, *Earnings Losses of Displaced Workers*, 83 AM. ECON. REV. 685 (1993).

13. The methodological approaches differ widely across studies. Some use a computable general equilibrium (CGE) model (see Jaime De Melo & David Tarr, *Welfare Effects of US Quotas in Textiles, Steel and Autos*, 72 REV. ECON. & STATISTICS 489 (1990)). Others take into account the time and costs of retraining and job search in their estimation of adjustment costs (see Carl David & Steven Mastuz, *Should Policy Makers Be Concerned about Adjustment Costs?*, in THE POLITICAL ECONOMY OF TRADE, AID AND FOREIGN INVESTMENT (Devashisha Mitra & Arvind Panagariya eds., 2004)). Some studies suggest that the effect is different for developing countries (SAM LAIRD & FERNANDEZ DE COROBA, COPING WITH TRADE REFORMS: A DEVELOPING COUNTRY PERSPECTIVE ON THE WTO INDUSTRIAL TRADE NEGOTIATIONS (2006)).

14. *See* Steven Magee, *The Welfare Effects of Restrictions on US Trade*, 3 BROOKINGS PAPERS ECON. ACTIVITY (1972); Robert Baldwin, John Mutti & David Richardson, *Welfare Effects on the United States of a Significant Trade Reduction* 10 J. INT'L ECON. 405 (1980).

15. *See* Scott Bradford, Paul Grieco & Gary Hufbauer, *The Payoff to America from Global Integration*, in C. FRED BERGSTEN & THE INSTITUTE FOR INTERNATIONAL ECONOMICS, THE UNITED STATES AND THE WORLD ECONOMY: FOREIGN ECONOMIC POLICY FOR THE NEXT DECADE (2005); Carl Davidson & Steven J. Matusz, *Should Policy Makers Be Concerned about Adjustment Costs?*, in INTERNATIONAL TRADE AND WITH EQUILIBRIUM UNEMPLOYMENT (2010).

16. *See, e.g.*, JOSEPH STIGLITZ, MAKING GLOBALIZATION WORK (2006); DANI RODRIK, ONE ECONOMICS, MANY RECIPES: GLOBALIZATION, INSTITUTIONS, AND ECONOMIC GROWTH (2008).

17. Carl Davidson & Steven Matusz, *Globalization and Labour Market Adjustment: How Fast and at What Cost?*, 16(3) OXFORD REV. ECON. POLICY 42 (2000).

18. *See* GARY BANKS & JAN TUMLIR, ECONOMIC POLICY AND THE ADJUSTMENT PROBLEM ch. 3 (1986) [Banks & Tumlir].

19. *See* TREBILCOCK ET AL., *supra* note 2.

20. This provision itself was borrowed from similar provisions in previous bilateral trade treaties. The Treaty of Paris, which established the European Coal and Steel Community in 1951 to promote the integration of coal and steel production in western Europe, contemplated various forms of "orderly" adjustment in furtherance of this goal. The Treaty of Rome, which established the European Economic Community in 1957, provided for a social fund to help workers adjust to liberalized European trade. In the United States the Trade Expansion Act of 1962 provided for assistance to firms and workers to ease adjustments to tariff concessions agreed to in the Kennedy Round of multilateral trade negotiations. In Canada, the Canadian-American Automotive Agreement of 1965 (the auto

pact) provided for forms of adjustment assistance to firms and workers affected by the agreement. The General Adjustment Assistance Program, which Canada adopted in 1968, provided adjustment assistance to firms under import pressure as a result of Kennedy Round tariff cuts. These and other early examples of programs designed to address the adjustment costs of trade imports were generally not widely used, in part because of the high growth rates that characterized most industrialized economies throughout the 1950s and 1960s.

21. Henceforth, for the sake of conciseness, I use the term "adjustment costs."

22. Louis Kaplow, *An Economic Analysis of Legal Transitions*, 99 HAR. L. REV. 509 (1986) [Kaplow].

23. *See* Robert Howse & Michael Trebilcock, *Protecting the Employment Bargain*, 43 U. TORONTO L.J. 751(1993).

24. These possible market failures do not, of course, suggest that government is any better at ex ante allocation of risks of job loss from trade.

25. JON ELSTER, SOUR GRAPES: STUDIES IN THE SUBVERSION OF RATIONALITY (1983).

26. C.R. LEANA & D.C. FELDMAN, COPING WITH JOB LOSS: HOW INDIVIDUALS, ORGANIZATIONS AND COMMUNITIES RESPOND TO LAYOFFS (1992).

27. MICHAEL TREBILCOCK. THE POLITICAL ECONOMY OF ECONOMIC ADJUSTMENT, Royal Commission of the Economic Union and Development Prospects for Canada, Collected Research Studies (1985); John Quinn & Michael Trebilcock, *Compensation, Transition Costs, and Regulatory Change*, 32 U. TORONTO L.J. 117 (1982).

28. *See* CHRISTOPHER GREEN, INDUSTRIAL POLICY: THE FIXITIES HYPOTHESIS (1984); M. Olson, *Beyond the Measuring Rod of Money: The Unification of Economics and Other Social Sciences*, University of Toronto Faculty of Law, Law and Economics Workshop, 1985).

29. JOHN RAWLS, A THEORY OF JUSTICE (1971).

30. GUIDO CALABRESI, THE COSTS OF ACCIDENTS: A LEGAL AND ECONOMIC ANALYSIS 109 (1970).

31. SMITH, *supra* note 3.

32. Helen Milner, *The Political Economy of International Trade*, 2(19) ANNUAL REV. POLITICAL SCI. 114 (1999).

33. *See* Hadi Salehi Esfahani, *Searching for the (Dark) Forces behind Protectionism*, 57(2) OXFORD ECON. PAPERS 283 (2005); Richard Caves, *Economic Models of Political Choice*, 9(2) CAN. J. ECON. 284 (1976).

34. ROBERT BALDWIN, THE POLITICAL ECONOMY OF US IMPORT POLICY (1986).

35. *See* James Cassing, Arle Hillman & Ngo Van Long, *Risk Aversion, Terms of Trade Uncertainty and Trade Policy*, 3(4) J. WELFARE & ECON. 389 (1986); David Newbery & Joseph Stiglitz, *Pareto Inferior Trade*, 51(1) REV. ECON. STUDIES (1984).

36. *See* BALDWIN, *supra* note 34; Mancur Olson, *The Political Economy of Comparative Growth Rates, in* THE POLITICAL ECONOMY OF GROWTH (Dennis Mueller, ed.,1983).

37. DOUGLAS IRWIN, PETROS MAVROIDIS & ALAN SYKES, THE GENESIS OF THE GATT (2008) [Irwin, Mavroidis & Sykes].

38. Cassing et al., *supra* note 35.

39. IRWIN ET AL., *supra* note 37 (Terms-of-trade are defined as the price of a country's exports relative to its imports. Because a small country is generally unable to improve its terms-of-trade, it may seek to improve its access to foreign markets via multi- or bilateral

trade agreements. This theory also suggests that larger countries will want to set an "optimal" tariff. This "optimal" tariff will offset the losses from reduced volume of trade with an improvement in their own terms-of-trade).

40. IRWIN ET AL., *supra* note 37.

41. *Id.*

42. Paul Krugman, *What Should Trade Negotiators Negotiate About*, 35 J. ECON. LITERATURE 113 (1997).

43. *See* Wilfred Ethier, *Political Externalities, Nondiscrimination, and a Multilateral World*, 12 REV. INT'L ECON. 303 (2004). (The representatives tended to state that they wanted to access foreign markets).

44. IRWIN ET AL., *supra* note 37; *see more generally* Robert Putnam, *Diplomacy and Domestic Politics: The Logic of Two-Level Games*, 42 INT'L ORG. 427 (1988).

45. *Id.*

46. *Id.*

47. IRWIN ET AL., *supra* note 37, at 185.

48. *Id.*

49. This theory is associated with the work of Charles Kindleberger. *See* CHARLES KINDLEBERGER, THE WORLD IN DEPRESSION, 1929–1939 (1973).

50. However, some forms of trade, e.g., in armaments or conflict diamonds may exacerbate conflict.

51. *See* Edward Mansfield & Brian Pollins, *The Study of Interdependence and Conflict: Recent Advances, Open Questions, and Directions for Future Research*, 45 J. CONFLICT RESOLUTION 834 (2001).

52. Many authors assume that individual voters take their preferences from their role as consumers. (See Gene Grossman & Elhanan Helpman, *Protection for Sale*, 84 AM. ECON. REV. 833 (1994)). Other models of individual preferences contradict this. (*See* Wolfgang Maye, *Theoretical Considerations on Negotiated Tariff Adjustments*, 33 OXFORD ECON. PAPERS 135 (1981)).

53. *See* Wendy Takacs, *Pressure for Protection*, 19 ECON. INQUIRY 687 (1981); James Cassing, Timothy McKowen & Jack Ochs, The Political Economy of the Tariff Cycle, 80 AM. POLITICAL SCI. REV. 843 (1986); M. Wallerstein, *Unemployment, Collective Bargaining and the Demand for Protectionism*, 31 AM. J. POLITICAL SCI. 729 (1987).

54. Dani Rodrik, *The Limits to Trade Policy Reform in LDCs*, 6 J. ECON. PERSPECTIVES 87 (1992).

55. *Id.*

56. RICHARDSON, *supra* note 8.

57. The Uruguay Round Agreement permitted developed countries to phase in new tariff commitments over four years, and developing countries over six years. The EPA agreements between the EU and ACP countries envisage full implementation over 25 years. NAFTA generally adopted a 10-year phase-in period.

58. *See* Kaplow *supra* note 22; BANKS & TUMLIR, *supra* note 18.

59. Michael Mussa, *Dynamic Adjustment in the Heckscher-Ohlin-Samuelson Model*, 86(5) J. POLITICAL ECON. 775 (1978).

60. In an analysis of UK New Earnings Survey Panel Dataset, Haynes et al. found that wage changes for movers are almost always positive and greater than wage changes for stayers, which led the authors to suggest that the majority of the job changes were

resignations rather than layoffs. (Michelle Haynes, Richard Upward & Peter Wright, *Estimating the Wage Costs of Inter- and Intrasectoral Adjustment* (2710 CEPR Discussion Paper, 2000).

61. MARC BACCHETTA & MARION JANSEN, ADJUSTING TO TRADE LIBERALIZATION: THE ROLE OF POLICY, INSTITUTIONS AND WTO DISCIPLINES (World Trade Organization Special Study, 2003) [Bacchetta & Jansen].

62. Mussa, *supra* note 59.

63. Francois et al., *supra* note 9.

64. Joaquin Maudos, Jose Pastor & Francisco Perez, *Competition and Efficiency in the Spanish Banking Sector: The Importance of Specialization*, 12(7), APPLIED FIN. ECON. 505 (2002).

65. MICHAEL TREBILCOCK, UNDERSTANDING TRADE LAW (2011) at 4–6.

66. Krugman, *supra* note 42.

67. *See* KYLE BAGWELL & ROBERT STAIGER, THE ECONOMICS OF THE WORLD TRADING SYSTEM (2002).

68. RICHARDSON, *supra* note 8.

69. TREBILCOCK, *supra* note 65.

70. Additionally, within the GATT/WTO framework, countries are also able to impose restrictions to safeguard the balance-of-payments (Article XII and XVIII.B) when a country's external financial position has experienced an unsustainable deterioration. Tariff renegotiation is also contemplated in the GATT (Article XXVII), but this permanent change in tariff structure is not generally considered an appropriate response to a temporary adjustment problem.

71. TREBILCOCK, *supra* note 65, chap. 8.

72. *Id.* at 94.

73. Carl Davidson & Steven Matusz, *An Overlapping-Generations Model of Escape Clause Protection*, 12(5) REV. INT'L ECON. 749 (2004).

74. Alan Sykes, *The Safeguards Mess: A Critique of Appellate Body Jurisprudence*, 2 WORLD TRADE REV. 261 (2003).

75. DANI RODRIK, THE GLOBALIZATION PARADOX: DEMOCRACY AND THE FUTURE OF THE GLOBAL ECONOMY 83 (2011).

76. Sykes, *supra* note 74.

77. *Id.*

78. *See* Alan Sykes, *The Persistent Puzzles of Safeguards: Lessons from the Steel Dispute*, 7(3) J. INT'L ECON. LAW 523 (2004).

79. TREBILCOCK, *supra* note 65.

80. *See generally* MICHAEL TREBILCOCK, ROBERT HOWSE, AND ANTONIA ELIASON, THE REGULATION OF INTERNATIONAL TRADE ch. 11 (4th ed. 2012).

81. Canada 1989, xvii. Advisory Council on Adjustment. *Adjusting to Win.* Ottawa: Supply and Services Canada.] The council was chaired by A.J. Grandpre.

82. Francois et al., *supra* note 9.

83. *Id.*

84. *Id.*

85. *See* LORI KLETZER, JOB LOSS FROM IMPORTS: MEASURING THE COSTS (Institute for International Economics, 2001); Avraham Ebenstein, Ann Harrison & Margaret McMillan, *Estimating the Impact of Trade and Offshoring Using the Current Population Surveys* (NBER Working Paper, 2009).

86. *See more generally* VARIETIES OF CAPITALISM: THE INSTITUTIONAL FOUNDATIONS OF COMPARATIVE ADVANTAGE (Peter A. Hall & David Soskice eds., 2001) and Kathleen Thelen, *Varieties of Capitalism: Trajectories of Liberalization and the New Politics of Social Solidarity*, 15(1) ANN. REV. POLITCAL SCI. 137 (2012).

87. MORLEY GUNDERSON, ACTIVE LABOUR MARKET ADJUSTMENT POLICIES: WHAT WE KNOW AND DON'T KNOW (2003). Report prepared for the Ontario Role of Government Panel.

88. OECD 2005.

89. JAN BOONE & JAN VAN OURS, EFFECTIVE ACTIVE LABOR MARKET POLICIES (Centre for Policy Research, 2004).

90. James Heckman, Robert LaLonde & Jeffrey Smith, *The Economics and Econometrics of Active Labour Market Programs, in* HANDBOOK OF LABOUR AND ECONOMICS (1999) (This study found that, overall, active labor market programs have a positive impact on participants' labor market prospects; however the results vary widely across programs).

91. Gordon Betcherman, Karina Olivas & Amit Dar, *Impacts of Active Labor Market Programs: New Evidence from Evaluation with Particular Attention to Developing and Transition Countries* (World Bank Social Protection Discussion Paper Series 2004).

92. John Martin & David Grubb, *What Works and for Whom: A Review*, 8(9) SWEDISH ECON. POLICY REV. 56 (2001) [Martin & Grubb].

93. *See* C. Gorter & G. Kalb, *Estimating the Effect of Counseling and Monitoring of the Unemployed Using a Job Search Model*, 31 J. HUMAN RESOURCES 590 (1996).

94. Martin & Grubb, *supra* note 92.

95. *Id.*

96. David Card, Jochen Kluve & Andrea Weber, *Active Labour Market Policy Evaluations* 120(548) ECON. J. F452 (2010).

97. Heckman et al., *supra* note 90.

98. John Martin, *What Works among Active Labour Market Policies: Evidence from OECD Countries' Experiences*, 30(79) OECD ECON. STUDIES 113 (2000).

99. William Craig Riddell, *Human Capital Formation in Canada: Recent Developments and Policy Responses, in* LABOUR MARKET POLARIZATION AND SOCIAL POLICY REFORM 125–72 (Keith Banting & C.M. Beach eds., 1995).

100. P. TREH'RNING, MEASURES TO COMBAT UNEMPLOYMENT IN SWEDEN (1993).

101. Anders Forslund & Alan Krueger, *Did Active Labour Market Policies Help Sweden Rebound from the Depression of the Early 1990s?, in* RICHARD FREEMAN, BIRGITTA SWEDENBORG & ROBERT TOPEL, REFORMING THE WELFARE STATE: RECOVERY AND BEYOND IN SWEDEN (2010).

102. Kenneth Carling & Katarina Richardson, *The Relative Efficiency of Labour Market Programs: Swedish Experience from the 1990s*, 11(3) LABOUR ECON. 335 (2004).

103. Robert Fay, *Enhancing the Effectiveness of Active Labour Policies: Evidence from Programme Evaluations in OECD Countries* 22 (OECD Labour Market and Social Policy Occasional Papers No. 18, 1996).

104. Examples of trade-specific adjustment programs include the European Globalization Fund in the European Union and the Trade Adjustment Assistance program in the United States. The European Globalization Adjustment Fund (EGF) was implemented by the European Union in 2006. In order to be eligible for assistance from this fund, a request must be made by a member state indicating that at least 500 jobs have been lost in a firm or in a sector within a region due to changing world trade patterns. The fund

provides support in the form of job-search assistance, and training and job-search allowances to individuals participating in long-term remedial training programs. The US Trade Adjustment Assistance program is discussed below.

105. Michael Trebilcock, *The Political Economy of Economic Adjustment*, in ROYAL COMMISSION ON THE ECONOMIC UNION AND DEVELOPMENT PROSPECTS FOR CANADA (1985).

106. Kara Reynolds & John Palatucci, *Does Trade Adjustment Assistance Make a Difference*, 30(1) CONTEMPORARY ECON. POLICY 43 (2012).

107. *Id.*

108. *Id.*

109. Francois et al., *supra* note 9.

110. BACCHETTA & JANSEN, *supra* note 61.

111. *See generally* TREBILCOCK, HOWSE & ELIASON, *supra* note 80, ch. 11.

112. Kaplow, *supra* note 22.

Chapter 6

1. Figures reflect the average PSE for the 2008–2010 period (rounded to the nearest half percent) as estimated by the OECD; OECD, AGRICULTURAL POLICY MONITORING AND EVALUATION 2011: OECD COUNTRIES AND EMERGING ECONOMIES 278–79 (2011).

2. See discussion of policy instruments in EDWARD IACOBUCCI, MICHAEL TREBILCOCK & HUMA HAIDER, ECONOMIC SHOCKS: DEFINING A ROLE FOR GOVERNMENT 169–83 (2001).

3. This discussion of global trade measures is based on MICHAEL J. TREBILCOCK, UNDERSTANDING TRADE LAW 101 (2011).

4. *See, e.g.*, Cameron G. Thies & Schuyler Porche, *The Political Economy of Agricultural Protection*, 69 J. POLITICS 116 (2007).

5. Danielle Goldfarb, *Making Milk: The Practices, Players, and Pressures behind Dairy Supply Management* 20 (The Conference Board of Canada, 2009) (estimate for 2008); Statistics Canada, *Balance Sheet of the Agricultural Sector* (Catalogue no. 21-016-X, at 37 (Jan. 2011) (estimating the value of all agricultural quotas in Canada in 2008 at $30.2 billion); OECD, *Modernising Canada's Agricultural Policies*, OECD ECONOMIC SURVEYS: CANADA 141 (2008) (estimating the value of the dairy quota in 2006 to be $26 billion).

6. Gordon Tullock, *The Transitional Gains Trap*, 6 BELL J. ECON. 671 (1975).

7. For a detailed discussion of the program, see OECD, *supra* note 5; Goldfarb, *supra* note 5. *See also* Michael Hart, *Great Wine, Better Cheese: How Canada Can Escape the Trap of Agricultural Supply Management* (C.D. Howe Institute Backgrounder No. 90, Apr. 2005); Owen Lippert, *The Perfect Food in a Perfect Mess: The Cost of Milk in Canada* (Fraser Institute, Nov. 2001); William Robson & Colin Busby, *Freeing up Food: The Ongoing Cost, and Potential Reform, of Supply Management* (C.D. Howe Institute Backgrounder No 128, Apr. 2010); W.T. Stanbury, *The Politics of Milk in Canada* (The Fraser Institute, Aug. 30, 2002); Martha Hall Findlay, *Supply Management: Problems, Politics and Possibilities* (University of Calgary School of Public Policy, SPP Research Papers 5:19, June 2012).

8. Goldfarb, *supra* note 5, at 8–10. Robson and Busby argue that replacing average production costs in price-setting formulas with the costs of the most efficient producer would introduce a modicum of competition to the industry; *supra* note 7.

9. OECD, *supra* note 5, at 138.

10. Goldfarb, *supra* note 5, at 11. *See* Canadian Dairy Commission Act, RSC 1985, c C-15, s 8.

11. Goldfarb, *supra* note 5, at 11. For example, in 2009 dairy farmers' profit margins were 21 percent, compared with 3 percent for cattle farmers and 2 percent for pig and hog farmers; Statistics Canada, *Farm Financial Survey 2009*, at 55, 63, 47 (Catalogue no. 21F0008X, Mar. 2011).

12. *Id.* at 10; Lippert, *supra* note 7, at 74.

13. The current CDC head, Jacques Laforge, is a former CEO of Dairy Farmers of Canada (DFC), a producer group; this is typical. *See* Sylvain Charlebois, Wolfgang Langenbacher & Robert D Tamilia, *The Canadian Dairy Commission: An Empirical Survey on Its Relevance in Today's Civil Society*, 10 INT'L FOOD & AGRIBUS. MGMT. 81, 83 (2007).

14. Goldfarb, *supra* note 5, at 8; Lippert, *supra* note 7, at 27.

15. *See, e.g.*, OECD, *supra* note 5, at 139.

16. Goldfarb, *supra* note 5, at 19; Lippert, *supra* note 7, at 29-30.

17. Statistics Canada, *Dairy Cows by Province on January 1st* (Table 003-0032, Sept. 14, 2011);: http://www.statcan.gc.ca/tables-tableaux/sum-som/l01/cst01/prim50a-eng.htm Canadian Dairy Information Centre.

18. *See* Al Mussell & Ted Bilyea, *At Odds with Stated Objectives: Increasing Industrial Milk Prices in Canada* 8 (George Morris Centre Special Report, July 16, 2008); Goldfarb, *supra* note 5, at 21.

19. Goldfarb, *supra* note 5, at 20.

20. Richard Barichello, John Cranfield & Karl Meilke, *Options for Reform of Supply Management in Canada with Trade Liberalization*, 35 CAN. PUBLIC POLICY 203, 210 (2009).

21. Goldfarb, *supra* note 5.

22. By comparison, the Canadian federal deficit was $23.5 billion in the 2012 fiscal year; *Federal Deficit $23.5B, Early Data Shows*, CAN. PRESS (May 25, 2012), online http://www.cbc.ca/news/business/federal-deficit-23-5b-early-data-shows-1.1270817.

23. World Trade Organisation, *Tariff Download Facility*, online http://tariffdata.wto.org/Default.aspx?culture=en-US.

24. Przemyslaw Kowalskil, *The Canadian Preferential Tariff Regime and Potential Economic Effects of Its Erosion*, *in* TRADE PREFERENCE EROSION: MANAGEMENT AND POLICY RESPONSE 132 (Bernard M. Hoekman, Will Martin & Carlos Alberto Primo Braga eds., 2009).

25. *See, e.g.*, MICHAEL J. TREBILCOCK, ROBERT HOWSE & ANTONIA ELIASON, THE REGULATION OF INTERNATIONAL TRADE ch. 12 (4th ed. 2012).

26. Demand for dairy products in Canada is only moderately elastic; see Goldfarb, *supra* note 5, at 28.

27. Marcel Boyer & Sylvain Charlebois, Economic Note: *Supply Management of Farm Products: A Costly System for Consumers* 3 (Montreal Economic Institute, Aug. 2007).

28. Between 1995 and 2009 the overall consumer price index rose 39 percent, as did food prices generally, while dairy prices rose 51 persent; Robson & Busby, *supra* note 7, at 6.

29. This amount is the producer single commodity transfer figure, reflecting only commodity-specific transfers from taxpayers and consumers to milk producers. As the amount of taxpayer subsidization of dairy producers is nearly negligible, this figure reflects a wealth transfer from consumers rather than from consumers and taxpayers. OECD, *supra* note 1, at 301.

30. *Id.*

31. OECD, *supra* note 5, at 140. *See also* Goldfarb, *supra* note 5; James Milway et al., *The Poor Still Pay More: Challenges Low-Income Families Face in Consuming a Nutritious Diet* 9 (Institute for Competitiveness and Prosperity & Open Policy Ontario, Dec. 2010).

32. Goldfarb, *supra* note 5, at 14.

33. *See* OECD, *supra* note 1, at 300.

34. A recent study noted that the average retail price of four liters of whole milk in 2012 is 260 percent of that in the United States ($5.92 higher); Findlay, *supra* note 7, at 9.

35. OECD, *supra* note 5, at 140.

36. Statistics Canada estimates that the population of Canada was 34,126,181; *Statistics Canada, Population by Year, by Province and Territory* (CANSIM, Database, Table 051-0001), online http://www.statcan.gc.ca/tables-tableaux/sum-som/l01/cst01/demo02a-eng.htm (accessed Sept 14, 2011).

37. Statistics Canada, "Food and Other Selected Items, Average Retail Prices" (CANSIM, Table 326-0012 and Catalogue 62-001-X, June 22, 2012), online. http://www.statcan.gc.ca/tables-tableaux/sum-som/l01/cst01/econ155a-eng.htm

38. Milway et al., *supra* note 31, at 12. *See also* The Frontier Centre for Public Policy, "Marketing Boards and the Poor: Let Them Drink Soda Pop"(Fax from the Frontier FF171, Oct. 29, 2001); Lawrence Solomon, *Dairy Farmers are Milking Canadian Consumers*, NAT'L POST (Jan. 16, 2001), online http://urbanrenaissance.probeinternational.org/2001/01/16/dairy-farmers-are-milking-canadian-consumers.

39. Milway et al., *supra* note 31, at 9.

40. Boyer & Charlebois, *supra* note 27, at 2; Goldfarb, *supra* note 5, at 14 (noting that consumer prices rose in line with inflation from 1998 to 2004 and faster than inflation from 2004 to 2008)

41. Statistics Canada, *Food Available Adjusted for Losses by Major Group, Per Person—Dairy and Eggs* (Table 2-4), *in* FOOD STATISTICS (Catalogue No 21-020-XWE, May 27, 2010), online. http://www.statcan.gc.ca/pub/21-020-x/2009001/t016-eng.htm

42. Health Canada, *Canada Food Guide* (Sept. 2011), online http://www.hc-sc.gc.ca/fn-an/food-guide-aliment/index-eng.php.

43. United States Department of Agriculture, *Dairy Health Benefits and Nutrients*" (ChooseMyPlate), last visited November 2012:online http://www.choosemyplate.gov/food-groups/dairy-why.html.

44. Boyer & Charlebois, *supra* note 27, at 3.

45. Statistics Canada, *supra* note 11, at 47.

46. Lars Osberg, *A Quarter Century of Economic Inequality in Canada: 1981–2006*, at 25 (Canadian Centre for Policy Alternatives, Apr. 2008).

47. Statistics Canada, *supra* note 11, at 47.

48. "If you made more than $63,350 in 2007, you made more than 90% of Canadian taxfilers;" Armine Yalnizyan, *The Rise of Canada's Richest 1%*, at 10 (Canadian Centre for Policy Alternatives, Dec. 2010). That year dairy farmers averaged above $97,000 in net income (after interest charges, family wages, etc.); Statistics Canada, *supra* note 11, at 47. In 2009, the year of the latest Farm Financial Survey, dairy farmers' net income was on average $108,000; *id.*

49. Yalnizyan, *supra* note 48, at 11.

50. Population figures rounded to the nearest integer and calculated using figures in Statistics Canada, *supra* note 36.

51. Statistics Canada, *supra* note 17.

52. In 2010, total agricultural support from taxpayers and consumers (PSE) amounted to an estimated $7.65 billion, of which $3.587 billion, or 47 percent, went to dairy farmers. OECD, *supra* note 1, at 301.

53. Statistics Canada, *Snapshot of Canadian Agriculture* (2006), *available at* http://www.statcan.gc.ca/ca-ra2006/articles/snapshot-portrait-eng.htm.

54. *Id. See also* OECD, *supra* note 5, at 141.

55. OECD, *supra* note 5, at 143

56. *See supra* note 1. In 2010 alone, PSE was 7 percent in the United States, 18 percent in Canada, and 20 percent in the European Union; OECD, *supra* note 1, at 278–79.

57. *See* Laura Dawson, *Can Canada Join the Trans-Pacific Partnership? Why Wanting It Is Not Enough* (C.D. Howe Institute Commentary No. 340, Feb. 2012); Michael Gifford, *Golden Opportunities and Surmountable Challenges: Prospects for Canadian Agriculture in Asia* (Canadian Council of Chief Executives, Apr. 2012); Findlay, *supra* note 7.

58. Quoted in Hart, *supra* note 7, at 6.

59. *See id.* at 1; Bill Dymond & Michael Hart, *Navigating New Trade Routes: The Rise of Value Chains, and the Challenges for Canadian Trade* 1 (C.D. Howe Institute Commentary no 259, Mar. 2008).

60. Findlay, *supra* note 7, at 13.

61. Daniel Schwanen, *Go Big or Go Home: Priorities for the Canada-EU Economic and Trade Agreement* (C.D. Howe Institute Backgrounder No 143, Oct. 2011).

62. Agriculture and Agri-Food Canada, *An Overview of the Canadian Agriculture and Agri-Food System 2012*, at xiii (Public Works and Government Services Canada, Publication 11660E, Mar. 2012).

63. *See* Al Mussel & Larry Martin, *Canadian Dairy Export Subsidies and the WTO Appellate Decision: Dairy Market Expansion in Limbo* (Special Report, The George Morris Centre, Feb. 2000).

64. Canada's dairy exports totaled $252 million in 2011; Canadian Dairy Information Centre, *Canadian Dairy Exports* (July 2012), online http://www.dairyinfo.gc.ca/index_e.php?s1=pb&s2=trade . Overall agriculture exports in Canada amounted to $35.5 billion in 2010; Agriculture and Agri-Food Canada, *supra* note 62. As noted above (note 40), Canadian dairy consumption is in decline, dropping in 2009 to its lowest level since 1975. Additionally, in the face of inflated dairy prices, imports of milk alternatives have risen significantly relative to domestic milk production; Informa Economics, *An International Comparison of Milk Supply Programs and Their Impacts* 11 (prepared for International Dairy Foods Association, Washington, DC, Sept. 2010).

65. Canadian dairy exports account for a mere 1 percent of the world export trade, whereas New Zealand controls roughly 36 percent of it. Canada's and the EU's share of world dairy exports both dropped over the 1996–2010 period, while countries such as the United States and New Zealand, with partial or no dairy price support, have seen their market share rise; Informa Economics, *supra* note 64, at 11–12.

66. *See* Goldfarb, *supra* note 5, at 2–3.

67. *Id.* at 6.

68. Stanbury, *supra* note 7, at 15–16.

69. *See, e.g.*, MICHAEL TREBILCOCK, DOUGLAS HARTLE, ROBERT PRICHARD & DONALD DEWEES, THE CHOICE OF GOVERNING INSTRUMENT 9–10 (1982).

70. MANCUR OLSON, THE LOGIC OF COLLECTIVE ACTION: PUBLIC GOODS AND THE THEORY OF GROUPS, Harvard Economic Studies CXXIV (1971).

71. Gary S. Becker, *A Theory of Competition among Pressure Groups for Political Influence*, 98 Q. J. Econ. 371, 395 (1983).

72. Canadian Dairy Commission (CDC), *Number of Farms with Shipments of Milk or Cream on August 1st* (AIMIS Table, June 12, 2012), online: Canadian Dairy Information Centre. http://aimis-simia-cdic-ccil.agr.gc.ca/rp/index-eng.cfm?action=pR&r=220&pdctc=]

73. Stanbury, *supra* note 7, at 10.

74. *Supra* note 36.

75. There were 12,965 dairy farms in 2010; CDC, *supra* note 72. This number was divided into the total $3.587 billion in single commodity transfers to dairy producers in 2010; OECD, *supra* note 1.

76. Stanbury, *supra* note 7, at 16. *See also* Findlay, noting that many politicians admit privately that supply management should be dismantled, but say "'politically, it's not possible' [or] 'there are too many votes at stake;'" *supra* note 7, at 2.

77. *See, e.g.*, Charlebois et al., *supra* note 13, at 86–87.

78. OECD, *supra* note 5, at 143.

79. TREBILCOCK ET AL., *supra* note 25, at 327–28.

80. *See, e.g.*, discussion in IACOBUCCI ET AL., *supra* note 2.

81. Informa Economics, *supra* note 64, at 3, 7.

82. *See* Hart, *supra* note 7, at 4–5; Stanbury, *supra* note 7, at 11–12.

83. TREBILCOCK ET. AL., *supra* note 25, at 327. *See also* Hart, *supra* note 4, at 4.

84. Barry Wilson & Peter Finkle, *Is Agriculture Different? Another Round in the Battle between Theory and Practice*, in *Agricultural Trade: Domestic Pressures and International Tensions* 17 (G. Skogstad & A.F. Cooper eds., 1990).

85. *See, e.g.*, Informa Economics, *supra* note 64 (concluding that dairy supply control programs in the European Union and Canada "have not reduced price volatility or slowed the decline in farm exits," "have constrained dairy industry and job growth," have "created an economic incentive for imports," and may have limited dairy consumption growth in those countries). For a discussion of communitarian values in this context see Trebilcock & Howse, *supra* note 25 at 328; Stanbury, *supra* note 7, at 11–12; Hart, *supra* note 7, at 4.

86. Megumi Naoi & Ikuo Kume, *Explaining Mass Support for Agricultural Protectionism: Evidence from a Survey Experiment during the Global Recession*, 65 INT'L ORG. 771 (2011).

87. *See, e.g.*, Alan MacIsaac, *The Case for Supply Management*, 31(3) CAN. PARL. REV. 18, 19 (2008).

88. *See, e.g.*, Robson & Busby, *supra* note 7, at 1; *but see* Findlay, *supra* note 7.

89. SC 2011, c 26.

90. Findlay, *supra* note 7, at 25.

91. Robson & Busby, *supra* note 7, at 1; Jean-Francois Minardi, *What Does the Future Hold for Quebec Agriculture?* 5–6 (Fraser Institute, Fraser Alert, Feb. 2009); Stanbury, *supra* note 7, at 17 ("Quebec wields enormous power in Ottawa....[It] loves to see those large income transfers...to each of its dairy farmers").

92. Al Mussell, *Does Canada Need to Dismantle Supply Management in the Trans-Pacific Partnership?* at 6 (George Morris Centre, June 2012). See also the discussion of the

contribution of federalism and other institutional features of local political systems to the entrenchment of agricultural protectionism in Thies & Porche, *supra* note 4.

93. See Tullock, *supra* note 6.

94. *See, e.g., supra* note 7.

95. Robson & Busby, *supra* note 7. See also Barichello et al., *supra* note 20.

96. Michael Trebilcock, *The Choice of Governing Instrument: A Retrospective, in* DESIGNING GOVERNMENT 68 (P. Eliades, M.M. Hill & M. Howlett eds., 2005).

97. *See* TREBILCOCK ET AL., *supra* note 69, at 18 ("Frequently voters seem satisfied with illusionary benefits and not antagonized by real though indirect ('hidden') costs").

98. *But see* Stanbury, *supra* note 7; Findlay, *supra* note 7. Martha Hall Findlay, for example, downplays the political difficulty of dairy reform, citing the dwindling number of dairy farmers, and their concentration in ridings that were not marginal in the most recent election and in which they are outnumbered by export-oriented farmers. This view may overemphasize numerical advantages and downplay many of the political factors discussed above. However, though her article suggests the risks to politicians of proposing reform are "negligible" (at i) she concedes that one must "mobilize" non–supply-managed farmers and "rally the ire of the consumers" to benefit from their support.

99. A restaurant group recently set up an online and media campaign, Free Your Milk, offering facts about the high price of dairy in Canada compared to the United States and elsewhere; Canadian Restaurant and Foodservices Association, *Free Your Milk* (Oct. 2011), *available at* http://freeyourmilk.ca. In response, the Dairy Farmers of Canada (DFC) started a counter-campaign called Stand Up For Your Milk (yourmilk.ca). Similarly, in 2004 the DFC carried out and publicized a survey claiming to show that Canadians pay less for dairy than Americans, though a critical paper argued that the survey's "methodological inconsistencies did not warrant such a sweeping conclusion" and that the survey's aim was to desensitize consumers to high consumer prices; Charlebois et al., *supra* note 13, at 91.

100. *See* Charlebois et al., *supra* note 13.

101. Between 1992 and 2009 dairy farm numbers fell almost uniformly in Canada, the United States, and the European Union, at a rate of roughly 60 percent, while farm numbers fell just 20 percent in New Zealand, an undistorted market; Informa Economics, *supra* note 64, at 5.

102. Charlebois et al., *supra* note 13, at 86–87.

103. *Id.* at 86. Though supply management keeps farm gate prices (which processors pay) double or triple world dairy prices (see Goldfarb, *supra* note 5, at 12–13), the Dairy Processors Association of Canada website describes supply management in a positive light; DPAC, *Regulatory Framework* (Mar. 8, 2012), *available at* http://www.dpac-atlc.ca/framework.php. A key member of DPAC, Agropur, is run by dairy farmers; Goldfarb, *supra* note 5, at 5. *See also* Findlay, *supra* note 7, at 9–10 (noting that export restrictions imposed by the WTO because of supply management limit global opportunities for processors).

104. Findlay, *supra* note 7, at 14.

105. *See, e.g.*, Gifford, *supra* note 57.

106. Nor is the support of such farmers' groups assured. For example, the Canadian Pork Council, a producer group, has publicly pushed for increased access to foreign markets under prospective trade deals, but at the same time, its executive director, Martin Rice, has argued that poultry supply management is good for pork producers as it "contributes to pork's higher market share" in Canada; Martin Rice, *Discussion: Canadian*

Pork Council, in Proceedings of the Fourth Agricultural and Food Policy Systems Information Workshop: Economic Harmonization in the Canadian/US/Mexican Grain-Livestock Subsector 157–59, 157 (R.M.A. Lyons, Ronald D. Knutson & Karl Meilke eds. Dec. 1998).

107. Naoi & Kume, *supra* note 86, at 791 ("our finding suggests that even subtle manipulation to draw citizens' attention to one aspect of their lives can substantially change the landscape of coalitions in the global economy").

108. David Strömberg has offered empirical evidence to support this idea: in a study of radio use in 3,000 US counties in the 1930s, he found that counties with a larger share of radios were more successful in attracting government relief funds; *Radio's Impact on New Deal Spending*, 119 Q.J. Econ. 189 (2004); *see also* Timothy Besley & Robin Burgess, *The Political Economy of Government Responsiveness: Theory and Evidence from India*, 117 Q.J. Econ. 1415 (2002); Andrea Prat & David Strömberg, *The Political Economy of Mass Media* 45 (Centre for Economic Policy Research Discussion Paper No DP8246, Feb. 2011); David Strömberg, *Mass Media Competition, Political Competition, and Public Policy*, 71 Rev. Econ. Stud. 265, 269 (2004).

109. Strömberg, *supra* note 108. Mass media profits depend largely on advertising revenues, which in turn depend in part on the larger size of the market reached; *see* Trebilcock et al., *supra* note 68, at 15. Further, although the fixed cost of producing a story or a single newspaper may be high, the variable cost of delivering news to more consumers is lower, resulting in increasing returns-to-scale; Strömberg, *supra* note 108, at 2.

110. For example, as Canada negotiated entry to talks toward the TPP in late 2011 and early 2012, media reporting on the issue appeared to increase substantially.

111. In New Zealand farmers recognized that heavy subsidies were not sustainable; OECD, *supra* note 5, at 144. In Australia, farmers in the major "industrial milk" state of Victoria supported removal of supply management, as it was less profitable for farmers who made milk for processing (in contrast to fluid milk); *id.* In addition, rapid growth in the importation of dairy products from countries such as New Zealand increasingly undercut support for industrial milk, and the decision of the Victoria government to deregulate made supply management systems in other states unviable. The impetus for reform was a competition policy review that concluded that milk price controls did not provide a net benefit to the community. Eighty-nine percent of Victoria dairy farmers then voted in favor of a deregulation proposal. *See* David Harris, *Industry Adjustment to Policy Reform: A Case Study of the Australian Dairy Industry* 15 (Australia Rural Industries Research and Development Corporation, Publication No 05/110, Aug. 2005).

112. *See* Colin Busby & Daniel Schwanen, Commentary: *Putting the Market Back in Dairy Marketing* 374 (C.D. Howe Institute, 2013).

113. *See, e.g.*, Mussell, *supra* note 92, at 7.

114. Harris, *supra* note 111, at xi.

115. *Id.*

116. *Id.* at xi–xii.

117. *Id.* at 1, 15.

118. *Id.* at 16.

119. *Id.*

120. Valentin Petkantchin, *Reforming Dairy Supply Management in Canada: The Australian Example* 4 (Montreal Economic Institute, Jan. 2006). Prices for generic brand milk fell 16 percent within a year; Harris, *supra* note 111, at 30.

121. Harris, *supra* note 111, at 30.

122. *Id.* at 58.

123. Robson & Busby, *supra* note 7, at 8.

124. *Id.* at 8–9.

125. According to the model; *id.* at 9.

126. Another study presents a third way, the "two-quota option." Farmers would have the choice to trade-in for new quotas by selling old quotas at full price to a government agency and simultaneously buying cheaper new quotas that entailed no price support; Barichello et al., *supra* note 20, at 213–14. This proposal, which requires government funds to buy out much of the value of "old" quotas, seems likely to be highly unattractive to governments, especially in lean economic times.

127. Stanbury, *supra* note 7, at 18.

128. In the Australian states where farmers were most reliant on the supply management system before deregulation, 85 percent of respondents to a survey said that transition assistance was important to their restructuring decisions; Harris, *supra* note 111, at 43.

129. In the 2010–2011 year 2.721 billion liters of fluid milk were sold; Canadian Dairy Information Centre, *Fluid Milk Sales in Canada* (Sept. 22, 2011), http://www.dairyinfo.gc.ca/index_e.php?s1=dff-fcil&s2=proc-trans&s3=mcs-vlc&s4=fluid&page=fluidca online.

130. Robson & Busby predict this, *supra* note 7, at 9.

131. Given that supply management provides approximately 60.5 percent of gross dairy farm receipts in Canada (see *supra* note 30 and accompanying text), an early drop in retail prices of this size seems not overly optimistic.

132. Export taxes are permitted under Article XI of the General Agreement on Tariffs and Trade 1994, 15 April 1994, 1867 UNTS 187, 33 ILM 1153.

133. *See* TREBILCOCK, *supra* note 3, at 110–11.

134. Frank I. Michelman, *Property, Utility, and Fairness*, 80(6) HARV. L REV. 1165 (1967).

135. Harris, *supra* note 111, at 24.

136. Barichello et al., *supra* note 20.

137. *See* Kenrick Jordan, *The Canadian Wine Industry: A Summary View* (Special Report from BMO Capital Market Economics, July 6, 2011); Hart, *supra* note 7, at 6–7.

Chapter 7

1. This case study draws extensively on Michael Trebilcock, *The Law and Economics of Immigration Policy*, 5 AM. L. & ECON. REV. 271 (2003), Michael Trebilcock & Matthew Sudak, *The Political Economy of Emigration and Immigration*, 81 N.Y.U. L. REV. 234 (2006), and MICHAEL TREBILCOCK, ROBERT HOWSE, & ANTONIA ELIASON, THE REGULATION OF INTERNATIONAL TRADE ch. 19 (4th ed. 2012).

2. INTERNATIONAL ORGANIZATION FOR MIGRATION, ABOUT MIGRATION (2008).

3. JOEL TRACHTMAN, THE INTERNATIONAL LAW OF ECONOMIC MIGRATION: TOWARD THE FOURTH FREEDOM (2009).

4. *See* Bob Hamilton & John Whalley, *Efficiency and Distributional Implications of Global Restrictions on Labour Mobility: Calculations and Policy Implications*, 14 J. DEV. ECON. 61 (1984).

5. Jonathan Moses & Bjørn Letnes, *The Economic Costs to International Labour Restrictions: Revisiting the Empirical Discussion*, 32 WORLD DEV. 609 (2004); WORLD

BANK INDEPENDENT EVALUATION GROUP, ASSESSING WORLD BANK SUPPORT FOR TRADE 1987-2004, at 31 (2006). For a recent excellent survey of the effects of immigration on receiving countries, sending countries, and immigrants themselves, see IAN GOLDIN, GEOFFREY CAMERON, & MEERA BALARAJAN, EXCEPTIONAL PEOPLE: HOW MIGRATION SHAPED OUR WORLD AND WILL DEFINE OUR FUTURE ch. 6 (2011); Michael Clemens, *Economics and Emigration: Trillion-Dollar Bills on the Sidewalk?* (Centre for Global Development, Working Paper 264, 2011).

6. Hamilton & Whalley, *supra* note 4, at 73–74.

7. *See* Alan Winters & Terrie Walmsley, *Relaxing the Restrictions on Temporary Movements of Natural Persons: A Simulation Analysis*, 20 J. ECON. INTEGRATION 688 (2005); LANT PRITCHETT, LET THEIR PEOPLE COME: BREAKING THE GRIDLOCK ON INTERNATIONAL LABOUR MOBILITY (2006); DANI RODRIK, THE GLOBALIZATION PARADOX: DEMOCRACY AND THE FUTURE OF THE WORLD ECONOMY 266–72 (2011).

8. *See* Douglas Massey, *America's Immigration Policy Fiasco: Learning from Past Mistakes*, 142 *Daedalus* 5, 6 (summer issue 2013))

9. *See* TRACHTMAN, *supra* note 3, ch. 6

10. *See* World Bank, *Overview*, THE WORLD DEVELOPMENT REPORT 2000/2001: ATTACKING POVERTY 3 (2000).

11. *See* Clemens, *supra* note 5; PRITCHETT, *supra* note 7.

12. For more detailed reviews of the welfare effects of immigration, see Trebilcock & Sudak, *supra* note 1; TRACHTMAN, *supra* note 3, ch. 2

13. *See, e.g.*, TERESA HAYTER, OPEN BORDERS: THE CASE AGAINST IMMIGRATION CONTROLS (2000).

14. This is plainly the case given that the modern welfare state provides materially for its own indigent very generously compared to those facing far greater deprivation in many developing countries. Adam Smith long ago recognized the tendency to care more strongly for those closest to us and less strongly for those more removed. *See* ADAM SMITH, THE THEORY OF MORAL SENTIMENTS (Prometheus Books, 2000) (1759); see especially part VI, section II, ch. I, entitled "Of the Order in which Individuals Are Recommended by Nature for Our Care and Attention."

15. A study by George Borjas, Richard Freeman & Lawrence Katz, *How Much Do Immigration and Trade Affect Labor Market Outcomes?* 62–63, 1 BROOKINGS PAPERS ON ECONOMIC ACTIVITY 1 (1997) finds that the adverse labor market impacts of immigration are concentrated primarily on high-school dropouts.

16. *See*. MICHAEL ADAMS, UNLIKELY UTOPIA: THE SURPRISING TRIUMPH OF CANADIAN PLURALISM 13, 14, 17 (2007).

17. *See* JULIAN SIMON, THE ECONOMIC CONSEQUENCES OF IMMIGRATION 377–84 (2d ed. 1999).

18. *See* Noel Gaston & Douglas Nelson, *Immigration and Labour-Market Outcomes in the United States: A Political Economy Puzzle*, 16 OXFORD REV. ECON. POLICY 104 (2000); *see also* NOEL GASTON & DOUGLAS NELSON, THE WAGE AND EMPLOYMENT EFFECTS OF IMMIGRATION: PERSPECTIVES FROM LABOUR AND TRADE ECONOMICS (2000); Howard Chang, *The Economic Impact of International Labour Migration: Recent Estimates and Policy Implications*, 16 TEMPLE POLI. & CIV. RIGHTS L. REV. 321 (2007); PHILIPPE LEGRAIN, IMMIGRANTS: YOUR COUNTRY NEEDS THEM ch. 3, 4, 5, 6, 7 (2006).

19. *See* THE NEW AMERICANS: ECONOMIC, DEMOGRAPHIC, AND FISCAL EFFECTS OF IMMIGRATION (James Smith & Barry Edmonston eds., 1997).

20. *See* Gaston & Nelson, *supra* note 18.
21. MADELINE ZAVODNY, IMMIGRATION AND AMERICAN JOBS (2011).
22. Heidi Shierholz, *Immigration and Wages* (Economic Policy Institute Briefing Paper 255, Feb. 2010).
23. VIVEK WADHWA, THE IMMIGRANT EXODUS: WHY AMERICA IS LOSING THE GLOBAL RACE TO CAPTURE ENTREPRENEURIAL TALENT 22, 33 (2012).
24. *See* VIVEK WADHWA, ANNALEE SAXENIAN & F. DANIEL SICILIANO, THEN AND NOW: AMERICA'S NEW IMMIGRANT ENTREPRENEURS (Oct. 2012).
25. The "NRC study" is in THE NEW AMERICANS, *supra* note 19.
26. *Id.* at 334.
27. Michael Greenstone & Adam Looney, *Ten Economic Facts about Immigration* (The Hamilton Project, Brookings Institute, Sept. 2010).
28. OECD, INTERNATIONAL MIGRATION OUTLOOK ch. 3 (2013).
29. GEORGE BORJAS, HEAVEN'S DOOR: IMMIGRATION POLICY AND THE AMERICAN ECONOMY, (1999).
30. Jeffrey Reitz, *Immigrant Success in the Knowledge Economy: Institutional Change and the Immigrant Experience in Canada 1970–1975*, 57 J. SOCIAL ISSUES 579 (2001); Jeffrey Reitz, *Immigrant Employment Success in Canada*, 8 INT'L MIGRATION & INTEGRATION 11 (2007) and 8 INT'L MIGRATION & INTEGRATION 37 (2007).
31. Arnold De Silva has found that earnings of refugees and economic immigrants differ initially but converge rather quickly in the Canadian labor market. De Silva argues that in Canada, the single most important determinant of labor market success is age and that skills-based screening may be largely ineffectual. *See* Arnold De Silva, *Earnings of Immigrant Classes in the Early 1980s in Canada: A Reexamination*, 23 CAN. PUB. POLICY 179 (1997); for a more recent and detailed evaluation, see CHARLES BEACH, CHRISTOPHER WORSWICK & ALAN GREEN, TOWARD IMPROVING CANADA'S SKILLED IMMIGRATION POLICY: AN EVALUATION APPROACH (2011).
32. *See* Michael Trebilcock, *The Case for a Liberal Immigration Policy, in* JUSTICE IN IMMIGRATION (Warren Schwartz ed., 1995).
33. For a discussion, see Peter Schuck, *Immigration Law and the Problem of Community, in* CLAMOR AT THE GATES 285–307 (Nathan Glazer ed., 1985). *See also* PETER SCHUCK, CITIZENS, IMMIGRANTS AND IN-BETWEENS: ESSAYS ON IMMIGRATION AND CITIZENSHIP (1998).
34. *See, e.g.*, Howard F. Chang, *Immigration Policy, Liberal Principles, and the Republican Tradition*, 85 GEO. L.J. 2105 (1997).
35. Pursuant to Australia's "White Australia" immigration policy, it was very difficult for non-Europeans to be admitted to Australia prior to the mid-1970s. *See, e.g., The Abolition of the White Australia Policy: The Immigration Reform Group Revisited* (Nancy Viviani ed.) (Centre for the Study of Australia Asia Relations, Working Paper No. 65, Faculty of Asian and International Studies, Griffith University, Queensland, June 1992). For a historical account of racial and ethnic discrimination in the Canadian immigration policy context, see NINETTE KELLEY & MICHAEL TREBILCOCK, THE MAKING OF THE MOSAIC: A HISTORY OF CANADIAN IMMIGRATION POLICY (2d ed. 2010).
36. *See* MICHAEL WALZER, SPHERES OF JUSTICE (1983).
37. *Id.* at 61–62; *see also* SAMUEL HUNTINGTON, WHO ARE WE? THE CHALLENGES TO AMERICA'S NATIONAL IDENTITY (2004).
38. *See* ARTHUR M. SCHLESINGER, JR., THE DISUNITING OF AMERICA 17–18 (1992). *See also* Robert Putnam, *E Pluribus Unum: Diversity and Community in the 21st Century*, 30

Scandinavian Political Studies 137 (2007), reporting empirical findings in the United States that more diverse communities exhibit lower levels of trust and lower levels of investment in various forms of social capital (a "hunkering down" effect); Amartya Sen, who is critical of the Blair government's proposals in the United Kingdom to provide public funding of private religious schools: Amartya Sen, Identity and Violence: The Illusion of Destiny 13, 117–19 (2006); and Paul Collier, The Exodus: How Immigration is Changing our World (2013), arguing that large, growing unabsorbed immigrant diasporas in developed countries, importing failed social models from their home countries, may undermine collective commitments of mutual regard and support and the provision of public goods.

39. Charles Hirshman, *The Contributions of Immigrants to American Culture*, 142 Daedalus 26 (summer issue 2013).

40. *See* Joseph Carens, *Aliens and Citizens: The Case for Open Borders*, 47 Rev. Politics 251 (1987).

41. *See* Robert Nozick, Anarchy, State and Utopia (1974).

42. *See* Alvaro Vargas Llosa, Global Crossings: Immigration, Civilization, and America (2013).

43. *See* John Rawls, A Theory of Justice (1971).

44. However, it is important to note that in later writings Rawls ascribed a very limited role to the application of principles of distributive justice among nations in the absence of a global government to enforce the social contract: Rawls, The Law of Peoples (1999)—a position strongly contested among other liberal philosophers: *see, e.g.*, Thomas Pogge, *The Incoherence between Rawls's Theories of Justice*, 72 Fordham L. Rev. 1739 (2003).

45. *See* Carens, *supra* note 40, at 256.

46. *See* Massey, *supra* note 8

47. Jagdish Bhagwati has long advocated a liberal approach to encouraging foreign students to stay on in the United States after they have completed their formal education. *See, e.g.*, Jagdish Bhagwati, *The False Alarm of Too Many Scientists*, in A Stream of Windows: Unsettling Reflections on Trade, Immigration, and Democracy 363 (Jagdish Bhagwati ed., 1998).

48. *See* Trebilcock & Sudak, *supra* note 1, at 240–67; Alejandro Portes & Adrienne Celaya, *Determinants and Consequences of the Brain Drain*, 142 Daedalus 70 (summer issue 2013).

49. *See* De Silva, *supra* note 31.

50. *See* Massey, *supra* note 8.

51. *See* Ayelet Shachar, *The Race for Talent: Highly Skilled Immigrants and Competitive Immigration Regimes*, 81 N.Y.U.L. Rev. 148 (2006); Wadhwa, *supra* note 23.

52. *See* Michael Porter, *Clusters and Competition: New Agendas for Companies, Governments and Institutions*, in On Competition (Michael Porter ed., 1998).

53. *See* Jeffrey Reitz, The Warmth of the Welcome (1998).

54. *See supra* note 38.

55. *See* Wadhwa, *supra* note 23, for a detailed set of proposals for liberalizing US admission policies for skilled workers, including temporary workers.

56. *See* Kelley & Trebilcock, *supra* note 35, ch. 11; Naomi Alboim, *Adjusting the Balance: Fixing Canada's Economic Immigration Policies* (Maytree Foundation, July 2009);

Naomi Alboim & Karen Cohl, *Shaping the Future: Canada's Rapidly Changing Immigration Policies* (Maytree Foundation, Oct. 2012).

57. *See* MICHAEL ADAMS, UNLIKELY UTOPIA: THE SURPRISING TRIUMPH OF CANADIAN PLURALISM, *supra* note 16 at 13, 14, 17 (2007),

Chapter 8

1. However, even for those who would contest these premises, much of the discussion below may still serve as an illustrative example of the problem of transition costs.

2. For a recent, masterful review of the evidence on the causes and consequences of global warming and possible policy responses thereto, see William Nordhaus, *The Climate Casino: Risk, Uncertainty, and Economics for a Warming World* (2013). The sheer volume of international meetings, agreements, and treaties suggests at least an elite acceptance of climate change concerns. *See, e.g.*, Joyeeta Gupta, *A History of International Climate Change Policy*, 1(5) WILEY INTERDISCIPLINARY REVS.: CLIMATE CHANGE 636–53 (2010). With respect to the possibilities of international agreement and coordination, see Robert O. Keohane & David G. Victor, *The Transnational Politics of Energy*, 142(1) DAEDALUS 97 (2013).

3. ROGER A. PIELKE, THE CLIMATE FIX: WHAT SCIENTISTS AND POLITICIANS WON'T TELL YOU ABOUT GLOBAL WARMING 32–34 (2010); Hal Harvey, Franklin M. Orr & Clara Vondrich, *A Trillion Tons* 142(1) DAEDALUS 8 (2013); Gunnar Luderer et al., *Economic Mitigation Challenges: How Further Delay Closes the Door for Achieving Climate Targets*, 8 ENVIRON. RES. LETT. 034033 (2013).

4. *Id.*

5. *See, e.g.*, JEFFREY D SACHS, COMMON WEALTH: ECONOMICS FOR A CROWDED PLANET (2008).

6. It should be recognized that arguments for a zero-growth economy have been advanced and that these proposals, if adopted, could go a long way to addressing many of the concerns regarding climate change discussed herein. However, the focus on developed industrial nations implies that such an approach can, in the short-to-medium term, serve only as a partial solution. Carbon emissions from developing economies will remain a strong driver of climate change independent of the actions of the West; *see, e.g.*, PETER A. VICTOR, MANAGING WITHOUT GROWTH: SLOWER BY DESIGN, NOT DISASTER (2008).

7. PIELKE, *supra* note 3, at 60; DIETER HELM, THE CARBON CRUNCH: HOW WE ARE GETTING CLIMATE CHANGE WRONG—AND HOW TO FIX IT ch. 11(201).

8. *See, e.g.*, ERIC A. POSNER & DAVID WEISBACH, CLIMATE CHANGE JUSTICE (2010); Yoram Margalioth & Yinon Rudich, *Close Examination of the Principle of Global Per-Capita Allocation of the Earth's Ability to Absorb Greenhouse Gas*, 14 THEOR. INQ. L. 191–206 (2013). Warwick J. McKibbin & Peter J. Wilcoxen, *The Role of Economics in Climate Change Policy*, 16(2) J. ECON. PERSPECTIVES 107 (2002).

9. Yoram Margalioth, *Tax Policy Analysis of Climate Change*, 64 TAX L. REV. 63 (2010).

10. Although such an approach may stop the exploitation of particularly "dirty" sources of fossil fuels at the margins. However, the sheer scale of capital investment required to facilitate fossil fuel extraction (e.g., refineries, pipelines) implies that production levels are likely to be inelastic, at least in the short and medium terms.

11. *See, e.g.*, MANCUR OLSON, THE LOGIC OF COLLECTIVE ACTION: PUBLIC GOODS AND THE THEORY OF GROUPS (1971) (1965).

12. *See* HELM, *supra* note 7, at ch. 8.

13. *See generally* MICHAEL J. TREBILCOCK & JAMES S.F. WILSON, THE PERILS OF PICKING TECHNOLOGICAL WINNERS IN RENEWABLE ENERGY POLICY (2010).

14. PIELKE, *supra* note 3; JEFFREY SIMPSON, MARK KENNETH JACCARD & NIC RIVERS, HOT AIR: MEETING CANADA'S CLIMATE CHANGE CHALLENGE (2007).

15. Matthew C. Nisbet, *Communicating Climate Change: Why Frames Matter for Public Engagement*, 51(2) ENVIRONMENT: SCI. & POLICY FOR SUSTAINABLE DEV. 12, 14 (2009).

16. An alternative mandate-based approach would be the imposition of emissions caps at the consumer level, for example for clothes dryers or air conditioners, as has been done in the United States.

17. Joseph E. Aldy & Robert N. Stavins, *Using the Market to Address Climate Change: Insights from Theory & Experience*, 141(2) DAEDALUS 45+ at 2–4 (2012).

18. *Id.*

19. TREBILCOCK & WILSON, *supra* note 13.

20. For example, Green suggests that such an approach may signal "that care for the environment should be viewed as a price, rather than a responsibility—if someone is willing to pay the price (forego a subsidy for driving a fuel-efficient car), they have no further responsibility"; Andrew Green, *You Can't Pay Them Enough: Subsidies, Environmental Law, and Social Norms*, 30 HARV. ENVT'L L. REV. 407, 408 (2006).

21. Aldy & Stavins, *supra* note 17, at 2–4.

22. TREBILCOCK & WILSON, *supra* note 13.

23. Aldy & Stavins, *supra* note 17, at 7.

24. HELM, *supra* note 7.

25. This, of course, is a mitigating consideration only. In the absence of preventative measures, energy intensive activities such as heavy manufacturing would be likely to "leak" to less regulated jurisdictions.

26. *See, e.g.*, Ian W.H. Parry, *Are Emissions Permits Regressive*, 47 J. ENVTL. ECON. & MGMT. 364 (2004); Daniel A. Farber, *Pollution Markets and Social Equity: Analyzing the Fairness of Cap and Trade*, 39(1) ECOLOGY L.Q. 1 (2012).

27. For an overview of the relative strengths and weaknesses of the two, see Ann E. Carlson & Robert W. Fri, *Designing a Durable Energy Policy*, 142(1) DAEDALUS 119 (2013); Anthony D. Owen, *Economics Instruments for Pollution Abatement: Tradable Permits Versus Carbon Taxes*, in ENERGY ECONOMICS AND FINANCIAL MARKETS 91–106 (André Dorsman, John L. Simpson, & Wim Westerman eds., 2013).

28. *See, e.g.*, Erick Lachapelle, Christopher P. Borick & Barry Rabe, *Public Attitudes toward Climate Science and Climate Policy in Federal Systems: Canada and the United States Compared*, 29(3) REV. POLICY RESEARCH 334, 348 (2012). Additionally, it has been estimated that in the United States an upstream approach focused on fuels would allow 98 percent coverage with only a few thousand firms needing to be covered (coal mines, refineries, oil importers, etc.) as opposed to millions of end-retailers. Aldy & Stavins, *supra* note 17. As a further incentive to reduce emissions, it would also be possible to implement a downstream crediting system complementing the upstream tax for those who actively engage in sequestration.

29. Some commentators suggest that regardless of initial allowance distribution, trading can lead to them being put to their highest-value use: "covering those emissions that are the most costly to reduce and providing the incentive to undertake the least costly

reduction." Aldy & Stavins, *supra* note 17, at 8. This suggestion, however, is at odds with the wealth of empirical support for prospect theory. Specifically, this theory suggests, inter alia, that initial endowments do matter as "The value of a good to an individual appears to be higher when the good is viewed as something that could be lost or given up than when the same good is evaluated as a potential gain." Daniel Kahneman, *Maps of Bounded Rationality: Psychology for Behavioral Economics*, 93(5) AM. ECON. REV. 1449, 1457 (2003).

30. Aldy & Stavins, *supra* note 17. Banking and borrowing of allowances has also been suggested as a way to introduce flexibility while maintaining overall GHG reduction goals.

31. PIELKE, *supra* note 3, at 50–58.

32. McKibbin & Wilcoxen, *supra* note 8, at 118. For a discussion of the idea of an emissions "budget" more generally, see: Harvey, Orr & Vondrich, *supra* note 3.

33. POSNER & WEISBACH, *supra* note 8.

34. Luc Bovens, *A Lockean Defense of Grandfathering Emissions Rights*, in THE ETHICS OF GLOBAL CLIMATE CHANGE 133 (Denis Arnold ed., 2011).

35. A regulatory scheme of this type has the effect of attaching a price to carbon. At the same time, it would assign ownership of the right to emit carbon in a manner that would require producers in developed industrial countries to then buy back those credits in order to maintain anything close to current levels of production.

36. McKibbin & Wilcoxen, *supra* note 8, at 115.

37. POSNER & WEISBACH, *supra* note 8; *see also* STEVE VANDERHEIDEN, ATMOSPHERIC JUSTICE: A POLITICAL THEORY OF CLIMATE CHANGE 107 (2008), cited in MARGALIOTH & RUDICH, *supra* note 8, at 203-04.

38. For example, if A owns property on a river and B dams the river, submerging A's property, the intuitive reaction is that B must compensate A for the loss. Maldives, a series of islands in the Indian Ocean, is expected to suffer catastrophically in a "business as usual" scenario, up to and including total submersion. The analogy here would seem to be that whoever can be identified with "B" in this scenario ought to compensate the Maldives ("A"). This, however, raises the problem of remoteness.

39. JOHN RAWLS, THE LAW OF PEOPLES: WITH "THE IDEA OF PUBLIC REASON REVISITED" (2001); *see* MARGALIOTH & RUDICH, *supra* note 8, at 198-99; *c.f.* Thomas W. Pogge, *The Incoherence between Rawls's Theories of Justice*, 72 FORDHAM L. REV. 1739 (2003).

40. Louis Kaplow, *Horizontal Equity: Measures in Search of a Principle*, 42(2) NAT'L TAX J. 139 (1989); *see also* MARGALIOTH & RUDICH, *supra* note 8. For a concise overview of this line of reasoning, see Bovens, *supra* note 34, at 124–26.

41. Henry Shue, *Subsistence Emissions and Luxury Emissions*, 15(1) L. & POLICY 39–60 (1993); MARGALIOTH & RUDICH, *supra* note 8, at 200-01.

42. It does, however, pose a problem with respect to implementation, presenting a classic collective action problem. If Canada were to impose a price on carbon emissions it would be negatively affecting the global competitiveness of its primary resource exports—approximately $200 billion per year (NATURAL RESOURCES CANADA, IMPORTANT FACTS ON CANADA'S NATURAL RESOURCES (2011))—by increasing the costs of extraction and/or processing. In the absence of a global scheme for pricing carbon, this would seem to be economically and politically disastrous as well as unfair.

43. MARGALIOTH & RUDICH, *supra* note 8, at 14 citing Bovens, *supra* note 34, at 130–36; c.f. POSNER & WEISBACH, *supra* note 8, at 135, arguing that the loss of a legal right to the use

of the commons ought to be compensated even in the absence of traditional use (i.e. a loss of a right is a loss of a right).

44. MARGALIOTH & RUDICH, *supra* note 8, at 203.

45. For example, in Canada, 80 percent of individuals believe in the legitimacy of climate change science. However, this masks substantial regional variation. For example, 85 percent and 83 percent of those surveyed in Quebec and British Columbia, respectively, agreed with the statement while only 66 percent and 68 percent agreed with it in Alberta and Saskatchewan. It is, one would imagine, no coindicence that the latter two provinces have substantial fossil fuel deposits.

46. Lachapelle et al., *supra* note 28, at 339–40.

47. *See, e.g.*, Aldy & Stavins, *supra* note 17; Lachapelle et al. *supra* note 28, at 341–42.

48. This issue is discussed in greater detail below.

49. Lachapelle et al., *supra* note 28, at 349, 351.

50. Indeed, an Olsonian-Public Choice understanding of federalism would suggest that subnational units would face serious barriers to collective action. See, generally, GEORGE TSEBELIS, VETO PLAYERS: HOW POLITICAL INSTITUTIONS WORK (2002).

51. Lachapelle et al., *supra* note 28, at 346.

52. However, both provinces have abundant water power, and the prospect of exploiting more water power; vigorous GHG policies nationally and continentally will likely be to their advantage. Thus, they may be leading by example at least partly out of self-interest.

53. This is a textbook example of a two-level game: see Robert D. Putnam, *Diplomacy and Domestic Politics: The Logic of Two-Level Games*, 42(3) INT'L ORG. 427 (1988).

54. Douglas M. Brown, *Comparative Climate Change Policy and Federalism: An Overview* 29(3) REV. POLICY RESEARCH 322 (2012).

55. JONAS PONTUSSON, INEQUALITY AND PROSPERITY: SOCIAL EUROPE VS. LIBERAL AMERICA (2005).

56. Brown, *supra* note 54, at 329. More generally, electoral time horizons are likely to play a role as well. Policy initiatives that will effectively deal with climate change tend to have time lines best expressed in decades, much longer than the four-to-five- year electoral cycles that politicians must generally cope with. However, it is unclear whether the relatively minor variations across countries have any effect.

57. Aldy & Stavins, *supra* note 17, at 23.

58. *Id.*

59. SIMPSON ET AL., *supra* note 14, at 103.

60. *Id.* at 43, 98.

61. *Id.* at 70.

62. Maxwell T. Boykoff & Jules M. Boykoff, *Climate Change and Journalistic Norms: A Case-Study of US Mass-Media Coverage*, 38(6) GEOFORUM 1190 (2007).

63. ANTHONY LEISEROWITZ, FIGHTING CLIMATE CHANGE: HUMAN SOLIDARITY IN A DIVIDED WORLD 3 (United Nations Development Project, 2007).

64. *See, e.g.*, CHARLES E. LINDBLOM, POLITICS AND MARKETS: THE WORLD'S POLITICAL ECONOMIC SYSTEMS (1977); EDWARD S HERMAN & NOAM CHOMSKY, MANUFACTURING CONSENT: THE POLITICAL ECONOMY OF THE MASS MEDIA (1988); JEFFREY D SACHS, THE PRICE OF CIVILIZATION: ECONOMICS AND ETHICS AFTER THE FALL (2011).

65. Russell B. Korobkin & Thomas S. Ulen, *Law and Behavioral Science: Removing the Rationality Assumption from Law and Economics*, 88 Cal. L. Rev. 1051 (2000).

66. MARGALIOTH & RUDICH, *supra* note 8 at 193.

67. LEISEROWITZ, *supra* note 63, at 35.

68. PIELKE, *supra* note 3; Nisbet, *supra* note 15; Anthony Leiserowitz, *Climate Change Risk Perception and Policy Preferences: The Role of Affect, Imagery, and Values* 77(1) CLIMATIC CHANGE 45, 56 (2006); LEISEROWITZ, *supra* note 63, at 35. For example, 92 percent of Americans are aware of global warming, 74 percent believe it is real and already underway, and 76 percent believe it to be a somewhat or very serious problem. Nonetheless, it is consistently ranked near the bottom of lists of priorities for government to address.

69. PIELKE, *supra* note 3, at 47–50, 58.

70. LEISEROWITZ, *supra* note 63, at 16.

71. *Id.* at 8.

72. Leiserowitz, *supra* note 68, at 56, 63; *see generally* DANIEL YANKELOVICH, COMING TO PUBLIC JUDGMENT: MAKING DEMOCRACY WORK IN A COMPLEX WORLD (1991).

73. PIELKE, *supra* note 3; *c.f.* Jon A. Krosnick & Bo MacInnis, *Does the American Public Support Legislation to Reduce Greenhouse Gas Emissions?*, 142(1) DAEDALUS 26 (2013). Appeals to ethical principles that sidestep environmental issues by juxtaposing them with human rights issues have also been advanced. One notable example of this is the "Ethical Oil" campaign aimed at garnering public support for Alberta's oil sands—a particularly environmentally costly source of fossil fuel—by portraying the environmental costs as marginal compared to alternative sources of oil from countries with poor human rights records.

74. Nisbet, *supra* note 15, at 17. With regard to the social construction of climate change more generally, see THE SOCIAL CONSTRUCTION OF CLIMATE CHANGE: POWER KNOWLEDGE NORMS DISCOURSES, (Mary E. Pettenger ed., 2013).

75. Korobkin & Ulen, *supra* note 65, at 1086–88; *see generally* Kahneman, *supra* note 29.

76. It is also notable that less than 15 percent of individuals in either country cite scientific research as their primary reason for believing that global warming exists, thus casting doubt on the effectiveness of "truth" in affecting public opinion. Lachapelle et al., *supra* note 28, at 341–42.

77. Nisbet, *supra* note 15, at 15.

78. Examples include the chemical disaster in Bhopal, India, the *Exxon Valdez* oil spill in Alaska, and the astounding images of ozone depletion, all of which, argues Nisbett, were vital components in triggering collective action to address the problems. *Id.*

79. Aldy & Stavins, *supra* note 17.

80. Brown, *supra* note 54, at 329.

81. Leiserowitz, *supra* note 68, at 49–50.

82. Dan M. Kahan, Hank Jenkins-Smith & Donald Braman, *Cultural Cognition of Scientific Consensus*, 14(2) J. RISK. RFS 147, 156 57 (2011).

83. *Id.*

84. Lachapelle et al., *supra* note 28, at 340–41.

85. SIMPSON ET AL., *supra* note 14, at 206.

86. *Id.*

87. TRACEY EPPS & ANDREW J GREEN, RECONCILING TRADE AND CLIMATE: HOW THE WTO CAN HELP ADDRESS CLIMATE CHANGE 89–91 (2010).

88. If a carbon tax was initially imposed at a relatively low level, say $25/ton, and gradually increased over time, not only is this acclimatization likely, but the economic impacts

of increased producer costs will be more gradual. This, in turn, should enable the desired reallocation of investments to occur in a more efficient manner, thereby smoothing the transition. *See, e.g.*, PIELKE, *supra* note 3.

89. Think, for example of the rhetorical gymnastics used by political leaders to avoid calling new sources of revenue taxes; terms such as "user fee" and "health premium" come to mind.

90. Aldy & Stavins, *supra* note 17, at 20.

91. *See, e.g.*, PAUL E. WAGGONER, FOREST INVENTORIES: DISCREPANCIES AND UNCERTAINTIES (Resources for the Future, 2009); Roger Sedjo & Molly Macauley, *Forest Carbon Offsets: Challenges in Measuring, Monitoring and Verifying* 54(4) ENV'T.: SCI. & POLICY FOR SUSTAINABLE DEVELOPMENT 16 (2012).

92. Aldy & Stavins, *supra* note 17.

93. SIMPSON ET AL., *supra* note 14.

94. This bias would probably be less important in systems where elected officials have a more active role in crafting policy options (e.g., the United States) as opposed to bureaucrats (e.g., Westminster systems).

95. Michael J. Trebilcock, *Trade Policy and the Environment*, in UNDERSTANDING TRADE LAW 161, 167–68 (2011).

96. Paul-Erik Veel, *Carbon Tariffs and the WTO: An Evaluation of Feasible Policies*, 12(3) J. INT'L ECON. L. 749, 749, 751–55 (2009); EPPS & GREEN, *supra* note 87. However, the ability of a crabon tariff to prevent leakage has recently been challenged by Jean-Marc Burniaux, Jean Chateau & Romain Duval, *Is There a Case for Carbon-Based Border Tax Adjustment? An Applied General Equilibrium Analysis*, 45 APPLIED ECON. 2231–2240 (2013).

97. Veel, *supra* note 96, at 793–95.

98. For example, the political attraction to a Corporate Average Fuel Economy standard in the United States as a means of increasing fuel efficiency rather than a gasoline tax, in spite of the economic forecasting that suggests the latter could accomplish the same goals at a lower cost. It would, however, do so in a much more visible way and was therefore deemed to be, at best, a second-best option. Aldy & Stavins, *supra* note 17.

99. Parry, *supra* note 26, at 365. This in turn can have adverse effects on labor supply.

100. Lachapelle et al., *supra* note 28, at 350.

101. *Id.*

102. SIMPSON ET AL., *supra* note 14, at 211; Margalioth, *supra* note 9, at 70.

103. Indeed, Margalioth has suggested that a harmonized global carbon tax whose revenues are remitted to the government of the territory of origin would be an effective and politically viable means of addressing climate change. Margalioth, *supra* note 9.

104. SIMPSON ET AL., *supra* note 14, at 213.

105. Margalioth, *supra* note 9.

106. In particular, there is a risk that these revenues may be more or less directly returned to affected industries via de facto subsidies or tax breaks in other areas.

107. Parry, *supra* note 26, at 365.

108. Farber, *supra* note 26, at 21.

109. Gilbert E. Metcalf, *Market-Based Policy Options to Control U.S. Greenhouse Gas Emissions*, 23(2) J. ECON. PERSPECTIVES 5, 19–20 (2009); Parry, *supra* note 26, at 365–66.

110. That being said, an initial allocation of permits on the basis of historical emissions levels could be used as a means of establishing a carbon market by having freely distributed permits expire over time as a means of phasing in carbon pricing.

111. Farber, *supra* note 26, at 24.

112. Aldy & Stavins, *supra* note 17, at 10.

113. *Id.*

114. A ceiling and a floor together are often referred to as a price "collar."

115. *See, e.g.*, Aldy & Stavins, *supra* note 17; Lachapelle et al., *supra* note 28.

116. As a result of, inter alia, confirmation bias and the availability heuristic. *See, e.g.*, Leiserowitz, *supra* note 68; Korobkin & Ulen, *supra* note 65.

117. For example, public opinion data indicates that opposition to the imposition of a carbon tax decreases and support increases when phrased with a specific price (in this case $15/ton) rather than in the abstract. This, holds Lachapelle, "may be taken as evidence of how little respondents understand concerning the cost implications of various climate policies and an aversion individuals have toward taxation in general, which may potentially be alleviated when they are provided information regarding the (in this case, modest) costs involved" (Lachapelle et al., *supra* note 28, at 348.). One might reasonably expect similar effects to result from the presentation of information that brings home and/or concretizes the impacts of climate change.

118. Leiserowitz, *supra* note 68, at 64.

119. Nisbet, *supra* note 15, at 15–17.

120. Kahan et al., *supra* note 82.

121. For example, McKibbin and Wilcoxen suggest that "A treaty that makes heavy demands on national sovereignty, or that requires large transfers of wealth from one part of the world to another, is unlikely to be ratified or, if ratified, is likely to be repudiated sooner or later. No international agency can coerce countries to comply with a climate change agreement they find significantly inconsistent with their national interest." *supra* note 8, at 115. *See also* POSNER & WEISBACH, *supra* note 8.

122. PIELKE, *supra* note 3, at 109.

123. See ALAN M. JACOBS, GOVERNING FOR THE LONG TERM: DEMOCRACY AND THE POLITICS OF INVESTMENT (2011).

124. HELM, *supra* note 7.

125. *See generally*, ANDREW GREEN & TRACEY EPPS, RECONCILING TRADE AND CLIMATE CHANGE (2010); Paul-Erik Veel, *Carbon Tariffs and the WTO: An Evaluation of Feasible Policies*, 12 J. INT'L ECON. L. 749 (2009); Henrik Horn & Petros C. Mavroidis, *To B(TA) or Not to B(TA)? On the Legality and Desirability of Border Tax Adjustments from a Trade Perspective*, 34(11) WORLD ECON. 1911 (2011).

126. *See* Farber, *supra* note 26.

Chapter 9

1. *See* H.W. ARNDT, ECONOMIC DEVELOPMENT: THE HISTORY OF AN IDEA (1987).

2. *See* AMARTYA SEN, DEVELOPMENT AS FREEDOM (1999).

3. DOUGLASS C. NORTH, UNDERSTANDING THE PROCESS OF ECONOMIC CHANGE 67 (2005); *see also* MATT ANDREWS, THE LIMITS OF INSTITUTIONAL REFORMS IN DEVELOPMENT: CHANGING RULES FOR REALISTIC SOLUTIONS (2013).

4. See Mariana Prado & Michael Trebilcock, *Path Dependence, Development, and the Dynamics of Institutional Reform*, 59 U. TORONTO L.J. 341 (2009); MICHAEL TREBILCOCK & MARIANA PRADO, WHAT MAKES POOR COUNTRIES POOR? 25–40 INSTITUTIONAL DETERMINANTS OF DEVELOPMENT (2011); DARON ACEMOGLU & JAMES ROBINSON, WHY NATIONS FAIL: THE ORIGINS OF POWER, PROSPERITY AND POVERTY (2012).

5. *See, e.g.*, Paul Pierson, *Increasing Returns, Path Dependence, and the Study of Politics*, 94 AM. POLITICAL SCI. REV. 251 (2000).

6. MICHAEL J. TREBILCOCK & RONALD J. DANIELS, RULE OF LAW REFORM AND DEVELOPMENT: CHARTING THE FRAGILE PATH OF PROGRESS CH. 1 (2008); Kevin Davis & Michael Trebilcock, *The Relationship between Law and Development: Optimists versus Skeptics*, 56 AM. J. COMP. LAW 895 (2008).

7. TREBILCOCK & DANIELS, *supra* note 6; TREBILCOCK & PRADO, *supra* note 4, at ch. 2.

8. Marina Ottaway, *The Post-War "Democratic Reconstruction Model": Why It Can't Work.* (Paper presented at United States Institute for Peace, 2002).

9. Dani Rodrik, *Feasible Globalizations* (KSG Working Paper Series RWP02-029, Harvard University, 2002), *available at* http://web.hks.harvard.edu/publications/workingpapers/citation.aspx?PubId=935 at 6–8. *See also* DANI RODRIK, ONE ECONOMICS, MANY RECIPES: GLOBALIZATION, INSTITUTIONS, AND ECONOMIC GROWTH ch. 5, 6 (2007); *see also* Francis Fukuyama, *Development and the Limits of Institutional Design* (Global Development Network, Jan. 20, 2006); FRANCIS FUKUYAMA, STATEBUILDING: GOVERNANCE AND WORLD ORDER IN THE 21ST CENTURY (2004).

10. *See* Mariana Prado & Ana Carolina Chasin, *How Innovative Was the Poupatempo Experience in Brazil? Institutional Bypass as a New Form of Institutional Change*, 5 BRAZILIAN POLITICAL SCI. REV. [2011].

11. *See* Thomas Heller, *An Immodest Postscript*, in BEYOND COMMON KNOWLEDGE: EMPIRICAL APPROACHES TO THE RULE OF LAW (Erik Jensen & Thomas Heller eds., 2003); Mariana M. Prado, *Institutional Bypass: An Alternative to Development Reform* (Apr. 19, 2011), *available at* http://ssrn.com/abstract=1815442.

12. *See* Michael Trebilcock, *Journeys across the Divides*, in THE ORIGINS OF LAW AND ECONOMICS: ESSAYS BY THE FOUNDING FATHERS (Francesco Parisi & Charles Rowley eds., 2005).

13. This can be true even in post-conflict societies; *see* Susan Rose-Ackerman, *Corruption and Post-Conflict Peace-Building*, 34 OHIO N.U. L. REV. 405 (2008).

14. This section draws on the analysis in Ronald J. Daniels & Michael J. Trebilcock, *The Political Economy of Rule of Law Reform in Developing Countries*, 26 MICH. J. INT'L L. 99 (2004).

15. Resistance to reform can also be higher if there is uncertainty regarding the identity of potential beneficiaries. The uncertainty is higher in large-scale reforms: Dani Rodrik & Raquel Fernandez, *Resistance to Reform: Status Quo Bias in the Presence of Individual-Specific Uncertainty*, 81 AM. ECON. REV. 1148 (1991).

16. How much instability these reforms should generate—that is, how much room for constant contestation would be good for future reforms—is a topic that deserves further research. For an insightful analysis, see Susan Rose-Ackerman, *Was Mancur a Maoist? An Essay on Kleptocracy and Political Stability*, 15 ECON. & POLITICS 163 (2003).

17. See, for instance, how informal institutions for contract enforcement in the footwear industry resisted the changes brought by an open trade regime when NAFTA

was implemented in Mexico: Christopher Woodruff, *Contract Enforcement and Trade Liberalization in Mexico's Footwear Industry*, 26 WORLD DEV. 979 (1998).

18. SEN, *supra* note 2, at 148

19. AMARTYA SEN, THE IDEA OF JUSTICE (2009), particularly chapters 15 and 16.

20. Adam Przeworski, *Democracy and Economic Development, in* THE EVOLUTION OF POLITICAL KNOWLEDGE: DEMOCRACY, AUTONOMY, AND CONFLICT IN COMPARATIVE AND INTERNATIONAL POLITICS (Edward D. Mansfield & Richard Sisson eds., 2004). For the African experience, SEE MARTIN MEREDITH, THE FATE OF AFRICA—A HISTORY OF FIFTY YEARS OF INDEPENDENCE (2005); for the Latin American experience, see MICHAEL REID, FORGOTTEN CONTINENT (2007); and for the Asian experience, see Minxin Pei, *The Puzzle of East Asian Exceptionalism*, 5(4) J. DEMOCRACY 90 (1994).

21. LARRY DIAMOND, THE SPIRIT OF DEMOCRACY: THE STRUGGLE TO BUILD FREE SOCIETIES THROUGHOUT THE WORLD (2008).

22. FREEDOM HOUSE, FREEDOM IN THE WORLD 2010: GLOBAL EROSION OF FREEDOM (2010).

23. Kevin Davis & Michael Trebilcock, *The Relationship between Law and Development: Optimists versus Skeptics*, 56 AM. J. COMP. L. 895 (2008).

24. Thomas Carothers, *The End of the Transition Paradigm*, 13(1) *Journal of Democracy* 5 (2002). *See also* THOMAS CAROTHERS, AIDING DEMOCRACY ABROAD (1999); THOMAS CAROTHERS & DIANE DE GRAMONI, DEVELOPMENT AID CONFRONTS POLITICS: THE ALMOST REVOLUTION (2013).

25. DIAMOND, *supra* note 21, at ch. 4.

26. *Id.* at 60.

27. *See* Michael Trebilcock & Poorvi Chitalkar, *From Nominal to Substantive Democracy: The Role and Design of Election Management Bodies*, 2 L. & DEV. REV. 179 (2009).

28. FREEDOM HOUSE, *supra* note 22.

29. *See, e.g.*, ROBERT PUTNAM, MAKING DEMOCRACY WORK: CIVIC TRADITIONS IN MODERN ITALY (1994); Peter B. Evans, *Government Action, Social Capital and Development: Reviewing the Evidence on Synergy*, 24 WORLD DEV. 1119 (1996); and PETER B. EVANS, EMBEDDED AUTONOMY (1996).

30. Francis Fukuyama, *Social Capital, Civil Society, and Development*, 22 THIRD WORLD Q. 7 (2001); *see also* Shan Berman, *Civil Society and the Collapse of the Weimar Republic*, 49 WORLD POLITICS 401 (1997).

31. Authoritarianism comes in almost as many shades as democracy, ranging from pro-development soft authoritarianism to grossly tyrannical or repressive kleptocracies.

32. FUKUYAMA, *supra* note 9.

33. Oona Hathaway, *The Case for Promoting Democracy through Export Control*, 33 HAR. J.L. & PUB. POLICY 17 (2010).

34. This discussion of property rights and development is largely derived from Michael Trebilcock & Paul-Erik Veel, *Property Rights and Development: The Contingent Case for Formalization*, 30 U. PENN. J. INT'L L. 397 (2008).

35. HERNANDO DE SOTO, THE MYSTERY OF CAPITAL: WHY CAPITALISM TRIUMPHS IN THE WEST AND FAILS EVERYWHERE ELSE 218 (2000).

36. De Soto, *id.*, at 35.

37. *See* David Kennedy, *Some Caution about Property Rights as a Recipe for Economic Development*, 1 ACCOUNTING, ECONOMICS & L., article 3, at 42–48 (2011).

38. *See* Daniel Fitzpatrick, *Evolution and Chaos in Property Rights Systems: The Third World Tragedy of Contested Access*, 15 YALE L.J. 996 (2006), who argues that the greater the divergence between state law and local norms, the more likely it is that attempts to enforce exclusionary claims will lead to open access rather than an authoritative property rights regime. He argues that legal and normative pluralism is a particularly common phenomenon in the Third World and is often accompanied by institutional pluralism—a fragmentation of the state into competing agencies and levels of government, and that in circumstances of legal, normative, and institutional pluralism efficient property rights regimes will not necessarily emerge.

39. *See* Harold Demsetz, *Toward a Theory of Property Rights*, 57 AM. ECON. REV. 347 (1967).

40. Kennedy, *supra* note 37, at 53, 54.

41. KENNETH W. DAM, THE LAW-GROWTH NEXUS: THE RULE OF LAW AND ECONOMIC DEVELOPMENT (2006).

42. DE SOTO, *supra* note 35.

43. *See* Sharun Mukand & Dani Rodrik, *In Search of the Holy Grail: Policy Convergence, Experimentation, and Economic Performance*, 95 AM. ECON. REV. 374 (2005) (which argues for implementation of appropriate policies and institutional arrangements at the local level).

44. For a classic paper exploring the importance of avoiding drastic imposed changes, see Charles Lindblom, *The Science of "Muddling Through,"* 19 PUB. ADMIN. REV. 79 (1959). *See also* JAMES C. SCOTT, SEEING LIKE A STATE: HOW CERTAIN SCHEMES TO IMPROVE THE HUMAN CONDITION HAVE FAILED (1998).

45. *See* Michael Trebilcock, *Communal Property Rights: The Papua New Guinea Experience*, 34 U. TORONTO L.J. 377 (1984).

46. *Id.* at 412–13.

47. For interesting examples relating to this point, see SCOTT, *supra* note 44; ANDREWS, *supra* note 3. *See also* Rachel Kranton & Anand Swamy, *The Hazards of Piecemeal Reform: British Civil Courts and the Credit Market in Colonial India*, 58 J. DEV. ECON. 1 (1999) (discussing how reform led to increased competition among lenders, and the resulting effects on the farmers of India).

48. Using data from the United States, Canada, and other Western countries, Lueck and Libecap have published empirical studies showing that a centralized, uniform land demarcation system is economically superior to an incremental, decentralized metes and bounds system. We cannot assume, however, that such a system would be successful in many developing nations today: Gary D. Libecap & Dean Lueck, *The Demarcation of Land and the Role of Coordinating Property Institutions*, 119 J. POLITICAL ECONOMY (June 2011), *available at* http://www.jstor.org/stable/10.1086/660842; Gary D. Libecap & Dean Lueck, *Land Demarcation Systems*, *in* RESEARCH HANDBOOK ON THE ECONOMICS OF PROPERTY LAW (2011). *But see, contra*, Fitzpatrick, *supra* note 38.

49. *See generally* Daniel Fitzpatrick, *Best Practice Options for the Legal Recognition of Customary Tenure*, 36 DEV. & CHANGE 449 (2005); Trebilcock, *supra* note 45; Kathrine Dixon, *Property: Mobilizing Land in Papua New Guinea the Melanesian Way*, 31 HAR. EVNTL REV. 219 (2007).

50. *See* ELINOR OSTROM, GOVERNING THE COMMONS: THE INSTITUTIONS FOR COLLECTIVE ACTION (1990).

51. Lant Pritchett & Michael Woolcock, *Solutions Where the Solution Is the Problem: Arraying the Disarray in Development, in* REINVENTING FOREIGN AID (William Easterly ed., 2008).

52. *See* ANDREWS, *supra* note 3; THOMAS CAROTHERS & DIANE DE GRAMONT, DEVELOPMENT AID CONFRONTS POLITICS: THE ALMOST REVOLUTION (2013); NINA MUNK, THE IDEALIST: JEFFREY SACHS AND THE QUEST TO END POVERTY (2013).

53. CAROTHERS & DE GRAMONT, *supra* note 52.

Chapter 10

1. *See* JONATHAN HAIDT, THE RIGHTEOUS MIND: WHY GOOD PEOPLE ARE DIVIDED BY POLICIES AND RELIGION (2012).

2. *See* LOUIS KAPLOW & STEVEN SHAVELL, FAIRNESS VERSUS WELFARE (2006).

3. Plessy v. Ferguson 163 U.S. 537 (1896).

4. Brown v. Bd. of Education 347 U.S. 483 (1954).

5. *See* Charles Lindblom, *The Science of "Muddling" Through*, 19 PUB. ADMIN. REV. 79 (1959); Charles Lindblom, *Still Muddling, Not Yet Through*, 39 PUB. ADMIN. REV. 517 (1979).

6. FRIEDRICH HAYEK, THE ROAD TO SERFDOM (1994).

7. *See, e.g.*, JODY FREEMAN & MARTHA MINOW, GOVERNMENT BY CONTRACT: OUTSOURCING AND AMERICAN DEMOCRACY (2009).

8. JAMES C. SCOTT, SEEING LIKE A STATE: HOW CERTAIN SCHEMES TO IMPROVE THE HUMAN CONDITION HAVE FAILED (1998); *see also* Lindblom, *supra* note 5 (both articles).

9. AMY GUTMANN & DENNIS THOMPSON, THE SPIRIT OF COMPROMISE: WHY GOVERNING DEMANDS IT AND CAMPAIGNING UNDERMINES IT (2012).

10. *Id.* at 204.

11. Michael Walzer, *Political Action: The Problem of Dirty Hands*, 2 PHILOSOPHY & PUB. AFFAIRS 160, 161 (1973).

12. *See* Steven Shavell, *On Optimal Legal Change, Past Behavior and Grandfathering*, 37 J. LEGAL STUDIES 37 (2008).

13. *See* Betty Fladeland, *Compensated Emancipation: A Rejected Alternative*, 42 J.S. HISTORY 169 (1976).

14. Richard Lipsey & Kelvin Lancaster, *The General Theory of Second Best*, 24 REV. ECON. STUDIES 11 (1953). In the context of this book, liberalizing immigration policies while maintaining protectionist trade policies may lead to too much immigration and too little trade from a social welfare perspective.

15. See more generally on arguments commonly invoked for policy stasis, ALBERT O. HIRSCHMAN, THE RHETORIC OF REACTION: PERVERSITY, FUTILITY, JEOPARDY (1991).

{ INDEX }

advocacy coalitions, 28
Afghanistan, 6, 142, 143, 158
agricultural protectionism, 4, 81–82, 84, 87, 90. *See also* Canada's dairy supply management regime
American Dream, 44, 48, 60, 157
American Recovery and Reinvestment Act of 2009, 78
American Taxpayer Relief Act of 2012, 58
Arab Spring, 6, 143
asylum seekers, 100, 111–12
Australia
 agricultural protectionism, 81
 climate change policy, 126, 127, 130
 dairy supply management, 84, 90, 91, 94
 immigration policy liberalization, 98, 99, 104
 public pensions, sustainability of, 37
 trade liberalization, 66, 76
Australian-New Zealand Closer Economic Cooperation Treaty, 66
availability heuristic, 22
 carbon abatement measures, 126, 129, 130, 134

Bacchetta, Marc, 72, 79
Bagwell, Kyle, 73
Baldwin, Robert, 70
Barichello, Richard, 94
Baumgartner, Frank, 25
behavioral economics, 22, 129
bias, explanations of political behavior, 22
 carbon abatement measures, 127, 129, 130, 131, 135
Bismarck, Otto von, 151
Blume, Lawrence, 12
Borjas, George, 102
Bowles, Erskine, 56
Brown v. Board of Education, 154
Buchanan, James, 17
Burman, Len, 58
Busby, Colin, 89, 92

Calabresi, Guido, 69
Canada. *See also* Canada's dairy supply management regime
 agricultural protectionism, 81

climate change policy, 123, 124, 125, 126, 127, 130, 131, 133
 immigration policy liberalization, 98, 99, 102, 104, 109, 112, 115
 public pensions, sustainability of, 32, 34, 35, 37, 38
 trade liberalization, 64, 66, 75, 76, 77
Canada's dairy supply management regime, 4, 82–88, 156
 Alberta, 83
 Canada-US Free Trade Agreement, 95
 Canadian Dairy Commission (CDC), 83
 Canadian federalism, 88
 Canadian Parliament, 87, 88
 communitarianism, 87, 94
 compensation
  policy options for compensation and mitigating opposition to reform, 90–93
  transition cost mitigation challenges, 89–93
  uncompensated dismantling and disaffection costs, 94
 Comprehensive Economic Trade Agreement, 86
 critical junctures, 94
 effects of dairy scheme, 84–86
 export-oriented farmers, 4, 86, 89, 94
 Fair Representation Act, 88
 free market system, 84, 89, 91, 92
 limiting imports, 83–84
 lock-in substantial reductions in out-of-quota tariffs, 94–95
 OECD analysis, 84
 Ontario, 83, 85, 88
 Peterson, Jim (Canadian Trade Minister), 85
 political geography, 88
 price setting boards, 83, 84
 proposed reform, phase in approach, 94–95
 Public Choice theory, 86–87
 public sympathy, 87–88, 94
 Quebec, 83, 85, 88
 quotas, 4, 82–83, 88–89, 91–92, 94–95
 reform challenges, overcoming, 88–93
  compensation and transition assistance policy options, 92–93

Canada's dairy supply management regime
  (*Cont'd*)
  compensation and transition cost
    mitigation challenges, 89–93
  dismantling supply management
    options, 91–92
  economic considerations, 90
  framing efforts, 90
  full impact approach, 91
  minor reform options, 90–91
  persuading the public, 89–90
  phased approach, 91–92, 93
  public sentiment, 89–90
  social welfare perspective, 90
  reforms, lock-in substantial reductions in
    out-of-quota tariffs, 94–95
  setting milk production levels, 83
  status quo, 82, 87, 89
  structure of supply management
    scheme, 82–84
  transitional gains trap, 82, 88
  Trans-Pacific Partnership (TPP), 86, 94
  Whelan, Eugene (Federal agriculture
    minister), 88
  WTO 2002 decision, scheme found to be
    export subsidy, 86
Canada-US Free Trade Agreement, 66, 95
Canadian-American Automotive Agreement
  of 1965, 65n20
carbon abatement costs, allocation, 123–24
carbon abatement measures, political factors
  affecting, 125–31
  availability heuristic, 126, 129, 130, 134
  behavioral economics, 129
  bias, 127, 129, 130, 131, 135
  economic factors, 126
  electoral systems, 126–27
  environmental factors, 126
  federalism, 126–27
  geographical factors, 125
  ideational (public opinion), 128–29
  institutional, 126–28
  journalistic presentation of global warming,
    127–28
  lack of public understanding and
    misperception of issues, 128–29
  low prioritization, reasons for, 128–29
  political viability of policies, 127
  predisposition of individuals, 130–31
  psychological, 129–31
  structural, 125–26
  2008 economic crisis, impact, 126, 128, 130
  types of world view, 130
carbon pricing, 121–22, 126, 131, 132, 135, 136
Card, David, 77
Carens, Joseph, 106–7

Carothers, Thomas, 143–44
China, 66, 121, 125, 137
Civil Right Act of 1964, 154
climate change policy, 5–6, 119–37, 157–58
  Australia, 126, 127, 130
  basic uncertainty of, 122
  border tax adjustments, domestic
    producers, 132
  Canada, 123, 124, 125, 126, 127, 130, 131, 133
  cap-and-trade system, 5–6, 121, 122, 127, 131,
    134, 136, 157
  carbon abatement costs, allocation, 123–24
  carbon abatement measures, political factors
    affecting, 125–31
  carbon pricing, 121–22, 126, 131, 132,
    135, 136
    revenue neutral carbon pricing, 132–33, 137
  carbon tariffs and equity, 132, 136–37
  compensation and mitigation, primary
    problems, 122
  developing countries, perspective of, 123
  endowment effect, 124, 125
  ethical and political demands, 132
  ethical considerations, 122–25
  framing strategy and climate change
    messages, 135
  global warming, 22, 120, 126, 127–29
  GlobeScan survey (1999), 129
  grandfathered permits and exemptions,
    133–34
  informational strategy to combat low
    prioritization, 134–35
  information and exhortation, 120
  Intergovernmental Panel on Climate
    Change, 129
  international community, level of
    participation, 119–20
  international human rights obligations, 124
  "iron law of climate change," 128, 129
  journalistic presentation of global warming
    issue, 127–28
  justifying different emissions levels (equal
    per-capita emissions), 124–25
  liability for past emissions, 122–24
  mandates, 120–21
  moral compulsion, 136
  moral culpability, 123
  moral duty, 124
  policy instruments available to address carbon
    emissions, 120–22
  price ceilings, floors, and collars, 134
  Prisoner's Dilemma, 136
  psychological explanations of behavior,
    129–31, 135
  public attitudes, changing, 136
  Public Choice theory, 120, 136

public opinion, 128–29, 133
revenue neutral carbon pricing, 132–33, 137
self-interest, 120, 125, 128
status quo, 122, 125, 127, 130
structural elements, 134
subsidies, 121
subsidization of green technology, 121
taxes and permits, 131
transition strategies, 131–35
zero-growth economy, 21, 119n6
Collier, Paul, 115
Common Agricultural Policy (CAP) (EU), 81, 82
communitarianism, 14–15
    Canada's dairy supply management regime, compensation necessity and politics of dairy, 87, 94
    immigration policy liberalization, 104–6, 107
    trade liberalization, 68–69
compensation
    explicit government compensation, 2
    normative theories of political process for and against compensation or mitigation of transition costs, 9–17
    political process, theories of compensation or mitigation of transition costs, 7, 9–30
    positive theories of the political process, role of compensation and other mitigation transition strategies in, 17–20
    slavery, 1
    socially desirable policy changes, compensation as strategy for expansion of, 7
    trade liberalization, 66–67
    utilitarianism, compensation formula, 13
compromise, virtues of incrementalism and, 153–55
corrective justice, 15
Cranfield, John, 94

dairy supply management. *See* Canada's dairy supply management regime
Davidson, Carl, 65, 74
demoralization costs, 13
    mortgage interest deductibility (MID), reform options/strategies, 54
    public pensions, sustainability of, 36, 40, 41
De Soto, Hernando, 145, 147
developing countries, institutional reform. *See* institutional reform in developing countries
Diamond, Larry, 143
Dictator Game, 23–24
distributive justice, 68, 107n44, 124, 130
Doha Round negotiations, 85

Downs, Anthony, 17
economics of politics, 17–18
EC Treaty, Title IV, 99
efficiency theories, 9–13
    adverse selection problems, 10, 12
    fiscal illusion, 11
    government policy changes, consequences of, 10
    Kaldor-Hicks conception of efficiency, 11, 13
    majoritarian political system, 11–12
    mortgage interest deductibility (MID), distortion of efficiency critiques, 51–53
    Pareto conception of efficiency, 11, 13, 16
    political economy perspective, 11–13
    private insurance markets, 9–11, 12
    trade liberalization, economic efficiency, 66–68
    Tyranny of the Majority, 12, 152–53
Egypt, 6, 142, 143, 158
eminent domain case, 12, 14, 19, 56
endowment effect, 22
    climate change policy, 124, 125
    immigration policy liberalization, 106
    trade liberalization, 68, 70
environmental regulations, 2
Epstein, Richard, 16–17, 158
European Union
    agricultural protectionism, 81
    climate change policy, 127
    immigration policy liberalization, 99, 104, 107, 113
    public pensions, sustainability of, 31, 37
    trade liberalization, 77

feckless pluralism, 144
federalism
    Canadian federalism, 88
    and climate change, 126
    Olsonian Public Choice understanding of, 126n50
    and voting procedures, 21
Feldstein, Martin, 57–58
Fifth Amendment ("Takings Clause"), 6, 15, 16–17, 29
fiscal illusion, 11, 16
Fischel, William, 12–13
framing
    Canada's dairy supply management regime, overcoming reform challenges, 90
    climate change messages, 135
    elite and popular reactions, 27–28
    ideational explanations of political behavior, 25
Francois, Joseph, 64
free market system, 84, 89, 91, 92
free-rider problem, 16, 70

General Agreement on Tariffs and Trade
    (GATT), 70–71
  Article XIX, 65, 73
Geneva Conference on Trade (1944), 70
Geneva Convention (1951 UN Convention
    Relating to the Status of Refugees),
    98, 107, 112
George, David Lloyd, 153
German Aussiedler citizenship policy, 104
Germany
  immigration policy liberalization, 104, 112
  trade liberalization, 76
Glaeser, Edward, 49–51
Goldin, Jacob, 51
government regulatory schemes, 26–27
grandfathering, 2
  climate change policy, grandfathered permits
    and exemptions, 133–34
  mortgage interest deductibility (MID), reform
    options/strategies, 57, 61
  public pensions, grandfathering of
    existing benefit recipients, 32, 38–40,
    41, 42
gun control law reform proposals, 2
Gutmann, Amy, 155

Hamilton, Bob, 98
Hanson, Andrew, 52
Harris, David, 91
Hayek, Friedrich, 154
Heckman, James, 77
Helm, Dieter, 121, 136–37
Hollande, Francois, 31, 39

ideational explanations of political
    behavior, 24–25
  carbon abatement measures, 128–29, 130–31
immigration policy liberalization, 97–117
  actual or perceived losers, 97, 100
  adverse selection problems, 109
  asylum seekers, 100, 111–12
  barriers, prevailing immigration policies,
    99–107, 114
  classical free trade theory, 97
  communitarianism, 104–6, 107
  decentralized approach, 108–13
  economic perspectives and evaluations,
    99–104
  endowment effect, 106
  family preference immigration, 111
  family sponsorship of immigrants, 98, 100,
    103, 104, 107, 111, 114
  fiscal effects in host countries, 101–2
  Geneva Convention (1951 UN Convention
    Relating to the Status of Refugees),
    98, 107, 112

  global and nationalistic welfare functions,
    99–100
  global economic welfare, 99–100, 114
  highly skilled immigrants, 5, 28, 99, 101–2,
    103, 115, 117
  illegal immigration, 98, 100, 101, 103–4, 108,
    112–13, 115, 117
  implications for existing immigration policies,
    102–4, 107
  independent applicants (sponsored
    immigrants), 98, 100, 103,
    108–11, 114
  knowledge-based economies, 98, 102, 115
  labor market effects in host countries,
    100–101
  liberalism, 106–7
  membership criteria, 105
  moral duty to admit, 104
  nation-state sovereignty, 105, 107
  neoclassical economic theory, 99
  non-economic perspectives, 104–7
  policy reforms, phased implementation, 98,
    107–17
    economic benefits, 114
    timing of reforms, 114–15
    US context, 116–17
  prevailing immigration policies, normative
    critiques of, 99–107
  primary immigrant receiving areas, 99
  quota system, 104, 107–8, 112
  refugees, 97, 98, 100, 107, 111–12
  social contract perspective, 106–7
  social programs, 97, 103, 108–9, 112, 113, 114
  student visas, 98, 110, 111, 116
  stylized facts about immigration policies in
    receiving countries, 98–99
  temporary workers, 5, 97, 98, 100, 101,
    112–13, 116, 117
  United States and, 98–99, 101–2, 104, 106,
    108, 109, 112, 115, 116–17
  utilitarian perspective, 106–7
incrementalism
  case study. *See* institutional reform in
    developing countries
  randomness, 140
  unintended effects or consequences, 153–54
  virtues of compromise and, 153–55
India, 66, 125, 137
individual rationality, 26
institutional explanations of political
    behavior, 20–22
  arrangement and internal logics of
    institutions, 28–29
  carbon abatement measures, 126–28
  feedback mechanisms, 22n63
  path dependence phenomenon, 21–22

randomness, 21–22
rational choice institutionalism, 20
unintended outcomes, 21–22
veto players concept, 21
institutional reform in developing countries, 6, 139–49, 158
   Afghanistan, 6, 142, 143, 158
   Arab Spring, 6, 143
   conventional transition paradigms, questionable assumptions, 143–44
   country characteristics and generalizations, 144
   critical junctures, 140, 141, 142
   democratic reform and development, 143–45
   differing political regimes, 144–45
   dominant power politics, 144
   Egypt, 6, 142, 143, 158
   feckless pluralism, 144
   Freedom House, 2010 report, 143
   Iraq, 6, 142, 143, 158
   Libya, 6, 143, 158
   mutually reinforcing mechanisms, 140, 141, 142
   new constitutionalism, 143
   path dependence theory, 140, 142
   property rights and development, 145–49
   randomness, 140
   rule of law, reform and development, 141–43
      approaches, 141
      institutional bypass strategy, 142
      institutional interdependence, 141
      range of conceptions, 141
      switching costs, 142–43
   self-reinforcement mechanisms, increase in switching costs, 140
   status quo, 142, 148, 158
   structural features, 144
   switching costs, 140, 142–43
   theories of development, 139
Intergovernmental Panel on Climate Change, 129
Internal Revenue Service, 45
international example, post-conflict nation building exercises, 2–3
Iraq, 6, 142, 143, 158
"iron law of climate change," 128, 129
Irwin, Douglas, 70

Jacobs, Alan, 23, 31, 34, 35–36, 39–41
Jansen, Marion, 72, 79
Japan
   agricultural protectionism, 81
   trade liberalization, 65, 77
Jim Crow laws, 154
Joint Committee on Taxation, 44, 53, 54
Jones, Bryan, 25

Kahan, Dan, 130
Kaldor-Hicks conception of efficiency, 11, 13
Kaplow, Louis, 9–11, 12, 13, 16, 17, 29, 66, 79, 124, 152, 158
Kennedy, David, 147
Kennedy Round of multilateral trade negotiations, 65n20
Kluve, Jochen, 77
knowledge-based economies, 98, 102, 115
Korea, 77
Krugman, Paul, 70, 73

LaLonde, Robert, 77
land use regulations or controls, 2
Leisorwitz, Anthony, 135
Levmore, Saul, 15
liberalism and social contract theory, 106–7
libertarian paternalist approach, 38
libertarian theories of the state, 16–17
Libya, 6, 143, 158
Lindblom, Charles, 154
Listokin, Yair, 51
Locke's natural rights theory of property rights, 16

Mann, Roberta, 44
Martin, John, 77
Matusz, Steven, 65, 74
Mavroidis, Petros, 70
McKibbin, Warwick, 123
Meilke, Karl, 94
Michelman, Frank, 13, 36, 54
MID. *See* mortgage interest deductibility (MID) reform
Morrow, Rebecca, 56
mortgage interest deductibility (MID) reform, 3–4, 43–61, 157
   addressing externalities, MID ineffective in, 50–51
   American Dream, 44, 48, 60
   Code Sec. 163(h)(1), 48
   criticism of MID, 44
   distribution by income class, 54
   efficiency critiques of the MID, distortion of, 51–53
      allocation of homes among taxpayers, 52–53
      investment choices, 52n73
      mortgage debt interest rates, 52
   election to itemize, 44–45
   equity critique of the MID, 53, 54
   first-time homebuyers, 3, 46, 52, 56, 60, 157
   first-time homebuyers' credit (FTHBC), 56
   foreclosures, 46, 56, 60
   history of the deductibility of home mortgage interest, 46–48

mortgage interest deductibility (MID) reform (*Cont'd*)
  home ownership rates, 48, 51
  inefficient and inequitable claims, 51–53
  itemizing deductions, 44–49, 51–53, 57–58, 59, 60
  justifications for subsidizing home ownership, positive and negative externalities, 49–50
  in choice of renting *versus* owning a home, 49–50
  from consuming more or better housing, 49
  legislative origins of the MID, 46–48
  marginal tax rate, 3, 43, 47, 48, 52–53, 57, 58, 59, 60, 157
  mechanics of the MID, 45
  miscellaneous itemized deductions, 45n20
  1913 income tax statute, 46
  policy case against the MID, 48–53
  politics leading to the codification of the MID, 48
  qualified residence interest, 43n2, 45
  real estate industry contributions to Congress in 2008, 44
  reform options/strategies, 53–59
    affected constituencies, 54–55
    classes of strategies for reforming the MID, 56–59
    demoralization costs, 54
    grandfathering, 57, 61
    phase outs of the MID over time, 58, 60–61
    potential risks of policy changes, 55–56
    raising the standard deduction, 58–59
    repeal of the MID, 56, 57, 59–60
    replace the MID with a credit, 56
    Social Security benefits, 54
    transitional gains trap, 54–55
  standard deduction, 44–45, 47–48, 53, 58–59, 60
  tax code, 43, 44, 46–48, 50, 56, 61
  US Financial crisis of 2008, 52
  zero-bracket exemption, 46
Mussa, Michael, 72

National Research Council (NRC), 101
National Tax Association survey, 44
neoclassical economic theory, 63, 99
New Deal agencies, 47
New Deal legislation, 16
New Zealand
  agricultural protectionism, 81
  Australian-New Zealand Closer Economic Cooperation Treaty, 66
  Canada's dairy supply management regime, 86, 90
Nirvana fallacy, 155

Nisbet, Matthew, 120, 129, 135
normative theories of political process for and against compensation or mitigation of transition costs, 9–17
  communitarianism, 14–15
  corrective justice, 15
  efficiency theories, 9–13
  Fifth Amendment ("Takings Clause"), 16–17
  fiscal illusion, 11, 16
  libertarian theories of the state, 16–17
  social contract theories, 14
  utilitarianism, 13
North, Douglass, 139
North America
  climate change policy, 127, 130
  trade liberalization, 66, 75, 77
North American Free Trade Agreement (NAFTA), 7, 66
Norway
  agricultural protectionism, 81
Nozick, Robert, 106

OECD countries
  active labor market policies (ALMPs), 76
  agricultural protectionism, 81
  Canada's dairy scheme, effects, 84
  Canadian Public Pension Plan, 38–39
  fiscal effects of immigration, 102
  public pension sustainability problems, 32–34, 38–39
Olson, Mancur, 17
Olsonian Public Choice understanding of federalism, 126n50
Organisation for Economic Co-operation Development. *See* OECD countries

Pareto efficiency concept, 2, 11, 13, 16, 94
Parsons, Craig, 20, 24
Pastor, Jose, 72
path dependence, 6, 21–22
  institutional reform in developing countries, 140, 142
pensions. *See* public pensions
personal sacrifices, 23, 28
  climate change policy, 120, 128
  trade liberalization, 64
Pielke, Roger, 128, 136
Plessy v. Ferguson, 154
political behavior, alternative explanations of, 20–29
  advocacy coalitions, 28
  arrangement and internal logics of institutions, 28–29
  framing of an issue, elite and popular reactions, 27–28
  government regulatory schemes, 26–27

ideational explanations of political
  behavior, 24–25
implications of alternative explanations for
  transition policies in the political
  process, 26–29
individual rationality, 26
institutional explanations of political
  behavior, 20–22
organized interest groups, 28
psychological explanations of political
  behavior, 22–24
Public Choice theory, 26
scale of proposed policy change, 27
structural explanations of political
  behavior, 20
political process, theories of compensation or
  mitigation of transition costs, 7, 9–30
normative theories, 9–17
political behavior, alternative explanations
  of, 20–29
positive theories, 17–20
Public Choice theory, 17–20
positive theories of the political process, role of
  compensation and other mitigation
  transition strategies in, 17–20
implications for transition policies, 18–19
limitations, 19–20
mortgage interest deductibility (MID), 49–50
Posner, Eric, 123
postponed implementation, 2
  case study. *See* climate change policy
Poterba, James, 53
Prisoner's Dilemma, 73, 136
private insurance, 10, 12, 67, 109
Producer Support Estimate (PSE)
  agricultural protectionism, 81
professional qualifications, 2
property rights and development, 145–49
  dead capital, 145
  dependence on context, 147
  economic benefits, 145–46
  formalizing of property rights regimes, 146–48
  informal regimes, 147
  Locke's natural rights theory of property
    rights, 16
  sporadic and voluntary formalization system,
    148–49
  systemic state-led formalization program,
    148–49
psychological explanations of political
  behavior, 22–24
availability heuristic, 22, 126, 129, 130, 134
behavioral economics, 22, 129
bias, 22
climate change policy, 129–31, 135. *See also*
  carbon abatement measures

Dictator Game, 23–24
endowment effect, 22, 68, 70, 106, 124, 125
group dynamics and policy changes, 23
personal sacrifices, 23, 28, 64, 120, 128
Public Choice theory and self-interest
  assumption, 7, 17–18, 23–24, 26, 41,
  120, 125, 128, 151
trade liberalization, 68
Ultimatum Game, 23–24
Public Choice theory, 17–20
Canada's dairy supply management
  regime, 86–87
climate change policy, 120, 136
economics of politics, 17–18
implications for transition policies, 18–19
limitations, generally, 19–20
Olsonian Public Choice understanding of
  federalism, 126n50
public pensions, sustainability of, 39–41
self-interest assumption and, 7, 17–18, 23–24,
  26, 41, 120, 125, 128, 151
trade liberalization, 67, 69–70
public opinion. *See* ideational explanations of
  political behavior
public pensions, sustainability of, 3, 31–42, 157
age, increasing eligibility (pensionable age),
  32, 34–37
benefits, 34–35
criteria, 35–36
intertemporal consequences of reform,
  34, 35–36
losers, 36–37
policy investment, 35–36, 39, 40
benefit payment reductions, 34
Canada, 32, 34, 35, 37, 38
demoralization costs, 13, 36, 40, 41
European Union, 31, 37
France, 31, 37, 39
grandfathering of existing benefit recipients,
  32, 38–40, 41, 42
individual accounts, 34
intertemporal consequences of reform,
  34, 35–36
libertarian paternalist approach, 38
lifespan
  average, 33, 34, 37
  increasing, 36
losers, options for dealing with, 37–39
normative analysis, 39–41
OECD countries, 32–34, 38–39
old age support ratio, 32–33
pay-as-you-go system, 32, 33, 35, 111
phase-in implementation of reforms, 32, 38,
  39–42, 157
Public Choice theory, 39–41
redistributive transition strategy, 37–38

public pensions, sustainability of (*Cont'd*)
  Sarkozy reform, 39
  sustainability problem, 32–33
    causes, 32–33
    diminished fertility, 33
    lifespan, 33, 34, 36, 37
    old age support ratio, 32–33
    transition strategies, proposed policy reforms, 33–38, 157
    United Kingdom, 35, 37, 39
    United Nations, lifespan predictions, 33
    United States, 32, 34, 39
      Social Security retirement benefits, 32, 35, 39
Putnam, Robert, 115

Quinn, John, 11

randomness, 21–22
  incrementalism, 140
Rawls, John, 14, 41, 68, 106, 107n44, 124
Reagan, Ronald, 48
refugees, 97, 98, 100, 107, 111–12
Reitz, Jeffrey, 102
revenue neutral carbon pricing, 132–33, 137
Ricardo, David, 63
Richardson, J. David, 64–65
Robson, William, 89, 92
Rodrik, Dani, 71, 74, 141
Rubinfeld, Daniel, 12
rule of law reform and development, 141–43

Schlesinger, Arthur Jr., 105–6, 115
self-interest assumption, 7, 17–18, 23–24, 26, 151
  climate change policy, 120, 125, 128
  public pensions, sustainability of, 41
Sen, Amartya, 115, 143
Shapiro, Jesse, 49–51
Shavell, Steven, 12, 152
Shaviro, Daniel, 17, 52, 55, 57
Simpson, Alan, 56
Simpson, Jeffrey, 131
Sinai, Todd, 53
slavery, abolition of, 1, 153–54, 159
Slavery Abolition Act of 1833, 1, 153
Slave Trade Act of 1807, 153
Smith, Adam, 63, 69
Smith, Jeffrey, 77
social contract theory, 14, 41, 68, 157
  eminent domain case, 14
  fairness of phase-in, 41
  liberalism and, 106–7
  Rawls, John, 14, 41, 68, 106, 107n44, 124
socially desirable policy changes, compensation as strategy for expansion of, 7
Spain, 72

Staiger, Robert, 73
Stanbury, W.T., 92
status quo, 1, 6, 7, 153, 155
  Canada's dairy supply management regime, 82, 87, 89
  climate change policy, 122, 125, 127, 130
  as default option, 7
  immigration policy liberalization, 104
  as impeding reforms, 6
  institutional reform in developing countries, 142, 148, 158
  mortgage interest deductibility (MID), 46, 51, 54, 57, 60
  status quo bias, 17
  switching costs, 6
Stigler, George, 17
structural explanations of political behavior, 20
  carbon abatement measures, 125–26
  climate change policy, 134
  institutional reform in developing countries, 144
subsidies. *See* mortgage interest deductibility (MID) reform
Sunstein, Cass, 38
Sweden, 76, 77
switching costs, 6
  institutional reform in developing countries, 140, 142–43
Sykes, Alan, 70, 74

tax reform. *See* mortgage interest deductibility (MID) reform
Tax Reform Act of 1986 (TRA86), 48, 58
Thaler, Richard, 38
Thirteenth Amendment, 154
Thompson, Dennis, 155
Tokyo Round, 65
Trade Act of 1974, 78
Trade Adjustment Assistance (TAA) program, 78
trade liberalization, 4, 63–80, 157
  active labor market policies (ALMPs), OECD countries, 76
  adjustment costs
    measuring, 64–65
    policies, history of, 65–66
  Australia, 66, 76
  Canada, 64, 66, 75, 76, 77
  Canadian de Grandpré report, 75
  communitarianism, 68–69
  compensation for losses resulting from liberalization, 66–67
  dislocation costs, 64
  distributive justice, 68
  economic efficiency, 66–68
    adaptive preferences, 67–68

Index 215

bribery, 67
dislocated workers, 67–68
private incentives, 68
private insurance, absence of, 67
rationale for adjustment policies, 67
economic theories of multilateral trade agreements, 70
endowment effect, 68, 70
export-oriented producers, 4, 69, 73
foreign policy, free trade motivated by, 70–71
free-rider problem, 70
free trade, 63, 69, 70, 71, 73, 78
industrial subsidies, 79–80
Japan, 65, 77
labor market adjustment policies, 75–80
   active policies, 76–78
   classroom training, 77
   job-search assistance, 76–77
   on-the-job training, 77–78
   passive policies: the safety net, 75–76
   trade-specific adjustment programs, 78–79
lobbies, impact of, 70
neoclassical economic theory, 63
normative rationales for and against intervention, 66–69
North America, 66, 75, 77
personal sacrifices, 64
policy instruments, responses to costs of adjustment, 71–80
   economic Darwinism, 72
   gradualism, 72
   labor market adjustment policies, 75–80
   multilateral and bilateral trade agreements, 71
   reciprocity agreements, 73
   reversibility measures, 73–74
   safeguard mechanisms, 74
political considerations, 69–71
Prisoner's Dilemma, 73
private and psychological costs of change, 68
protectionism statistics, 64
Public Choice theory, 67, 69–70
regional trade pacts, 7, 66
terms-of-trade theory, 70
trade protectionism, 15, 64, 69–70, 71
United States, 71, 76, 77, 78
US debt crisis, 1980s, 71
transition cost mitigation strategies, 2–3, 151–59
   disparate nature of transition cost challenge, 158
   examples of costs associated with policy changes, 2–3
   explicit government compensation, 2
   grandfathering. *See* grandfathering
   institutional reform and incrementalism, 140, 153–55

   case study, developing countries and institutional reform. *See* institutional reform in developing countries
   international treaties, 7
   lessons from experience, 155–58
   phased implementation strategy, 2
   case studies
      Canadian dairy supply management regime. *See* Canada's dairy supply management regime
      immigration policy liberalization. *See* immigration policy liberalization
      mortgage interest deduction reform strategy. *See* mortgage interest deductibility (MID) reform
      sustainability of public pensions. *See* public pensions, sustainability of
      trade liberalization. *See* trade liberalization
   compensation and, 1
   postponed implementation, 2
   case study, climate change policy. *See* climate change policy
   social costs, 158
US Supreme Court, 6, 154
Trans-Pacific Partnership (TPP), 86, 94
Treasury Department, 47, 48
Treaty of Amsterdam, 99, 107
Treaty of Paris, 65n20
Treaty of Rome, 65n20
Tsebelis, George, 21
Tullock, Gordon, 17, 54, 82
2008 financial crisis
   carbon abatement measures, 126, 128, 130
   mortgage interest deductibility (MID), 52
Tyranny of the Majority, 12, 152–53
Tyranny of the Minority, 153

UK New Earnings Survey Panel Dataset, 72n60
Ultimatum Game, 23–24
unemployment insurance, 67, 75, 101, 109, 111
United Kingdom
   climate change policy, 121
   public pensions, sustainability of, 35, 37, 39
   trade liberalization, 76
United States
   agricultural protectionism, 81
   climate change policy, 123, 125, 126, 127, 129, 130–31
   immigration policy liberalization, 98–99, 101–2, 104, 106, 108, 109, 112, 115, 116–17
   public pensions, sustainability of, 32, 34, 39
   Social Security Retirement Benefits, 32, 35, 39

United States (*Cont'd*)
  trade liberalization, 71, 76, 77, 78
  US mortgage interest deductibility (MID).
    See mortgage interest deductibility
      (MID) reform
Uruguay Round, 66, 72n57, 73
US Constitution
  Fifth Amendment ("Takings Clause"), 6, 15,
    16–17, 29
  Thirteenth Amendment, 154
US debt crisis, 1980s, 71
US home mortgage interest deduction. *See*
  mortgage interest deductibility
    (MID) reform
US National Academy of Sciences, 100
US Trade Expansion Act of 1962, 78
utilitarianism, 13, 152, 155
  compensation formula, 13
  demoralization costs, 13, 36, 40, 41, 54
  distributive justice, 68
  fairness of phase-in, 41
  immigration policy liberalization, 106–7
  libertarianism and, 16

Veil of Ignorance, 14, 41, 68, 106
Ventry, Dennis, 47, 48, 53
veto players, 21, 28
  agricultural protectionism, 82, 88
Voith, Richard, 50
Voting Rights Act of 1965, 154

Wadhwa, Vivek, 101
Walzer, Michael, 105, 155
Weber, Andrea, 77, 149
Weinrib, Ernest, 15
Weisbach, David, 123
Whalley, John, 98
Wilberforce, William, 1, 153, 159
Wilcoxen, Peter, 123
Wilson, E.O., 129
Woerth, Eric, 31
World Trade Organization (WTO), 73,
  85, 132
World War I, 47
World War II, 85

zero-growth economy, 21, 119n6

www.ingramcontent.com/pod-product-compliance
Ingram Content Group UK Ltd.
Pitfield, Milton Keynes, MK11 3LW, UK
UKHW042006230426
12048UKWH00009B/584